# "Still They Remember Me"

## "eskᵂa·tte nəmihkawitəhaməkok kohsəssənawak"

# "Still They Remember Me"

A VOLUME IN THE SERIES
Native Americans of the Northeast
EDITED BY
Colin G. Calloway, Jean M. O'Brien, and Lisa T. Brooks

# "eskʷa·tte nəmihkawitəhɑməkok kohsəssənawak"

**CAROL A. DANA**

**MARGO LUKENS**

**AND CONOR M. QUINN**

PENOBSCOT TRANSFORMER TALES · VOLUME 1

UNIVERSITY OF MASSACHUSETTS PRESS · AMHERST AND BOSTON

Copyright © 2021 by Penobscot Nation Cultural and Historic Preservation Office
Printed in the United States of America
ISBN 978-1-62534-579-0 (paper); 580-6 (hardcover)
Designed by adam b. bohannon
Set in Gentium Plus and IT Marxiana
Printed and bound by Books International, Inc.
Cover design by adam b. bohannon
Cover art: *Half Length Portrait of Newell Lion,* from Sepck papers - 9-2-n. Courtesy of American Philosophical Society.

Library of Congress Cataloging-in-Publication Data

Names: Dana, Carol A., author. | Lukens, Margo, author. | Quinn, Conor M., author.
Title: "Still they remember me" / Carol A. Dana, Margo Lukens, and Conor M. Quinn.
Other titles: Native Americans of the Northeast.
Description: Amherst : University of Massachusetts Press, [2021] | Series:
    Native Americans of the Northeast | Includes bibliographical references
    and index. | English and Penobscot.
Identifiers: LCCN 2020053345 (print) | LCCN 2020053346 (ebook) | ISBN
    9781625345790 (paperback) | ISBN 9781625345806 (hardcover) | ISBN
    9781613768365 (ebook)
Subjects: LCSH: Penobscot Indians—Folklore. | Penobscot
    Indians—Language—Texts. | LCGFT: Folk tales.
Classification: LCC E99.P5 D36 2021 (print) | LCC E99.P5 (ebook) | DDC
    974.1004/9734—dc23
LC record available at https://lccn.loc.gov/2020053345
LC ebook record available at https://lccn.loc.gov/2020053346

British Library Cataloguing-in-Publication Data
A catalog record for this book is available from the British Library.

# CONTENTS

## "Still They Remember Me"
### PENOBSCOT TRANSFORMER TALES, TOLD BY NEWELL LYON TO FRANK SPECK

# ILLUSTRATIONS

# kči-wəliwəni (Acknowledgments)

We wish to thank the circle of people who have helped make this project possible and real. All have been with us on the journey, some longer than others, and all are connected to each other in some way.

To the spirit of our mutual friend, ssipsis

All the grandmothers: Monimkwehso, St. Anne, Edwina Mitchell, Lorraine Dana, Cheryl Francis, ssipsis, and many others

Newell Lyon and the Penobscot elders who spoke with him, and the Penobscot ancestors, *nəkanəsohsak,* who spoke with them

Our families, including Carol Dana's six children and fourteen grandchildren who inspired this project; Margo's husband, Ken Dupuis; John and Amy Lukens, the parents who raised her; and the Austin and Lukens grandparents who connect her to the nineteenth century; the Quinn, Carroll, Thomas, Arbuckle, Medley, and Denham families who give Conor Quinn so many relations, with special thanks to Richard Garrett and Martha Young (and their family) for introducing him to the Penobscot people, and to Steve Cayard and Angela DeRosa (and their family); and to Adrianne L. Hess and Caroline Hadilaksono, and also Rosa Noreen, Daniel Lawrence, and Erin Finn for love, friendship, and unstinting support; and to his generous web of friends and family in the Penobscot, Passamaquoddy, Wolastoqew/Maliseet, Mi'gmaw/Mi'kmaw, Wôpanâak, Mohegan, Abenaki, Montaukett, Shinnecock, Unkechaug, Makah, and Somali and Irish/Gaeltacht communities, and beyond

Lisa Brooks (Abenaki), professor at Amherst College, who first urged us to submit our idea to UMass Press

Brian Halley, most patient editor at UMass Press, Margaret Hogan, Sally Nichols, and Rachael DeShano

Donna Loring, Penobscot playwright, author, veteran of war and politics who helped connect us to the Penobscot Theatre project

Bari Newport, artistic director of the Penobscot Theatre, who imagined a new play for the Acadia Park Centennial and had the desire to pursue a viable connection between the Penobscot Nation and the Penobscot Theatre

Amy Roeder, who helped bring the script of *Transformer Tales: Stories of the Dawnland* into being and directed the premiere production at Penobscot Theatre Company's Dramatic Academy

William S. Yellow Robe, Jr., who inspired us to imagine plays in Penobscot language and culture

Andrea Perry and the administrators of the Broad Reach Fund of the Maine Community Foundation

Rick Pouliot and Judy Dow, Gedakina, Inc.

Maryanne Mattson and Red Empress Foundation

Kathy Pollard and her daughter, Ann Pollard Ranco

University of Maine, for Summer Faculty Research Fund support, and the McGillicuddy Humanities Center for support all the way from initial research to creating the index

Penobscot Nation Chief Kirk Francis

Former Penobscot Nation Vice-Chief Bill Thompson (great-great grandson of Newell Lyon), for early support of a National Endowment for the Arts grant for the production of the play *Transformer Tales: Stories of the Dawnland*

James Francis, Penobscot tribal historian and director of the Penobscot Nation Cultural and Historic Preservation Office (CHPO)

Jane Anderson, professor at NYU and specialist in indigenous cultural intellectual property law

Edwina Bear Mitchell, for consulting on stories

Gabe Paul, language resource person at CHPO, who had the good idea to solicit illustrations from Penobscot community artists

Carole Binette, director of trust services at the Penobscot Nation Tribal Office, for help with genealogical records

Joshua Woodbury, Penobscot Nation webmaster, for community email communications

Jennifer Neptune, Penobscot artist, museum curator, clear thinker, and wrangler of .pdfs

The late Tim Powell, director of the Center for Native American and Indigenous Research

Brian Carpenter, friend and senior archivist, Center for Native American and Indigenous Research, American Philosophical Society, Philadelphia

The staff at the Division of Rare and Manuscript Collections, Kroch Library, Cornell University, Ithaca, NY, especially Interim Reference Coordinator Eisha Neely

William Haviland, University of Vermont, *emeritus*

Celeste Cota, administrative support supervisor, University of Maine Department of English

Kate Walters, Deborah Smith, and Jason Charland, University of Maine Office of Research Development

Christel Peters, research communications coordinator, University of Maine Research, for a great photo session in our "office" at Tim Horton's in Old Town, ME

Laura Rosbrow-Telem, Maine News Service, publicnewsservice.org, for an excellent radio interview that got picked up by National Native News

Tim Horton's waitstaff at the now-shuttered Old Town/Stillwater, ME, shop who allowed us to treat the shop as our office one day per week

Governor's waitstaff, Old Town/Stillwater, ME, for letting us do the same after Tim's closed

Our contributing artists:

Martha Piscuskas (the fish weir)

Joshua Woodbury (the grasshopper)

Shannon Sockalexis (the rest of the chapter illustrations)

Margaret Pearce, who at the eleventh hour drew us a map of Gluskabe's world

Frank G. Speck, who made the first attempt with Newell Lyon's help

Frank T. Siebert, who persisted and worked closely with many speakers to come up with a more accurate account of the sound system of Penobscot language and developed the Penobscot orthography adopted by the Nation as its official writing system

This book is dedicated to the Penobscot generations yet to come, *kohsəssənawak.*

# Preface

I'm curled in darkness without form waiting, waiting for a special dawn
To be born to a people great and good
The people of the northeast land wood
My name is Gluscabe as the stories tell
All over our great country I did dwell
I taught alenape how to live in ages past
When they were so very young
Their livelihood was made to last
I didn't leave a detail undone
Now I watch and wait and see
How much people prolong their misery,
how much we adopt foreign ways,
and if you can truly forget together our days
I will return if you call my name
But slowly I hear your voices wane
Protect the peoples' ways
Don't let them be crushed,
Reducing lives to misery
My spirit dwells in every creature and tree
When you address the powers,
Think of me
I'm curled in darkness without form, waiting, waiting for a special dawn.

(1976)

This is for *kohsəssənawak,* our descendants, and *nəkanəsohsak,* our ancestors. We at Penobscot Nation look to publish the Transformer Tales because it contains the words of our ancestors. They told these tales as a way to transmit our values to the next generation. The stories will be an invaluable tool for those willing to learn Penobscot. This present generation has not heard the sounds of their language. In the 1980s there were twenty-five or so speakers on Indian Island in Maine, mostly Passamaquoddy. Two elderly native speakers of Penobscot died more than ten years ago. The Penobscot Nation Cultural and Historic Preservation Office (CHPO) continues efforts on revitalizing Penobscot language as the official language of the tribe, in the writing system devised by the linguist Frank T. Siebert, based on the International Phonetic Alphabet. We believe speaking Penobscot is a way to honor our ancestors and to remember them. Newell Lyon told these stories in our language almost a hundred years ago. He died on March 3, 1919, a few months after the anthropologist Frank G. Speck published the stories in the *International Journal of American Linguistics* (*IJAL*).

Stephen Krashen, a second language advocate, has stated that if you can read a language you can learn it. These texts are the legacy left to us from our relatives, via an anthropologist and linguist (Speck and Siebert). Conor Quinn has transcribed the stories in our official language, the written system devised by Siebert. Some people resist the idea of reading a Native language and writing it, but if you can read and write in your language, you are literate in it. Reading is our stepping stone to speaking Penobscot.

In our community we have done the stories as plays in grade schools and beyond. The main reason for this republication is the need in our community so that we may see it as well as hear it. We can put recordings of the stories on the web so that people can hear them. For years I have had a dream of teaching Penobscot in early childhood as well as in kindergarten through grade eight, born out of my work with Frank Siebert. Someday I hope it will be realized. The stories are cultural tools for us to learn our values and language.

We are presenting this new publication of the Penobscot Transformer Tales as told by Newell Lyon to Frank Speck because it has messages and teachings relevant to today. The messages are of conservation, environmental balance, and consideration for upcoming generations when making decisions. Transformer Tales chronicles a journey of Gluskabe, culture hero to the Penobscot and other Wabanaki tribes of the Dawnland (New England and the Maritimes). The way we impart our values to our youth is through storytelling. These stories are told traditionally in winter. Newell Lyon must have heard them numerous times to be able to commit them to memory, working with the elders on this process. Traditionally, stories have been told with each other's permission. Certain families hold certain stories. It would be great if all of our children became familiar with the old stories and if they were taught in the school as the stories' message is timeless for all people. Gluskabe's grandmother mentions when the rivers will become dangerous; we witness that with pollution in the rivers that poisons the fish and muskrat that we eat. As we read the stories, we see Gluskabe still at work on the land trying to bring about balance. That is what he did in the past. He taught us how to live and made way for us. He promises to return again in the future.

We have done plays in the past based on these stories, in Indian Island School and also at the Penobscot Theatre with a full cast. It was beautiful to hear the words given breath. By publishing the stories, they become widely available to our children and all children and people of all ages. We want to continue the cycle of our cosmogony of our people so that our youth will learn more about our traditional cultural values.

We are in an age of limited resources on earth with an expanding population. Our stories teach about conservation, which we always practiced as a matter of course. Hearing the stories every year, they become part of who we are and shape what we do. For many years, because mainstream society and education interrupted our culture, telling traditional stories was not a common practice. This book is a beginning, and a return to tradition. These stories contribute to the scholarly study of Penobscot as an Algonquian language in which there are few published tales such as these. This work will make the teaching of Penobscot easier and more accessible for those who are interested, a process so valuable to future students of the Penobscot language. The Penobscot Cultural and Historic Preservation Department will provide a link to the stories on the web, so one can hear as well as see the words. This will be an invaluable tool for future learners, in keeping with Grandmother Woodchuck's teaching to consider those who will come after us.

CAROL A. DANA
Indian Island, 2021

## NOTES

PAGE

xvi  *Frank G. Speck published the stories*: Speck, "Penobscot Transformer Tales."

xvi  *if you can read a language you can learn it*: Krashen, "The Input Hypothesis." Krashen's idea is that language acquisition happens when a language learner receives "comprehensible input," as in the form of a story that may already be familiar. He posits that "the learner improves and progresses along the 'natural order' when he/she receives second language 'input' that is one step beyond his/her current stage of linguistic competence" (420).

# "Still They Remember Me"

"esk$^w$a·tte nəmihkawitəhɑməkok kohsəssənawak"

"...nətah·ap' awen
otαwəsiwən
alohsete:
kʷaskʷačo·pa...."

[p208]

○ *ktatən*

"...n·eli-kawihlαt wikʷesk,
αkələpeməwal wəkʷaskʷtəhαn...."

[p174]

"...nə·
wikəya
askámi.

[p.

*kči-məkʷasəpemək
(mosatəpakamok / mosatəpəssək)*

"...mαlam pečihlαt
kčĭ-məkʷasəpemək,
etali-mskawαt
alənαpa...."

[p182]

*p a n a w a h p s k e w t ə kʷ*

*kkiniyo/
kkino*

"...na nihkʷαp wačo
ali-wiso kkiniyo...."

[p198]

*matakəməssək*

"...n·as·te
wəkʷəssakαkətahin
pekəssik...."

[p192]

*mosihkačik*

"...nihkʷαp ali-wih
mosihkači..."

[p196]

"...mečĭmi
wənenawelαmo
spətáhi
ahč nipáyi....

[p250

*kətahkina*

*wəlakəsəyal* ○

"...nə·tt' etali-pənahpskʷihlαk
wαpahpəskʷ.
eskʷa·tte nihkʷαp
wewinαkʷatol...."

[p196]

# Introduction

## A Brief History of Penobscot Stories in Print

At the turn of the twentieth century, when Newell Lyon agreed to tell the stories he knew to a visiting anthropologist, Frank Speck, Anglo-American authors had for the past two or three decades been collecting and publishing Penobscot and other Algonquian traditional stories. Some were of a more literary bent; others came from an academic ethnolinguistic perspective. Charles G. Leland published in 1884 the early collection *The Algonquin Legends of New England*, in which he credits the assistance of Abby Alger; she published her own volume, *In Indian Tents*, in 1897, which she dedicated to Leland. Both Alger and Leland also credited the work of Silas T. Rand, who collected Micmac stories throughout the nineteenth century. Leland's interest in Wabanaki traditions appeared to be primarily in the extent to which he could see connections (sometimes via far northern and Greenland indigenous traditions) to stories of "the Norsemen, as set forth in the Eddas, the Sagas, and popular tales of Scandinavia." This hobby horse led him to a 1902 collaboration with ethnolinguist John Dyneley Prince called *Kulóskap the Master and Other Algonkin Poems*, in which the two took turns making versified versions of the already anglicized stories from Leland's first book. The poems read more like the Anglo-Saxon poem *Beowulf* than anything from a Wabanaki language. From Leland's and Prince's perspectives, Penobscot and other Wabanaki people were "a rapidly perishing race—a race which fifty years from now will have hardly a single living representative."

Meanwhile, Penobscot writer Joseph Nicolar, a grandson of John Neptune, former representative to the Maine legislature and author of many newspaper columns under the penname "Young Sebattis," had taken matters into his own hands, publishing the versions of Penobscot stories he knew from his elders in his 1893 book *The Life and Traditions of the Red Man*. In the preface to his book, Nicolar wrote of his intention "to remove the fear that the life of the red man will pass away unwritten." He was responding to "a general desire among the people that some one ought to write it now if ever," "the people" being his own Penobscot. Although the book is narrated in English, Nicolar used Roman characters to represent the sounds of Penobscot language when he named places and beings in his versions of the stories. Clearly, Nicolar wanted to create linguistic and cultural bridges for anglophone readers (whether Penobscot or non-Native). He often drew attention to the Penobscot language in his newspaper columns; a good example from about 1887 can be found in *Dawnland Voices*, the 2014 anthology assembled by Siobhan Senier and editors from each of eleven New England tribal communities. In this particular column, Nicolar introduced readers to Penobscot placenames along Penobscot Bay and upriver to Old Town, and explained what the language tells about the importance of these places to Penobscot people; it is only one example of many more items he published in newspapers and other ephemeral media that can teach twenty-first-century readers more about the Penobscot language, history, and stories.

In the late nineteenth and early twentieth centuries, ethnology and anthropology departments at universities emphasized a process of "salvage," studies actuated by the belief that indigenous languages and peoples were quickly becoming extinct. In 1910, Prince published a short article on the Penobscot language, based on ten years of collection in Maine; it contains four stories, some phrases, and a glossary. Prince believed his work to be "the only large collection of Penobscot words and forms" to have been published at that point, although he refers the reader to Sébastien Rasles's [Rale's] seventeenth-/eighteenth-century dictionary of the Abenaki language for "the mother-tongue . . . the Old Abenaki." Prince's student at Columbia University Frank Speck had begun working on Penobscot at Indian Island, Maine, in 1907, publishing his first brief collection of Penobscot stories in 1915 in English.

It would take him a decade and a lot of help from Penobscot speakers to gain any familiarity with the language.

It has been noted that Anglo New Englanders have worked hard for a couple of centuries to create the mythology of their own "firstness" and the vanishing of the indigenous peoples of the places Anglos colonized. New England has only recently begun to integrate Native studies into school curricula; in Maine, despite the 2001 passage of LD291, "An Act to Require Teaching of Maine Native American History and Culture in Maine Schools," teachers still struggle to fulfill the requirement, which was never funded by the state legislature. However, people in tribal communities have not forgotten their history, stories, or written literature. Carol Dana remembers that back in the early 1980s Penobscot community member Lester Bassett brought a photocopy of the 1918 "Penobscot Transformer Tales" to Frank Siebert, the linguist who was at work on a dictionary of the Penobscot language. "Frank ignored it," Carol says. Decades earlier, Frank Speck had shared his own manuscript transcriptions of these tales with Frank Siebert while Siebert was building his writing system; perhaps in Siebert's mind, the published versions had nothing more to teach him. For Carol, however, the early publication contained important information about her language, as well as stories important to the people's well-being. She kept a copy, gave it to friends, and eventually began teaching the stories at Indian Island School in the 1990s. The photocopied 1918 version continued to circulate; the late James Neptune sold spiral-bound photocopies at the Penobscot Nation Museum, and the Penobscot Nation Cultural and Historic Preservation Office (CHPO) has continued to support local awareness by circulating copies as pamphlets to interested people on Indian Island.

Over the past decade, the CHPO has taken responsibility for guarding the Penobscot Nation's intellectual property, which has been a concern of Carol's for a long time. Director James Francis began working on articulating the guidelines while he was studying at the University of Maine; since then the nation has connected with New York University professor Jane Anderson, who specializes in processes for protecting indigenous intellectual property worldwide. In 2018, Penobscot Nation Tribal Chief Kirk Francis signed a memorandum of understanding with the president of the University of Maine regarding Penobscot cultural patrimony held at the university. In the document, the university recognized the sovereignty of the Penobscot Nation and agreed to support the creation of a process for reviewing proposed research projects involving the nation or materials belonging to the nation, parallel to the U.S. federal requirements for review of research by an institutional review board for the protection of human subjects. It takes time and clear communication to create processes that justly recognize tribal intellectual property. We are grateful to the editors at the University of Massachusetts Press, who worked with us to negotiate a contract for this book that gives the copyright and royalties to the Penobscot Nation, as well as oversight of any future projects involving the materials in the book.

## The Transformer Tales Play

Carol Dana is the instigator of this project. When she said, "We have to republish these stories," we had just finished a year of work concentrating on the first thirteen Penobscot Transformer Tales in the process of creating a script for public performance. This came about because the artistic director of our nearby professional theatre, Penobscot Theatre Company in Bangor, Maine, had expressed the desire to collaborate with Penobscot people on a theatrical production. Carol and I had to figure out how to make the process work with the Penobscot Nation. We began groundwork in the summer of 2015, and the aim was to have a production ready for the Acadia National Park Centennial celebration in August 2016. There were plenty of ways the process could have failed: the timetables of the Penobscot Theatre rehearsal schedule or the national park centennial could have been too short or prescriptive, the effort to create the script could have broken down over cultural differences, or the Penobscot writers and storytellers from Indian Island could have decided not to spend their time and energy for government and cultural institutions like the National Park Service or a mainstream theatre. Carol and I were most concerned that the show be something with which the theatre audience *and* the Penobscot people would be happy.

Late in the fall we gathered a group of about eight Penobscot people interested in the project to consider stories they thought would be important to tell. We imagined a play based on the life of our friend ssipsis, the Penobscot author, artist, and activist who had just passed away in October 2015. Carol suggested the Penobscot Transformer Tales, some of which are familiar to many people in the community and reach back into time immemorial. It felt right to concentrate on these stories; years before, ssipsis had given Carol her family's permission to retell the stories transmitted by their ancestor Newell Lyon. We chose the first thirteen of the Transformer Tales, which tell the story of Gluskabe's growth in wisdom and maturity and describe how he shaped Penobscot territory. We thought too that bringing the stories to audiences in the theatre would be an appropriate way to express a fundamental idea ssipsis had shared with Carol: that Gluskabe is the spirit of creativity.

It was fortunate that Carol and I already had a good basis for trusting each other because the visibility of the project raised the stakes. I knew Carol as a friend and poet; she knew my teaching on Native American literatures and had visited classes when my students read her work. Together we struggled to keep the presentation of the stories clear and respectful while still engaging a varied audience of theatergoers. We had the help of Amy Roeder, education director at Penobscot Theatre, to tighten dramatic elements of the script. Sometimes Amy and I misunderstood a story's purpose—why was Monimkwehso willing to make Gluskabe three different *amignagweh* (game bags) in response to his "shaman's wish?" Carol often preferred

Frank Speck's formal phrasing to our attempts at humor: "He wouldn't say that to an elder!" But when she began to show us how we could use the Penobscot language on every page of the script, then we had a guideline for the project and a cultural compass that we could completely trust. Our purpose was to give breath to the sounds of the language, to set Penobscot words and phrases in the dialogue of the play, so anglophone audiences could understand their meaning and also begin to be familiar with words we used over and over again: *nohkəmi* (grandmother), *nkʷenəss* (grandson), *kči-wəliwəni* (great thanks).

Carol's choice to incorporate Penobscot language into the script was a brilliant move. The young Penobscot Theatre Dramatic Academy students cast in the production of *Transformer Tales: Stories of the Dawnland* had an amazing experience. At first the language-learning part of the rehearsals seemed difficult and unlike anything they had ever heard. They gave Carol respectful attention; she showed them how to make flashcards for pronunciation and recorded audio lessons from each page of the script so the actors could listen and practice at home. It was demanding for English speakers, but the magic of theatre, of being onstage together, focused their attention on doing their best with the things that matter most: clear and correct speaking, caring for their scene partners, and contributing 100 percent to make the whole show a success. And the show made history: it was the first time the Penobscot language had been spoken from the stage of the Penobscot Theatre.

The language stuck with the students too. Those who came from the Penobscot Nation recognized words and phrases like *nohkəmi* and *nəmohsomi*, the words they use to address their own grandparents. Penobscot kids felt the privilege of bringing their traditions to center stage and celebrated the world premiere of *Transformer Tales* at their school on Indian Island, with all their relatives watching. On the other hand, kids who might never have met a Penobscot person before had new vistas as well as new friends. Amy Roeder told me that months after the show closed, a group of her theatre students doing a Chicken-Little-Sky-Is-Falling scene suddenly began to chant *kati-mehtkamike*, Gluskabe's warning to the animals from the second story telling them "the world is going to end." The Penobscot words came back to the students to express precisely what was happening in that dramatic moment.

We had just finished an interview about the play at WERU radio in Blue Hill, Maine, when Carol declared her desire to republish the Transformer Tales. She is most concerned with bringing young people in the Penobscot Nation back to their traditional language through these familiar stories. The project has led us on many journeys already, close to home and far away. We have thought deeply about the stories and learned more about Newell Lyon and his historical context. We have worked with several University of Maine classes to bring the teachings of these stories to their study of communication and literary history. After our friend Martha Piscuskas gave Carol her woodcut of the fishing weir, we invited Penobscot community members to contribute illustrations, and right away Josh Woodbury produced his grasshopper. We heard about a young woman, Shannon Sockalexis, who might be interested in drawing for us. Working with her we discovered a balance between Penobscot arts and a style influenced by Japanese *anime*. We feel this balance represents the contemporary reality of young Penobscot people, who incorporate many cultural influences into their lives and use unlimited artistic means to interpret fundamental aspects of the Penobscot worldview.

## Who Was Newell Lyon and How Were Penobscots Living during His Lifetime?

Research in Penobscot Nation genealogical records gives us some scant knowledge of the outlines of Newell Lyon's life. He was born in 1846 in Winterport, Maine, to Louis Lyon and Elizabeth Natannis Lyon. His mother was from the Penobscot community in Old Town, and his father, born in the Canadian province of New Brunswick, may have been from a Maliseet community. Newell Lyon and his sister, Mary, however, surely grew up in and around the Penobscot community at Indian Island. The year of Newell Lyon's birth was also the year of Henry David Thoreau's first trip to Maine, when he climbed Mount Katahdin; Thoreau was guided on two later trips by Penobscot men, Joe Aitteon and Joseph Polis, as he narrated in *The Maine Woods*. Thoreau's visits were part of a larger tourist interest in summer travel to Maine, which stimulated Penobscot economic and cultural participation: "Men, women, and children alike made canoes, baskets, snowshoes, and moccasins for the tourist trade and offered performance of traditional songs and dances."

By the late nineteenth century, though, making a living had become increasingly difficult for Penobscot people. Dams in the Penobscot River powered sawmills and other factories, but they prevented the migration of anadromous fish that had been among the Penobscots' most dependable foods. It was hard to find work in the Old Town mills because of white employers' racism, so men often had to relocate—sometimes with their whole families—to find work in lumbering, fishing, and transportation. After the turn of the twentieth century, Penobscot people who eked out livings as ferrymen or worked at the Oldtown Woolen Mill (built in 1889) found their traditional lifeways subject to taxes and restricted to limited seasons by the state's annual hunting and fishing licenses or the very expensive ten-dollar trapper's license. The choice may have amounted to being "cut off from their ancient sources of subsistence or [being] forced to break the law just to survive."

Newell Lyon, a gifted storyteller who had worked closely with his elders to learn the stories, would have been about sixty-one years old when Frank Speck came to Old Town in 1907 to do his linguistic research. Like his predecessor Joseph Nicolar, Lyon may have felt concern for the transmission of Penobscot cultural tradition and a motivation to help Speck transcribe and translate the stories because of encroachment by Anglo-American society, policy, and technology. During his own lifetime, Lyon would have seen the children on Indian Island begin to attend schools where

English was taught intentionally to exclude Penobscot, either at the island's elementary school, established in 1878 by the Sisters of Mercy, or at local public schools. At both, teachers used physical and emotional violence to destroy children's natural use of the Penobscot language. Language use eroded further during the boarding-school era; at least forty children from the Penobscot community went away to Pennsylvania to attend the Carlisle Indian Industrial School before it closed in 1918.

Women on Indian Island at the turn of the twentieth century enacted significant resistance to the erosion of Penobscot language use. Returning to Indian Island nearly two decades after closing his research project in Maine, Frank Speck observed "in 1936 the two married women of my host's family group speaking no English during my stay, but understanding it." Speck reflected that during his earlier stays, the "non-use of English" was widespread among the women there, despite their entrepreneurial interactions with tourists and even despite being married (in some cases) to anglophone Penobscot men. Although many young Penobscot people may have been speaking almost exclusively English even with their parents, the mothers and wives maintained a distrust of white people and valued "their own heritage of pride of tongue." This linguistically conservative attitude had support in a belief based in the stories that Speck claimed were common at the turn of the twentieth century: that Gluskabe was still making arrowheads in his place at *mehtakʷičihlɑk kətahkina* (the end of our land), getting ready to "return and expel the whites from the country." Not unlike the pan-Indian Ghost Dance movement of the late nineteenth century, the Penobscot tradition about Gluskabe's promise to return if the people needed him supported cultural and political resistance to Anglo-American encroachment.

In his introduction to his 1940 book *Penobscot Man*, Speck looked back at his Penobscot work in two stages: "The main investigation of Penobscot general ethnology begun in 1907 closed in 1914," when he located himself on Indian Island with the people, and sporadically "from 1914 to 1918, when occasion permitted, attention was focused upon the recording of myth texts and religious beliefs, shamanism, social organization, and decorative art, with the cooperation of Newell Lion [sic]." Presumably Lyon was observing the tradition that stories be told in winter, rather than summer. After all the years of their collaboration, Speck gave only one sentence to the fate of Newell Lyon: "He froze to death in the woods in 1918." According to tribal records, however, Lyon died on March 3, 1919, in the winter immediately following the journal publication of "Penobscot Transformer Tales." The location on his death certificate is recorded as "Birch Stream, Milford, Me," which flows into Sunkhaze Stream in the Sunkhaze Meadows, a traditional winter hunting ground to the east of Indian Island. Lyon was buried in the cemetery of St. Ann's Catholic Church on Indian Island on March 9, 1919.

Penobscot genealogical records show that Newell Lyon's direct and collateral descendants are part of the contemporary Penobscot community. His daughter, Theresa Camilla Lyon, who lived from 1890 to 1958, married four times and was known to young Penobscot people as "Auntie Camilla." She was a noted basket maker who specialized in sewing baskets, tool cases, and other fine work, including horsehair miniatures, woven using her own finger as a mold. Camilla's third child, William Thomas, was the father of the late author, artist, and activist ssipsis (1941–2015); it was ssipsis who gave Carol Dana permission to retell the stories of her great-grandfather Newell Lyon. ssipsis's three children continue to practice living traditions of basketry and other arts and leadership in the Penobscot Nation.

Carol Dana herself is a connected by marriage and by neighborly friendships lasting into this generation. Theresa Camilla Lyon's second husband, Henry Mitchell Francis, was previously married to Katherine Neptune. Among their children was Sylvester Francis, Carol's maternal grandfather. Carol's paternal grandparents lived next door to Auntie Camilla, and Carol heard that Camilla helped that family as their neighbor. In the next generation, ssipsis and Carol lived as neighbors and continued to help each other day to day with children and household work. Their friendship included their mutual concern for Penobscot tradition, language, and stories—and carried on the resistance to colonial erosion of Penobscot life.

## What Do the Stories Say about the Dawnland?

Across Algonquian literatures, there is almost uniformly a distinction between an *atlohkakan*, a sacred story dealing with how the world came to be, and the related actions of figures like Gluskabe, and an *ačəməwakan,* an "(ordinary) story," a genre that apparently includes most other kinds of story, be it news, personal history, ordinary people's encounters with the supernatural, and so on. Telling the sacred stories insures the continuation of the people in connection to the universe and actively fuels the universe. These Penobscot teachings socialize children into shared values and instruct them in how they are woven together in integral relationship with all other beings, animals, and the land itself.

Stories like these describe and connect to the span of natural history in the Dawnland region, the shape of the land, and the lifeways of the people who have made their home here for millennia. Elements of the Gluskabe stories may actually describe the changes—"tundra-like conditions [giving] way to more mixed vegetation"—that people living here at the end of the last ice age had to deal with. William Haviland explains that "as forests developed, other animals moved in. These included mastodons, the moose-elk . . . and woodland caribou. Some of these species, like the mammoth and mastodon, were impressively large," such as the large and threatening beasts that Gluskabe must overcome in these and other stories. Haviland suggests Penobscot traditional stories may indeed "contain the memories of a people whose ancestors witnessed what things were like in the immediate postglacial era" and reminds us that "today's Wabanaki are descendants of people who have been living in the region continuously for over 11,000 years." For contemporary people, too, the stories contain ancient knowledge about balanced and sustainable relationships between human beings and the rest of the world that will be important for our continued survival.

Bodies of water, islands, the ocean, high winds, mountains, the Penobscot River appear and take shape as Gluskabe grows and moves about the land. The stories point out specific features such as a rocky point, out of which he makes a stone canoe, or the overturned kettle that becomes Mount Kineo after Gluskabe cooks the meat of the great moose. Gluskabe takes on the task of softening the wind but goes too far when he temporarily disposes of the great bird (*kči-ssipəss*) who has been making the wind blow.

Penobscot literature and oral tradition all suggest that, as is common in many of the world's languages, people use kinship terms to address non-kin: with younger people respectfully addressing elders as *nohkəmi*, "my grandmother," and *nəmohsomi*, "my grandfather," and those elders addressing them in kind as *nkʷenəss*, "my grandchild," to show affection and connection; survival often depended on cooperation among relatives. Because these relationships have always been so integral to healthy life, family and teachers interested in reinforcing this traditional custom may want to point out these usages in the stories. Readers will also notice that we have titled the stories simply with numbers given in Penobscot language, preserving the order in which they were first published, but not the English titles created by Frank Speck.

From the start of the stories about Gluskabe, his grandmother Monimkwehso, the woodchuck, teaches him the importance of balance and creates technology for gathering food (*pesəkʷ*, literally "one"). Monimkwehso teaches him to hunt and fish, and she makes him his first bow and arrows when he is old (and hungry) enough. When he kills first a deer and then a bear, Monimkwehso perceives her grandson will be a person of great power and therefore carries great responsibility for *kohsəssənawak*, "our descendants." She teaches Gluskabe to build a canoe so he can expand their diet from freshwater fish and snared rabbits to include ducks that yield many more fat calories. This may represent Penobscot awareness of nutritional needs for healthy lives. But the young Gluskabe's desires keep him wishing for more and better tools.

By means of a "shaman's wish," Gluskabe gets his grandmother to create a magical *amignagweh,* a traditional Penobscot vessel made with a square bottom and a round opening, which Gluskabe wants to use as a game bag, made from her own hair. The idea that people with power can cause changes to happen by a simple act of thought is a recurrent theme in Penobscot literature—you see it again in the fifth story. But each time Gluskabe reacts overenthusiastically to the success of his technology— filling the game bag with all the animals (*nis,* "two") and tricking all the fish to take refuge in Monimkwehso's super-efficient fish weir (*nahs,* "three")—Monimkwehso realizes she must teach her grandson sustainable practices in taking animal life for food. She teaches him to consider the lives of those in future generations, for whom it is necessary to cultivate continuing sources of sustenance.

Despite the good influence of his grandmother, Gluskabe takes a while to learn the difference between creating change through trickery or fraud and creating it through negotiation. When he tries to stop the wind (*yew,* "four") by dropping the elderly Wind Bird into a mountain crevasse, it is a moment of such bad behavior that he tries to deny it later. The Wind Bird addresses Gluskabe as *nohsəss,* a word translated in Speck's original manuscript as "my grandson" and in the 1918 publication as "my grandchild," a term of endearment implying a mutually beneficial relationship. Instead of continuing to disrespect and fool the grandfather Bird, Gluskabe negotiates a balance of wind and calm when he realizes some wind is necessary for a healthy environment.

The story of Grasshopper and tobacco (*palenəskʷ* | *nɑn,* "five") takes place on a great island (*kči-mənahanok*); to get there, Gluskabe does several experiments with canoe design to create one that will travel efficiently enough on the ocean to make the long journey of three "looks" (*tekakɑpimək*, "as far as one can see"). Before setting out to Grasshopper's island, Gluskabe again uses his power of thought to ensure that Grasshopper will not be at home when he arrives. The Penobscot expressions for this are literally the ordinary verbs meaning "think," as in *n·wətəlitəhɑmɑn*, "then he thought him (causing him to . . .)," as in *n·wətəlitəhɑmɑn čɑlsal kiwohse*, "then by thinking he made Grasshopper walk wandering." When Gluskabe arrives at the island, he can tell Grasshopper is away from home because Grasshopper's habitual canoe parking spot is empty; the language names his beachfront launching spot (*wətahsitəmomək*), an area claimed by an individual or family as a traditional practice. Gluskabe's purpose is to relieve Grasshopper of all the stockpiled tobacco he has been hoarding and redistribute it for the people's medicinal and ceremonial use.

Gluskabe's growing sense of responsibility leads him to consider the difficulty of navigating on the rivers in the Dawnland, and to tame the currents and falls so that his descendants can paddle and portage more safely (*nəkʷətɑs*, "six"). Wabanaki people have continuously used the rivers as means of travel, as highways rather than boundaries.

Uugulubemo, the great Frog, has been guarding the water (*tɑ̀pawɑs*, "seven"): even today the presence of frogs is a sign that the water quality is good and clean. The problem is that Uugulubemo is out of balance, keeping all the water back until people die of thirst. Gluskabe must figure out how to make the frog give up the water he is hoarding. It is literally a watershed moment for the people: the end of the water famine creates the Penobscot River and all its tributaries. It is also the time that establishes the family relationship between Penobscot people and the creatures of the river—turtles, fish, and frogs, whose names are to this day the clan names of the community.

A great magic moose (*ktəhɑnətəwi-mos*) has been harassing people and preventing their hunting near a big lake, and they ask for Gluskabe's help (*nsɑsək*, "eight"). He promises to hunt the moose for them. Before he can kill the moose, *pohkačinskʷehso*, "Jug-Woman," crosses his path. He views her as a distraction, and she is insulted because he refuses to acknowledge her. Many coastal landmarks are created from Gluskabe's chasing of, butchering, and eating the moose: snowshoe marks (*matakamassak*), moose buttocks (*mosihkačik*), moose guts, his stone dog near Castine, and his cooking kettle overturned to become Kineo, the mountain in Moosehead Lake.

Gluskabe's challenge in the lodge of Winter (*nóli*, "nine") is caused by extreme winter weather conditions, deep snow that even buries the trees. For the trip north to see Winter, Gluskabe requests that Monimkwehso make him six pairs of snowshoes—two each of moose hide, deer hide, and caribou hide. Winter mocks him mercilessly, repeating Gluskabe's own words. This emphasizes Winter's cruelty, maybe depicting the mercilessness of winter winds that throw human words back down our throats. Left for dead by Winter and thrown out the door of the lodge, Gluskabe survives because of his intrinsic power when spring thaws him. The lesson is not to succumb to a cruel adversary, and to believe in your own power to revive in better conditions and come back with a plan.

Foxes pick on Monimkwehso while Gluskabe is away (*matala*, "ten")—the big lesson is about respecting elders, and the bad fox behavior is to trick her, blind her, and impersonate her grandson for whom she waits so eagerly. When Gluskabe returns, he is able to remove her blindness with herbal medicine (*naya·č katahsihpilal*, "I will treat you with medicine"). Even better, Gluskabe kills all but one of the foxes, leaving one alive for Monimkwehso to take her revenge—he ties it to a tree, and Monimkwehso gets the satisfaction of beating it with switches and scolding it for being so mean to her. When she releases him, the only surviving fox takes with him the lesson that he should be very shy around people, and especially not to disrespect the very oldest of us. Abuse of elders cannot be tolerated in the Dawnland.

The story of Gluskabe going to visit his father (nəkʷətənkaw, "eleven") begins with his continuing sense of purpose to moderate and balance the weather for his descendants. He asks his grandmother for the location of Summer, which Grandmother tells him is heavily guarded. She also tells him he must visit his father who, she says mysteriously, has one eye. As the listener learns later, Gluskabe prepares for dangers to come when he asks his grandmother to make seven balls out of strips of rawhide; he can only do this because his inner sight or premonition tells him what he will need. The story may help listeners to imagine future challenges, needs, or dangers, and to create safeguards against them. Before he arrives at his father's village, Gluskabe removes one of his own eyes, perhaps to create an immediate connection with his one-eyed father. The worst threat in this story comes from Gluskabe's elder brothers, who are jealous on his arrival. They pose him a series of challenges—smoking a pipe, playing the dish game—designed to dominate him. But his father, with his one eye, recognizes that Gluskabe has great power (kamač ktəhánəto) and warns them not to act carelessly toward their brother.

As soon as he wins the dish game, Gluskabe joins a group of people there who are dancing (nisənkaw, "twelve"). People do not welcome him because he is a stranger—Gluskabe twists the nose off the one who gives him a rude gesture, and he turns the girls who ignore him into toads. The dancers surround a vessel containing Summer, which they guard closely; however, using his wishing power to create darkness, Gluskabe is able to take Summer and escape. A group of fierce crows pursue him—the wrapped rawhide balls made by Monimkwehso come in handy as decoy "heads" for the crows to carry away, one after another—but the crows turn back when Gluskabe reaches the land of Winter. He retrieves his snowshoes and tries to find his missing eye; he ends up taking it back from Horned Owl, who sees and hunts in the darkness. Gluskabe completes his purpose to balance the power of Winter in a confrontation with the old man who froze him earlier in his house of ice. Gluskabe treats the old man as heartlessly as the old man treated him when he froze, mocking his pleas for mercy but keeping Summer close until the old man and his ice house melt completely away.

Back home, Gluskabe and his grandmother Monimkwehso celebrate that there will never be such a severe winter (*nsɑnkaw*, "thirteen"). Some archaeologists, like William Haviland, believe this moment in the cycle is a commemoration of the end of the last ice age, when glaciers receded to the north and revealed the Dawnland. This marks the end of the work Gluskabe set out to do, but both he and Monimkwehso lay in provisions for future struggles of their people: Gluskabe makes arrowheads, and Monimkwehso makes *nimɑwan*, convenient, nourishing "lunches" that each person can carry easily. The ongoing connection between Gluskabe and his descendants happens when they tell stories about him. Gluskabe's laugh signifies his recognition of how connected the people continue to be: *eskʷa·tte nəmihkawitəhaməkok,* "still they remember me!"

MARGO LUKENS

University of Maine, 2021

## NOTES

PAGE

1 *connections . . . to stories of "the Norsemen"*: Leland, *The Algonquin Legends of New England,* v.

1 *"a rapidly perishing race"*: John D. Prince, introduction, in Leland and Prince, *Kulóskap the Master and Other Algonkin Poems,* 40.

2 *"to remove the fear"*: Nicolar, *The Life and Traditions of the Red Man,* 95.

2 *a good example from about 1887*: "The Scribe of the Penobscots Sends Us His Weekly Message," in Senier et al., eds., *Dawnland Voices,* 219–222.

2 *"the only large collection of Penobscot"*: Prince, "The Penobscot Language of Maine," 184.

3 *the mythology of their own "firstness"*: See particularly Senier et al., eds., *Dawnland Voices,* 2–5; and O'Brien, *Firsting and Lasting.*

6 *the production of* Transformer Tales: Stories of the Dawnland: Penobscot Nation, "Transformer Tales."

7 *an interview about the play at WERU radio*: Roeder et al., "The Production of *The Transformer Tales Play.*"

8   *"Men, women, and children alike made"*: Kolodny, "A Summary History of the Penobscot Nation," 18–19.

8   *It was hard to find work in the Old Town mills*: Kolodny, "A Summary History of the Penobscot Nation," 19–21.

8   *traditional lifeways subject to taxes*: Speck, *Penobscot Man*, 302–303.

8   *"cut off from their ancient sources of subsistence"*: Kolodny, "A Summary History of the Penobscot Nation," 22.

9   *at least forty children from the Penobscot community*: Kolodny, "A Summary History of the Penobscot Nation," 19–20.

9   *"non-use of English" was widespread among the women*: Speck, *Penobscot Man*, 305, 4.

10  *"from 1914 to 1918 . . . attention was focused upon the recording of myth texts"*: Speck, *Penobscot Man*, 4.

10  *"Birch Stream, Milford, Me"*: Not to be confused with a larger stream by the same name that flows into the Penobscot River from the west, near Alton, Maine.

11  *"tundra-like conditions"*: Haviland, "Local Indians and the End of the Last Ice Age."

# Editing Principles and Design Choices, Transcription, and Translation

## Editing Principles and Design Choices

Our focus in making this book has been accessibility—in its transcriptions, in its translations, and in its layout/visual presentation. The Transformer Tales have technically been accessible to the Penobscot community since their 1918 publication, and indeed they have been circulated among Penobscots in print/photocopy/PDF form, especially in recent years. But the material itself, as well as a later in-depth grammatical analysis (Voorhis, *Grammatical Notes on the Penobscot Language*), was published by linguists for other linguists.

Even for linguists, the original text is challenging: it uses a very early twentieth-century Americanist transcription system—one different from the modern standard International Phonetic Alphabet, and different still from the spelling system designed by Frank T. Siebert, Jr., that has been officially adopted by the Penobscot Nation and broadly used in current learning materials and the *Penobscot Dictionary*.

The original publication layout is visually dense: it uses an interlinear translation followed by free-translation format that is familiar to most linguists, but its small print bristling with phonetic diacritics is still challenging to navigate, and even more so for the would-be everyday reader.

For beginners/learners in particular, we also recognize that a single polysynthetic verb (often with associated particles, etc.) is already a mass of information to grapple with. We first considered a layout with just one verb-based phrase (sometimes more, if two verbs are tightly linked) per left-hand page, with a right-hand page containing an English free translation facing it. This may yet be used in the future to present individual stories as standalone works aimed at young readers.

Here, however, space considerations have made us choose the next best option: presenting the language in units made of brief sentences or even clauses, with direct translations for each, and word-by-word breakdowns immediately below. Through this, the reader can still engage with the stories in digestible chunks, in a layout that does not visually ask them to move on to the next chunk until they are ready.

Toward this same goal of extreme simplicity/readability, we have not attempted to include the original 1918 text, which is already readily available to interested researchers. Original-text transcriptions are usually cited only as retranscriptions into the current standard Penobscot writing system form that they most directly suggest (see the Technical Notes for examples), to simplify discussions where the final transcription choice is uncertain or needs other explanation. Also toward simplicity and long-term access, citations here from the *Penobscot Dictionary* (and likewise the online *Passamaquoddy-Maliseet Dictionary*) are from the headword unless otherwise noted, as its most current manuscript is still in digital form with no fixed pagination. Material from the *Penobscot Legends* digital manuscript is similarly cited by story title only (Penobscot Nation, *Penobscot Legends*). Dictionaries from Sébastien Rasles (Dictionary of the Abenaki Indian Language), Joseph Aubery (*Father Aubery's French-Abenaki Dictionary*), and Gordon Day (*Western Abenaki Dictionary*) are cited by page number; all other citations are given in full form.

As a major audience here is young readers, we have chosen a raised dot · as the visually least obtrusive way to mark clitics, for example, *nə·* rather than the standard *nə=*. The casual academic reader might easily confuse this with the raised dot used by early Americanist and much Algonquianist work to mark vowel/consonant length, that is, what Frank G. Speck himself employed in the 1918 text. Since scholars of this era of linguistic documentation are used to adapting to idiosyncratic differences in transcription norms, we hope this slightly tricky but practically motivated departure will be understood. For explanations of the small-caps forms used with the raised dot, beyond those like ·WILL and ·WOULD, which generally mean what those English glosses suggest, and especially those like ·KA and ·EHT, which we have kept in Penobscot, see the Reader Guide to the Penobscot Language: Patterns of Relation.

As a perhaps more radical step on behalf of Penobscot-language learners, our policy has been to normalize most still-uncertain transcriptions in the main text to match our current understanding of the language, but also to carefully note each such case in the Technical Notes so that these questions are not silently elided and stay accessible to the interested researcher.

Also in this line, after each text we provide only a minimum of Reader Notes that address points needed for general-reader understanding; then, at the end of the book itself, we offer a set of more in-depth Technical Notes, arranged by story title. We do not attempt to reproduce all of the notes found in the 1918 version (some are questionable and/or quite dated) and include only those thought most helpful toward immediately understanding the text.

The 1918 version numbers each story and offers English-language titles for each but gives no Penobscot-language equivalents. Instead of attempting to create new Penobscot-language titles, we have simply used the Penobscot words for the number of each text. Our motivation here is that children in particular will be able to learn these numbers for their own sake and also use them as a simple and consistent way for complete beginners to refer to these stories in Penobscot itself. Note here that Penobscot has two expressions for 'five': *nan* is shared with most of the language's immediate neighbors, while *palenəskʷ*, literally 'one side of (a pair of) hands', is shared with Caniba and a few more distant relatives.

Overall, our aim here has been to offer the texts in a form that does not require the audience to assimilate to and internalize traditional academic-linguist norms. Instead, we have tried to give readers a clean, simple, and fairly minimalist presentation so that they can more easily build their own relationships with traditional Penobscot-language literature.

## Transcription

The texts here were originally created as retranscriptions of the 1918 publication version; they have now also been checked against Speck's original handwritten field notebook notes (Speck, Penobscot Texts). In both sources, sentence/clause breaks are not always clearly indicated (or justified). Ours are provisional, and we have erred on the side of adding periods and commas to make it easier for younger readers, especially for reading and performing aloud. In several cases it is not certain whether a word/phrase should be interpreted as belonging to the end of one clause or the beginning of the next. We usually follow the 1918 version translation in these instances. Very uncertain/unidentifiable forms are indicated by [?].

Transcription here generally follows the official writing system adopted by the Penobscot Nation. Designed by Frank T. Siebert, Jr., and used in his extensive documentation and analysis of the language, this appears to accurately represent the sounds of spoken Penobscot as we currently understand them, based on a critical appraisal of his work and other sources, especially the small set of audio recordings of first-language speakers. Unlike Siebert, we only mark accent on those forms where we have reason to think they do not follow the general pattern (subject to certain principled exceptions) of high pitch on the third-from-last "full" vowel (see Reader Guide to the Penobscot Language: Sounds, below). Siebert's low-pitch accent is also broadly predictable as what occurs on the first syllable (or often second, if the first vowel is a schwa) of words not meeting the above pattern and thus is likewise left unmarked.

We choose to write accents only minimally (and also in direct citations of Siebert's work) in large part because Speck's own transcription of pitch-accent is highly variable and not consistently reliable. Because our current model of accentuation in Penobscot still has many details to be worked out, we would rather leave the text here underspecified in this way and provide only the generalizations above, instead of adding a large set of newly created accent-marking that is not directly in or necessarily implied by the original text.

We do, however, generally follow Siebert in "overtranscribing" possible cases of /h/ followed by two consonants, for example, *kati-mehtkamike* 'it is going to be the end of the world', rather than the *kati-metkamike* more directly suggested by the 1918 text. It is still uncertain whether Penobscot generally uses such sound sequences, or if some speakers do and others do not. These kinds of sequences are solidly attested for fellow Eastern Algonquian languages like Munsee (as well as unrelated but closely neighboring languages like Kanien'kéha/Mohawk), even as Passamaquoddy-Maliseet, a language historically also spoken by many Penobscot speakers, does not allow them. Siebert did not originally transcribe them—which is unsurprising, since they would be probably the hardest feature of Penobscot for an English-based non-native speaker to detect reliably—but his later claim that they exist (and consequent transcription updates) might also just have been motivated by a fixed assumption that in Penobscot—but unlike in Passamaquoddy-Maliseet—morphemes with original /h/ + consonant do not lose that /h/ when (typically through vowel deletion) a further consonant follows. Our approach has been to restore potential /h/ of this kind, thinking it better to have a possibly spurious /h/ that can be omitted later, rather than leave it out, which would make it nearly impossible for future learners, teachers, and researchers to be aware of the issue at all for the relevant wordforms.

To his credit, Speck's early transcriptions, messy and glitchy as they sometimes are, also preserve valuable variations and phonetic details that are often lost in Siebert's heavily normalized/regularized transcriptions. Siebert at one point edited the common reductions and contractions of *ni·, nə·, n·* 'then', all to *ni*, and only later began to restore the originally documented forms. Speck in contrast appears to have always transcribed them directly, along with other comparable cases; for example his transcriptions reflect common elision phenomena like those seen in forms suggesting *kəyahč* as the collocation of *kəya* 'you' and *·ahč* 'also, too', and so on. Therefore, overall he gives us a much more direct sense of the actual surface-phonetic flow of the language.

A particular challenge here is that the /ɑ/ vowel is generally recorded by Siebert as non-nasal—as confirmed by audio recordings of several of the speakers he worked with. But Speck very frequently (though by no means consistently) noted it in Lyon's speech (and others) as nasal. This fits with early missionary documentation of the Kennebec Valley language (Caniba) to the immediate west, and with the well-established facts of the Western Abenaki and southern New England Algonquian languages as well—and also with one very early twentieth-century audio recording (on an aluminum disk) of what is unquestionably Penobscot speech, which also shows a clear, strong nasalization of this vowel.

In shifting to Siebert-based spelling, these kinds of variations are essentially silenced. Here and in the Technical Notes we try to address these silences, to help readers recover Newell Lyon's own speech as closely as possible to what he and Speck together recorded.

As is discussed in the Reader Guide to the Penobscot Language: Sounds, below, Penobscot does not fundamentally distinguish /b/ from /p/, /d/ from /t/, /g/ from /k/, and so on. The same single sound can come out as [b] or [p] (etc.) depending on the sounds next to it, and Speck transcribes using "b" or "p" accordingly. His practice is much easier for the English-based reader, and we at one point considered providing in each breakdown an additional line using a more English-familiar transcription with "b," "d," "g," and so on, along with more English-type spelling strategies for the vowels. This, however, would double the editorial work and make the breakdowns much more visually dense. And so we have somewhat reluctantly used only the official transcription system, trusting that readers will be able to work through and follow the explanation in the Sounds guide provided here. This is a thorny problem and not an easy choice, and we should note that the question of using a PTK-only kind of spelling versus a PTK + BDG-type spelling is not a problem of Penobscot itself but of the often unquestioned features of the European alphabetic tradition. The Penobscot spoken sound system follows a common and natural pattern that simply does not fit easily within the fundamental expectations of the Roman alphabet.

Speck's transcriptions show a variety of recurrent problems, mainly involving the sound contrasts that are most difficult for an English-based non-native-speaker transcriber. We therefore frequently restore cases of missing /h/ before a consonant, especially before /s/, and of consonants that either should be geminate or should not. Beyond this, Speck's most common problems are with vowels. In particular, while he is clearly aware of the distinct /a/, /α/, and /ə/ vowels, his transcriptions do not distinguish them reliably or accurately. Where needed, we restore them based on Siebert's transcriptions and/or sound-correspondences with related languages, and note cases where these emendations are still provisional.

Speck's unreliability regarding the /α a ə/ contrast is a particular problem in his four transcriptions of /-pa/ rather than the expected /-pα/ for the 'you (pl.)' Indicative endings, that is, he gives forms suggesting *kənəkkαnepa·č* (story 2), *kənəkkαne-pa* (story 3), *kəpəmαwəsolətipa* (story 3), *kkisi-nəpahkatawippa* (story 10), and *kənihlipa* (story 10). These may just be simple mishearings, or one or more such mishearings then led Speck to generalize /-pa/ as the form for this ending against an actual /-pα/. Alternatively, the ending may genuinely be /-pa/, as this is the historically more conservative form, attested in Western Abenaki and Caniba among others— while modern Penobscot (like Passamaquoddy-Maliseet and Mi'kmaw) have leveled out the vowel in favor of their reflex of Proto-Eastern Algonquian *ā, hence /-pα/

in Siebert's transcriptions. Since Lyon uses several other forms that appear to be distinctively shared with speech communities to the west of the Penobscot River, the /-pa/ possibility cannot be wholly ruled out. Here, as usual, we have edited to normalized -pα and again noted these cases individually.

More unexpectedly, Speck also often conflated /e/ and /i/, giving for example *ehkʷtahe*, literally 'stop beating him/her/them' (story 10), where the context can only support *ehkʷtahi* 'stop beating me'. Speck also sometimes struggled with the /kʷ/ versus /k/ contrast, not only word/syllable-finally, as one might expect, but occasionally even word-internally. We see this in his apparent hypercorrection of *mosolakəsəyal* 'moose guts' as *mosolakʷəsəyal*, *wəlakəsəyal* 'guts' as *wəlakʷəsəyal* (story 8), and several other forms. Genuine variation between /kʷ/ and /k/ seems to be vanishingly rare in Penobscot, and so we amend accordingly.

Perhaps the most vexing problem in Speck's materials is his treatment of word-initial /wə-/, both as a sound in general and as the common third-person element *wə-*. Words already beginning with /wə-/ contract with third-person *wə-* to form initial /o-/, a sequence otherwise rare in lexical items (*otene* 'town' is the only particularly common case). Speck seems to conflate initial /wə-/ and /o-/ in transcription, mainly as "u" or "wu", leading to some cases of uncertainty as to whether or not we are looking at the bare stem beginning with /wə-/ or its third-person possessed form beginning with /o-/, for example, *wətamαkanal* 'pipe (obviative)' versus *otamαkanal* 'his/her pipe (obviative)' (story 11). It should be noted that the sequence of *nə·* 'then; there; that (NI)' with word-initial /wə/ (mainly third-person *wə-*) is generally recorded by Speck as /nu/ or /no/. This highly frequent fusion is a point never noted in Siebert's documentation but is confirmed by audio recordings of speakers like Arthur Neptune, where this sequence indeed sounds like /no/. We represent this common form consistently and uniquely as *n·wə-*.

A further problem is presented by *wə-*. Before labials /w, m, p, kʷ/, *wə-* historically reduced to *ə-*, which then by a later general sound change became *a-*. Subsequently, however, the *wə-~a-* alternation seems to have become reshaped and/or variable, such that in more recently documented Penobscot, *wə-* itself again appears before labials in many cases. Lyon's stories show unquestionable examples of the original *a-* pattern (e.g., *amǝskamǝn* 'he found it') but also numerous cases of *wə-* before labials, for example, *wəmačin* '(then) he started off'. Occasionally we even see both options on the same stems, for example, with /m/: *wəmoskǝnan* '(then) he brought it out' (story 11) versus *amoskǝnan* '(then) he brought it out' (story 12), and *amǝskamǝn* 'he found it' (stories 7 and 8) versus *ahtɑmɑ wəmǝskamowǝn* 'he didn't find it at all' (story 12). However, many instances of expected *wə-* (or alternatively *a-*) before /w, m, p, kʷ/ are absent. It is not clear if this represents genuine variation within Lyon's speech or is simply based on Speck missing the very weak *wə-* before labials, a not unexpected possibility.

The most common case of this involves the stem *wikǝwɑm* 'house', which complicates the issue further: in Penobscot sources overall, it apparently can appear either with its initial /w-/ alternating as the pronominal marker itself (*nikǝwɑm* 'my house', *kikǝwɑm* 'your house', *wikǝwɑm* 'her/his house'), or, much less commonly, with that marker before it, that is, *nǝwikǝwɑm*, *kǝwikǝwɑm*, and *awikǝwɑm*/*\*wǝwikǝwɑm*. While *awikǝwɑm* and so on are attested, it is not clear if *\*wǝwikǝwɑm* and related forms exist at all. In these texts, Speck gives the form *awikǝwɑmǝwɑk* 'to their house' three times but also *wikǝwɑmǝwɑk* four times; however, in all of the published Lyon texts, we only find forms based on *nikǝwɑm* and *kikǝwɑm*, not *nǝwikǝwɑm* or *kǝwikǝwɑm*. In this volume we leave *wikǝwɑmǝwɑk*-type forms as is, assuming the *w-* is in fact the possessor marker, with the distribution of the *a-w-* variant still unexplained. The stem *wičəye-* '(fellow) brother' is similar, though it attests *w-* and *a-w-* variants only (see story 11 for both), with no known instances of *\*nǝwičəye* or *\*kǝwičəye*. So for these two particular stems we leave as is any forms that were transcribed with simple initial /w/.

There is very little evidence for any *wə-* before /w/ in Penobscot, though it appears to be attested for Western Abenaki. *Penobscot Legends* gives one instance of *wihkʷínɑkʷəsin* '[so] he was comical' (*wanɑkəmehsəwak*, story 1) that could notionally be a /wəw/ misheard as /w/, but also has *awihkʷínɑkʷəsin* '[cause] him to be a laughingstock' (*kəloskɑpe nɑkɑ kči-mɑčihlehso*). An isolated and uncertain instance of apparent /wə-w/ is the 1918 version (195) and original notes transcription /uwiʹgwomuk/ 'to his wigwam' (= this volume's [*mɑlam·te*] *wikəwɑmək* '[finally] at his house', story 4)—even as the same text also has simple /wiʹgwomuk/ 'to his wigwam' (= this volume's [*n·wəmɑčin*] *wikəwɑmək* '[(then) he started off] to his house', story 4). We have elected to level this one questionable case to the simple *w-* form.

We do not yet have a full clear story for this variation but do want to provide a consistent pattern for learners, and so the policy here is to represent expected *wə-* as (*a-*) before /w/, and as restored *wə-* elsewhere. (See the 1918 version for original forms with absent *wə-*.) Since we do not have a clear sense of what determines *a/wə-* alternations even where we see them (like *wəmoskɑnɑn* versus *amoskɑnɑn* above, etc.), this choice is provisional. In this volume, (*a-*) restoration applies specifically to some stems with the following initial elements:

| | |
|---|---|
| *wew-* | 'know(n)' |
| *wihkʷ-* | 'pull in/toward self; funny' |
| *wit-* | 'together with others' |
| *wiwən-* | '(circling) around' |

This applies only to about ten forms, primarily those using *wihkʷ-*.

A further issue involving initial sonorant + schwa sequences is the transcription of apparent *nəkʷasəpem* 'lake', where Siebert attests *məkʷasəpem*. Philip S. LeSourd, discussing the many attestations of an apparent reduced form *kʷasəpem*, suggests that "it would not be surprising if speakers who routinely dropped the first syllable of *mə̀kʷasəpem* went astray when they attempted to restore it, thus introducing alternative forms of this noun" (LeSourd, "The Passamaquoddy 'Witchcraft Tales,'" 489). This is a solid possibility. One other option involves the fact that word-initial nasal + sonorant often realizes in Penobscot as a syllabic nasal. So it is possible that Speck heard the syllabic nasal in /m̩kʷasəpem/ as a placeless nasal before /kʷ/ and then restored it as /nə/. Lyon himself (and other speakers) could in principle have done the same. Rasles offers a further form, *pek8âsebem* 'lac' (477), where *-8â-* is probably a typo for *-ð̂a-*, which does appear in *messi8ikki pekð̂asebémar añmañgânð̂ar* 'Il y a pêsche dans tous les lacs [= there is fishing in all the lakes]' (505). Together with Aubery's very similar *pék8azebem* [*sic*] 'lac' (332), this suggests a form *pkʷasəpem*, from a putative schwa-deleted preform *\*mkʷasəpem*, with the sporadic devoicing of the /m/ to /p/ in such clusters that also gives rise to *pkʷami* 'ice', from a Proto-Algonquian form in *\*/m-/*. In the face of this uncertainty, we normalize to *məkʷasəpem* and note accordingly.

Speck also seemed to have frequent problems hearing word-final consonants. This in turn seems to have fed some overgeneralizations/hypercorrections of certain grammatical forms. Most notable of these are his recurrent transcriptions suggesting *kohsəssənawa* 'our (incl.) descendants (obviative pl.)' or 'our (incl.) descendant (absentative singular)', where the context strongly suggests or indeed can only fit a simple *kohsəssənawak* 'our descendants'. We find a comparable example of this with *namehsa* for expected *namehsak* 'fish (pl.)' (story 3), and a strong suggestion that this is merely perceptual error in the entirely unexpected and unmotivated form *peməkisəka* for *peməkisəkahk* 'today' (story 13).

Issues with final /-k/ may in some way be tied to a set of unexpected mismatches in grammatical form, all found in story 11. Here, where an obviative plural is expected, we instead see apparent proximate plural forms *mosewayiyαk* 'ones made of moose-pelt' and *nolkewayiyαk* 'ones made of deer-pelt', and apparent proximate singular *makαlipəwayiye* 'one made of caribou-pelt':

*mαlam wəmehtkawα nisαkəmakəsəwa mosewayiyαk*
'eventually he wore out two pairs of moose-pelt snowshoes'

*mαlam mina wəmehtkawα nolkewayiyαk.*
'eventually again he wore out the deer-pelt ones'

*mαlam wəmehtkawα nəkʷətakəmakəsəwa makαlipəwayiye*
'eventually he wore out one pair of snowshoes of the caribou-pelt'

Oddly enough, however, we have not yet located in any Penobscot documentation any obviative plural forms, predicted to be *-iyα*. These apparent mismatches may be explainable as Lyon treating them as separate standalone elements: an appositive, an afterthought, or a consequence of fragmentary dictation. It is also possible that Speck miscorrected these to *-iyαk* and *-iye* based on he himself being uncertain about the presence or absence of a final /-k/ in other cases in the language, and/or overgeneralization of these patterns. (For a form that does not involve the obviative but does at least show agreement between two similar nominal elements, compare retranscribed Passamaquoddy *naka ktoliyan kmaksonok oposiyeyak* 'and you make [your] wooden shoes' (Prince, "A Passamaquoddy Aviator," 629), with *oposiyeyak* '[ones] of wood [prox. pl.]' matching *kmaksonok* 'your shoes'.)

Similarly, the 1918 version suggests *tepapo kči-pkənačo* for 'it was sitting inside a great bark container' (story 12), where the expected form is locative *kči-pkənačok* 'in a great bark container', rather than the unmarked stem. If Speck simply missed the final /-k/, this makes sense. We similarly find at least one instance of an entire missing locative syllable, that is, the 1918 version *pečihlɑt kčī-nəkʷasəpem* for 'when he got to a greeeat big lake' (story 8), which we normalize to locative *pečihlɑt kčī-məkʷasəpemək*. An important but less certain case is *mosihkɑči* 'Moose Rump' (story 8), a placename attested in the Andrew Dana versions of this story (see story 8 notes for details on these) as a locative *mosihkɑčik*, for example, as in the *Penobscot Legends* account's *ni·č nihkʷɑp, owa·tahk wačo nətəli-wihlɑ, mosihkɑčik* 'So now I shall name this mountain "At the Moose Rump"' (*kəloskɑpe nɑkɑ mos*). The context in Lyon's version is a similar naming context: *nihkʷɑp ali-wihtɑso mosihkɑči* 'Now it is called Moose Rump'. Since it is not explicitly a target of motion or location of position, it is hard to be certain that a locative would be absolutely necessary, but given Andrew Dana's usage and with Speck's established kinds of mishearings, the possibility that Lyon too said *mosihkɑčik* here cannot be readily ruled out.

One case shows a possible conflation of /-t/ and /-k/: *etali-pənahpskʷihlɑt* 'where it [dog] turned to stone' (story 8). The 1918 version suggests *etali-pənahpskʷihlɑk* 'where it [NI] turned to stone', which does not fit with *aləmoss* 'dog': the NA form *etali-pənahpskʷihlɑt* would be needed instead. Here Speck may simply have overgeneralized the previous *etali-pənahpskʷihlɑk*, referring to the NI guts, to this second transformation event. A final /-t/ is also apparently misheard as /-č/ in the 1918 version *pɑnihlɑč* for *tɑmɑ pɑnihlɑt* 'wherever she came to an opening' (story 8).

Speck also appears to be missing the final /-n/ in at least two Subordinative forms that would require it: *wətakʷečilɑkʷanewi* for *wətakʷečilɑkʷanewin* '(then) he tried moving his wings' (story 4) and *nə·kətɑtalahsimi* for *nə·kətɑtalahsimin* 'then you rest' (story 4), as well as *kənɑkkɑ-kəmotənɑmi* for possible secondary object form *kənɑkkɑ-kəmotənɑmin* 'you stole (it) all from me' (story 5)—these last two both occurring before a word-initial /n-/.

We see possible instances of grammatical leveling that may either be genuinely from Lyon or from Speck overgeneralizing. One possible case is *nipənal* 'Summer (obviative)' (story 12), where we might expect a form from an original NI verbal stem to use -*ol* as the variant of -*al* 'NI plural; obviative singular'. However, the *Penobscot Dictionary* gives *nìpənal*, *pàponal*, and *sìkʷanal* as the ordinary NI plurals of 'summer', 'winter', and 'spring', so this leveling may be established. In contrast, the 1918 version form suggesting *manalœmsənal* 'they (NI) are blown off by the wind' (story 4) is somewhat more likely a Speck transcription error, since we do find at least one comparable verbal form *kisikənol* 'they had grown', using -*ol* rather than -*al* (compare also Bécancour Abenaki *kəsəlœmsənol* 'the Wind [obviative]' (retranscribed from Speck, "Wawenock Myth Texts from Maine," 181), and so this we have amended in the main text.

**Translation**

In our new translation, made directly from the Penobscot text, we have worked to maintain a consistent translation of the same/similar forms wherever feasible, in order to help learners pick up on their meanings more directly. Also toward helping learners internalize Penobscot ways of expression, we have leaned in the direction of making the English conform to the literal Penobscot, even if this works out as slightly awkward English. Unlike Speck and Siebert, we have actively avoided using obscure, archaic, or high-register English in the pursuit of precise direct translation, again for the benefit of younger learners in particular.

Wherever the Penobscot forms were ambiguous for English translations—particularly for "she" versus "he" gender, which is not expressed in Penobscot and is only recoverable if other context (like kinship terms or other explicitly gendered terms like *winehsohs* 'old woman' and *mlohsəss* 'old man') provides that information—we have followed the 1918 version.

In the word-glosses, we have generally translated narrative-chaining Subordinative forms as '(then) . . .' or '(so) . . .' but omitted this if the phrase already includes an explicit 'then', 'and', 'so', or a comparable element. We have also consistently used '(group) ...' to highlight the special set of stem-formations that seem to imply an explicitly group-plural reading. The standard analysis for Eastern Algonquian languages with this morphology is that corresponding plain stems with nonsingular markings read as duals, while these special stems then read as (more-than-dual) plural. However, numerous cases of simple plain stems with necessarily more-than-dual readings occur. Chiefly these are stems whose semantics already imply more-than-dual participants—for example, stems meaning 'congregate', 'live as a village', and so on, or ones including more-than-two numerals or other quantificational elements—but not all observed exceptions to the standard analysis can be explained this way, so we remain agnostic as to what the actual semantic contrast may be.

The 1918 free translation texts (which follow each interlinear Penobscot-English translation) occasionally telescope or omit parts of the original Penobscot; here we have attempted to maintain as close to a word-for-word translation as possible.

To facilitate access to as broad an audience as possible, we intentionally avoid using technical terms in the Reader Notes and Reader Guides, but in the Technical Notes (and in this portion of the introduction) familiarity with general and Algonquian-specific linguistic terms is presupposed. We have however chosen to capitalize "Indicative," "Subordinative," "Independent," "Conjunct," and "Imperative" (as well as "Direct" and "Inverse") to draw the general linguist reader's attention to these terms' rather particular uses within Algonquian linguistics. (For the terms "NA" and "NI," see the Reader Guide to the Penobscot Language: Patterns of Relation, below.) All other technical terms remain lowercase.

# Reader Guide to the Penobscot Language
## *Patterns of Relation*

The Penobscot language is all about relations. For families wanting to help children to learn their language, getting familiar with just the few simple patterns described below, which show some key everyday relations, can help beginners recognize and understand those relations throughout all the stories. (Note: here expressions not from the stories are created as explanatory examples; they are based on but not directly from native-speaker sources.)

• Knowing just these two basic phrases,

|  |  |
|---|---|
| awen na? | 'Who is that?' |
| kek$^w$ ni? | 'What is that?' |

beginners can recognize not just WHO and WHAT, but also how 'that' is a different word depending on if it refers to people (*na*) or things (*ni*). Everything in Penobscot is either a NA-word or a NI-word: the two questions above are one of the easiest ways for beginners to learn this. (Here we name these patterns using words from the language itself, instead of confusing and often outdated or even inaccurate technical terms.)

We can see that the word for 'this' also has a NA-version, *owa* (vs. NI-version *iyo*), when Gluskabe asks his grandmother about the bear he has killed:

|  |  |
|---|---|
| awen owa? | 'Who is this?' |

Penobscot (like other Wabanaki languages) relates differently to animals, asking 'Who is this?' to identify an animal, unlike English 'What is this?'.

• Asking about a family relation also uses *na* 'that (NA/person)' and shows two new relations: *kikawəss* '*your* mother' and *nikawəss* '*my* mother':

kəya na kikawəss?      —αhα, nəya na nikawəss.
'Is that *your* mother?'      '—Yes, that is *my* mother.'

The pattern *nikawəss* '*my* mother', shows up often in the stories, as in:

nohkəməss '*my* grandmother'   nkʷenəss '*my* grandchild'

• This pattern of *kikawəss*, talking about YOU, versus *nikawəss*, talking about ME, happens again as

kolitəhαsi?      —αhα, nolitəhαsi.
'*You* are happy?'      '—Yes, *I* am happy.'

And we see this all coming together in just one phrase from Gluskabe:

kolαme, nohkəmi . . .      'You're right, *my* grandmother . . .'

Notice here with *nohkəmi* '(o) *my* grandmother!' (and *nəmohsomi* '(o) *my* grandfather!' etc.), the stories also show learners the traditional ways younger people address their elders.

• An essential pattern for Penobscot stories can be learned from a simple WHY question:

kekʷ weči-wəlitəhasəyan?          —_____, ni weči-wəlitəhasəya.
'Why are *you* happy?'          '—_____, that's why *I* am happy.'

This pattern picks out one *part* of the event, the reason WHY, and focuses on it, as opposed to the *kolitəhasi/nolitəhasi* '*you* are happy/*I* am happy' pattern above, which just talks about the *whole* event. Penobscot speakers can use this -wəlitəhasəyan/-wəlitəhasəya pattern to focus on/talk about other *parts* of an event, like WHO, WHAT, WHERE, or, very often, the time/WHEN, as in:

tɑn kʷenɑwəsəyan          'for however long *you* live'
eləmɑwəsəyan          'as *you* go on living'
etoči-talilǝkʷanewəyan          'at whichever point *you* move your wings'

Readers will very often see in the stories this exact pattern as used for NA, NI, and 'them':

pečohset          'when *he* (= NA) arrived (walking)'
etoči-wəlitəhɑsit          '*she* (= NA) was so happy'
etali-pənahpskʷihlɑk          'where *it* (= canoe = NI) turned to stone'
weči·č-kisɑwəsihǝtit          'so that *they* will be able to live'

• The simple relation of giving—and especially showing who you are giving it to—is possibly the central language pattern of Penobscot:

mili̇          'give *me* it'
mile          'give *her* it'

In the stories, we can see the *mili* pattern here:

| | |
|---|---|
| alihtawi | 'make *me* it' |
| kinɑkʷ·əka mili skaniminal | 'at least give *me* seeds' |
| tepat ehkʷtahi | 'so stop hitting *me*' |

• This pattern is central because, knowing just these four words related to *mili* and *mile*, a beginner can understand most relations in the language:

| | |
|---|---|
| kəmilin | 'you give *me* it'   (like *mili*) |
| kəmiləlǝn | 'I give *you* it' |
| kəmilɑn | 'you give *her* it'   (like *mile*) |
| kəmiləkon | 'she gives *you* it' |

For example, with the last two words above, a simple switch that follows the same relation as *kikawəss* for YOU versus *nikawəss* for ME shows exactly the same change of meaning here:

| | |
|---|---|
| nəmilɑn | '*I* give her it' |
| nəmiləkon | 'she gives *me* it' |

The *-n* at the end of all of these words expresses the 'it', the thing given. Without 'it', the rest of the relations are still the same, as in these examples from the stories:

| | |
|---|---|
| mina·tte·č kənamihi | 'You will see *me* again' |
| nəya·č kəwičohkeməl | 'I will help *you*' |

nəkati-namihα pəpon          'I want to see [*him*=] Winter'

nəmihkawitəhaməkok         'they remember *me*'

• Asking about *kikawəss* 'your mother' versus *nikawəss* 'my mother' has a simple pattern. As soon as we ask about someone else's mother—whose mother, her mother, and so on—an extra relation comes in:

awen *nilil* wikawəss*al*?      —sosehp *nilil* wikawəss*al*.

'Whose mother is that?'      '—That is Joe's mother.'

Instead of *na* 'that (NA)', Penobscot here uses *nilil* 'that (NA) in-relation-to . . .'. This *nilil* is matched by the ending in *wikawəssal* 'his/her mother'. What *nilil* means here is easiest to understand by comparing it with regular *na* 'that (NA)':

awen na?                   —sosehp na.

'Who is that?'           '—That is Joe.'

awen nilil?                 —sosehp nilil.

'Who is that [person in-relation-to]?'   '—That is Joe's [relation].'

Here *na* talks directly about that person; *nilil* talks about that person as in-relation-to someone, that is, in-relation-to the main person we are talking about (here: Joe). The relation could be an actual family relation, like *wikawəssal* 'her mother', *wkʷenəssal* 'her grandchild', and so on. Or, as this example from the stories shows, just being the other participant in the event (SAY), the fox here is in-relation-to Gluskabe:

nə·kəloskαpe wətihlαn kʷαkʷsəss*al*     'Then Gluskabe said to the [NILIL] fox . . .'

The *nilil* pattern shows us that at this point the main person is Gluskabe and the fox is only here in-relation-to him, as the one to whom he is talking.

For more than one person, *nihi* 'those (NA) in-relation-to' is used and again matched with the ending in *wəničana* 'her/his kids':

awen *nihi* wəničana?          —sosehp *nihi* wəničana.
'Whose kids are those?'        '—Those are Joe's kids.'

And again the stories show us the same thing:

wətihlαn awaassα . . .          '(then) he [= NA = Gluskabe] told the [NIHI] animals . . .'

Only NA-words use the *nilil/nihi* 'in-relation-to' pattern. NI-words do not. And in fact, if the *nilil* pattern is used with a NI-word, it does not mean 'in-relation-to' but just 'more than one': *ni sipo* 'that river' versus *nilil sipəwal* 'those rivers'. (This is one reason why knowing whether a word is NA or NI is so important in the language.) The *nilil/nihi* pattern—this special attention to relation(s)—is, as far as we know, not clearly found in any languages of the world except Penobscot and its fellow Algonquian languages.

• Penobscot also shows relations between events, using a pattern we have already seen. So from these two phrases we can see that the *-n* refers to 'it' or 'that'—the thing given:

kəmilin          'you give me it'
kəmilin ni       'you give me [it =] that'

The word *ni* 'that (NI)' can also refer to 'that place' (= 'there') or 'that time' (= 'then').

With the meaning 'then', it is said either as *ni* or as a shortened/reduced version *n(ə)·*, and used to connect the event to the ones before:

nə·monimkʷehso wətihlɑn . . .   '*then* Woodchuck said to him . . .'
nə·kɑloskɑpe oči-mɑčin.        '*Then* Gluskabe started off from there.'

As we saw above, when *ni/n(ə)·* is used, it is almost always matched with the *-n* that refers to it. So 'and then . . .' in Penobscot is usually *ni . . .-n*. Speakers often just use the *-n* without even the *ni/n(ə)·*, making the connection/relation between events still understood. This pattern is the most basic connector/linker in Penobscot story-telling.

• Also key to Penobscot storytelling is a small set of words that usually tuck in after the first word of a phrase. Storytellers use these to show their own relation to the event, or to help the listener more clearly relate to it. Some examples—all from the stories, except *·akʷa*, which shows something the speaker has only heard from others: it is generally common in Penobscot literature but unexpectedly rare in Lyon's tellings—are these:

nohkəmi, ɑtɑ·ka nəya kʷɑkʷsəss!        [·ka = established topic/'it's . . .']
'My grandmother, I am not a fox!'

tɑn·ɑskʷe eyit nipən?                  [·ɑskʷe = new/changed topic]
'Where (*however*) is the Summer?'

nihkʷɑp·əkahk . . .                    [·əkahk = contrasting topic]
'this time [*unlike before*] . . .'

yo·tahk ksenɑkan . . .                 [·ətahk = presenting a new topic]
'here was a weir . . .'

eskʷa nihkʷαp·te . . .                                    [·(t)te = intensifies meaning]
'still even *right* now . . .'

n(i)·akʷa . . .                                           [·akʷa = hearsay information]
'so *it is said* . . .'

ni·tt'·*eht* nəya nəkawinessa.                            [·eht = shows uncertainty]
'so *I guess* I must have been asleep'

These words are often not translated directly or at all into English versions of the stories. In the original Penobscot, however, storytellers use them constantly to carefully and clearly set up the speaker's and the listener's relations to the events of the story.

• The example here shows one other key way speakers relate to the events. The ending shows that the speaker did not directly witness the past event—they were not there or not awake/aware when it happened—and so can only suggest it:

nəkawines*sa*                                            'so I must have been asleep'

When a speaker does feel a direct relation to the past event—they were there when it happened, and so on—a different ending is used:

nəya·č mina kəpətəkohsaləl epəyanəpan     'I will walk you back again to where you (had) sat'

• One final feature of Penobscot that can help learners is knowing that the typical Penobscot word is often more like a two- (or more) word phrase in English. This is because many basic concepts that are separate, standalone words in English are expressed as word-endings in Penobscot. For example, 'walk' is just expressed by the italicized ending here and never stands as separate word—it is always in relation to where or how the person is walking:

| | |
|---|---|
| pəm*ohse* | 'she walks along' |
| al*ohse* | 'she walks to [there]' |
| wəč*ohse* | 'she walks from [there]' |
| pətək*ohse* | 'she walks back' |
| kiw*ohse* | 'she walks with no destination/wandering' |

A very common ending meaning anything from 'go, move' to even 'become, turn into' is shared between these words:

| | |
|---|---|
| n·wəmače*hlαn* | 'then he went off' |
| nə·ka wəpətəki*hlαn* | 'so then he headed back' |
| peči*hlαt* kəloskαpe | 'when Gluskabe arrived' |
| namehsi*hlα*wələtəwak | 'they (group) *turned into* fish' |
| čəkʷalsəwi*hlα*wələtəwak | 'they (group) *turned into* frogs' |
| toləpayi*hlα*wələtəwak | 'they (group) *turned into* turtles' |
| etali-pənahpskʷi*hlαk* | 'where it *turned into* stone' |
| tohki*hlαt* | 'when he woke up [=*became* awake]' |

The ending for 'jump' is used many times in the stories to create these vibrant words:

| | |
|---|---|
| wanαkik*ə*taho | 'she *jumped* up from sitting' |
| wətepik*ə*tahin | '(then) he *jumped* in [a vehicle]' |

| | |
|---|---|
| wəčawpikətaholətinα | '(then) they (group) *jumped* into the water' |
| n·wək^wəssakαkətahin | 'then he *jumped* across' |
| wənotekətahin | '(then) he *jumped* outside' |

As we can see, Penobscot speakers use this rich set of endings for different kinds of movement always in relation to an equally rich set of word-beginnings, ones that then convey the direction: along, to, from, back, away/off, up from sitting, into a vehicle, into water, across, out, and so on. Therefore, the two words below share the same expression for direction, '(heading) off', but each has a different ending, one that makes it clear what kind of movement/motion is used:

| | |
|---|---|
| n·wəmačehlαn | 'then he went [*by any movement*] off' |
| n·etoči-mαčepəyet | 'then when he *paddled* off' |

Through this one single pattern, almost any combination of movement and direction/path can be expressed by a single word in Penobscot.

Actions and results work the same way. An equally rich set of endings tell us how the main action is done. This one below means it is done (to a NA) with the hand(s), and the beginnings show the specific result (spooked, taken, marked, outside + visible, touched):

| | |
|---|---|
| wəkalapαnαn | '(then) he spooked him (*by hand*)' |
| awihk^wənαn | '(then) he took it [*by hand*]' |
| wəkisi-čilənαl | 'he has marked it *with his hand*' |
| amoskənαn | '(then) he brought it out [*by hand*]' |
| -kisi-samənαhk^w | '[so that] they cannot touch it' |

From here, it is even possible to expand the last expression to include which part of the body was affected:

wəsɑmihpskʷanenɑn          '(then) he touched them *on the back*'

So to understand even a seemingly complicated word like

nətəmiləkʷanehtehsiməkon      '(then) he hit me (against something)
                               breaking (my) wing'

only requires a few steps of relation. First, relationship of *nəmiləkon* 'she gives *me* it' (seen above, and here also showing the 'then . . .' meaning of *-n*). Then the words *nələkʷan* 'my wing' and *təmahikan* 'ax (lit. device for *severing*)'. And finally the part italicized above, which means the action is hitting a NA against something else.

These patterns of relation are just a few of many and so hopefully will give the reader a beginning sense of how Penobscot can build rich, complex words expressing a whole phrase or sentence's worth of meaning in one breath.

# Reader Guide to the Penobscot Language: Sounds

The standard Penobscot writing system can look intimidating at first. Instead of a chart matching Penobscot letters to English sounds—which can confuse more than it helps—here we introduce the spoken sounds themselves, with a few key points on how those sounds relate to each other, to English sounds, and to the standard writing system. With these few points, and especially a focus on rhythm and melody, you will be able to bring these stories back into voice, comfortably and fluently.

• Penobscot uses only six vowel sounds, five of which are shared with English:

| | | |
|---|---|---|
| mili | = give me (it) | mee-lee |
| mosok | = (more than one) moose [= "mooses"] | moo-zoog |
| nehe | = hey! | neh-heh |
| αhα | = yes | [see below] |
| ala | = or | ah-lah/aw-law/uh-luh |
| nətəp | = my head | n'-d'b |

The only non-English sound here is /α/, which is very close to English "bird" minus the r-sound. (Using "α" to write it is a holdover from early twentieth-century linguistics; modern linguists would use "ɤ").

The sound /ə/ is common in English but has no specific letter. It is the sound of the first "o" in "potato," that is, a weak, short sound, almost a blip. And in Penobscot, the shortness/weakness is what consistently tells this sound apart from the other five vowel sounds, which are always full and clear. (Unlike English, Penobscot /ə/ can be stressed; see below.)

• Putting real feeling into words depends most of all on their rhythm and melody. A lot of what gives spoken Penobscot such a distinctly melodic sound is its basic rhythm + melody pattern: putting a high pitch (here written "á," "í," etc.) on the third "full" vowel (= most cases of /i o e ɑ a/) from the end:

[3]  2  1        [3] 2 1       [3]  2  1

wɑ [pá] nah ki       [ó] te ne       wi [čóh] ke mi

'Wabanaki'       'town'       'help me!'

The only commonly non-"full" sound is /ə/. It is said quickly and weakly, and so on its own it is skipped for this rhythm + melody pattern. However, when there are two /ə/s in a row, the first is still weak/skipped but the second now acts like a "full" sound, and can even be stressed and given the high pitch:

[3]  2  1       [3]  2  1

pəmɑwə [sə́] wi no       peči-kəsəlɑm [sə́] nih ke

'person, human'       'a lot of wind came up'

The second example shows how /ə/ is also usually "full" after two consonants: here /ms-/. Both patterns share the simple fact that it is very natural to say /ə/ quickly/ weakly when it is just one on its own but not when they pile up together in pairs, or consonants are piled up before them.

• Penobscot phrases usually end in a high pitch, unlike English, which drifts down to a low pitch. So when said as standalone phrases, most words have an [UP-down-UP] melody that helps give Penobscot speech its distinctive musical quality.

• When reading longer words for/with children, a useful trick for confident and full-feeling rhythm is to start from the end of the word and then build up backward. With this approach, when you finally say the whole word, your mouth and mind literally know where they are headed:

pɑnawɑhpskéwɑtəwe        'speak Penobscot!'
we
təwe
wɑtəwe
skéwɑtəwe
wɑhpskéwɑtəwe
nawɑhpskéwɑtəwe
pɑnawɑhpskéwɑtəwe

It can also help to treat any long words as if they were just a series of shorter ones, and then finally bring them together—again with the distinctive Penobscot rhythm + melody pattern:

pɑna wɑhp skéwɑ təwe        →        pɑnawɑhpskéwɑtəwe

• Penobscot consonant sounds are all ones shared with English, but they can come in different combinations than English has. In particular, the /kʷ/ and /h/ sounds are basically identical to those in English—but unlike English, they do not need a vowel sound after them:

wikəyekʷ     'where you folks live'     wikəyek     'where we (but not you) live'
wee-g'-yegw                              wee-g'-yeg

/kʷ/ is very common at the ends of words. To be said clearly there, it only needs the lips rounded/stuck out in the exact same way as at the start of an English word like "queen" or "Gwen."

The /h/ sound without a vowel after it is a distinctive and common sound in Penobscot, but it is still basically just like English. It only needs to be said as a soft but clear whisper or breathing out after the vowel just before it:

| | | | |
|---|---|---|---|
| ihli | 'tell me!' | nətahki | 'my land' |
| eehh-lee | | n'dahh-kee | |

• Like other languages of the Northeast, Penobscot does not fundamentally distinguish these sound-pairs:

B vs. P       D vs. T       G vs. K       J vs. CH       Z vs. S

while English does. Instead, which sound (to English ears) is said follows a simple pattern of what comes naturally to the mouth. That is, these sounds come out as the first, softer version of each pair (BDGJZ) everywhere except when they are next to another consonant. Then the second, harder version (PTKCHS) is used:

| | | | | |
|---|---|---|---|---|
| kəloskɑpe 'Gluskabe' | tɑmɑ 'where' | kəloskɑpe 'Gluskabe' | péči 'even' | sipo 'river' |
| g'loos-kɑ-**beh** | **d**ɑ-mɑ | g'loos-kɑ-beh | beh-**jee** | **zee**-boo |
| | | | | |
| **p**kʷami 'ice' | **k**tatən 'Katahdin' | **k**tatən 'Katahdin' | **k**či- 'great' | **sk**ʷəte 'fire' |
| **p**kwah-mee | **k**tah-d'n | **k**tah-d'n | k**chee** | **sk**w'-deh |

Academic norms led the designer of the Penobscot writing system to write only /ptkčs/ in all contexts. This is a challenge for beginners: for them, it may be helpful to rewrite these as "bdgjz" as needed.

• Penobscot also has double-length sounds: /pp tt kk čč ss/. The /hp ht hk hč hs/ sound very similar to the English ear, as the /h/ is easy to miss, and in both sets, they come out as PTKCHS and not BDGJZ—but there is a simple trick to tell them apart. With /hp/ and so on, the vowel sound before it is much longer than usual. With /pp/ and so on, the vowel sound before it is much shorter than usual. You also "sit" on the P-sound much longer, like in English "lap-pad" or "black cat." So once again, the key is rhythm:

| wihke | 'fat' | wikke | 'she builds a house' |
| weehh-keh | | wick-keh | |
| | | | |
| mkasehs | 'old coal' | mkasess | 'crow' |
| mkah-zehhs | | mkah-sesss | |

• In combinations like /kč-, psk-, nt-/, and so on, Penobscot puts the most weight on the second sound, not the first one:

| kči- | 'great' | nsəta | 'three times' |
| kCHee (not KU-chee) | | nS'dah (not NU-s'dah) | |

The first sound is still said but only weakly. In running speech, it is usually tacked onto a vowel sound before it. That is, *iyo kki* 'this land' would be said [*i-yok-ki*].

• Overall, probably the most helpful and essential points for comfortably reading Penobscot aloud are knowing the six vowel sounds and the basic rhythm + melody pattern of the language.

CONOR M. QUINN
University of Southern Maine, 2021

# "Still They Remember Me"

## "eskʷa·tte nəmihkawitəhɑməkok kohsəssənawak"

**PENOBSCOT TRANSFORMER TALES**
**TOLD BY NEWELL LYON TO FRANK SPECK**

1

aclam kəloskɑpe tepəkil wəhisawehkəhən tɑpəyal nɑkɑ pahkʷal.

pesəkʷ

nətatlohkakan kəloskape.
nətatlohkakan
kəloskape

wikičik, monimkʷehso, nɑkɑ wkʷenəssal, kəloskape.
wikičik
monimkʷehso
nɑkɑ
wkʷenəssal
kəloskape

wəmačekənɑn, məsi kekʷəss wətakehkimɑn—
wəmačekənɑn
məsi kekʷəss
wətakehkimɑn—

eli-katonkemək, nɑkɑ eli-ahč-ɑmɑlot namehsak
eli-katonkemək
nɑkɑ
eli-ahč-ɑmɑlot
namehsak

—weči·č-kisɑwəsihətit.
weči·č-kisɑwəsihətit

*My story (is) Gluskabe.*
    my story/character
    Gluskabe

*They lived there, Woodchuck and her grandson, Gluskabe.*
    they lived, resided (there)
    Woodchuck
    and
    her grandson
    Gluskabe

*(So) she raised him, (and) she taught him everything—*
    (so) she raised him
    everything
    (so) she taught him

*how to hunt, and also how to fish for fish*
    how one hunts
    and
    also how one fishes for them
    fish(es)

*—so that they could live.*
    so that ·WILL they can live

mɑlam kəloskɑpe tepəkil wəkisawehkəhɑn ttɑpəyal nɑkɑ pahkʷal,

> mɑlam
> kəloskɑpe
> tepəkil
> wəkisawehkəhɑn
> ttɑpəyal
> nɑkɑ
> pahkʷal

nɑkɑ ohkəməssal wətihlɑn,

> nɑkɑ
> ohkəməssal
> wətihlɑn

"alihtawi ttɑpi nɑkɑ pahkʷal,

> alihtawi
> ttɑpi
> nɑkɑ
> pahkʷal

nəkati-katonalɑn nolke.

> nəkati-katonalɑn
> nolke

kis nəsiwɑtamən mahtəkʷehsəwiye nɑkɑ namehsəwiye."

> kis
> nəsiwɑtamən
> mahtəkʷehsəwiye
> nɑkɑ
> namehsəwiye

n·wəkiwohsɑn, wənihlɑn nolkal.

> n·wəkiwohsɑn
> wənihlɑn
> nolkal

*Eventually Gluskabe was big enough to be able to use a bow and arrows,*
    eventually
    Gluskabe
    he was big enough
    (for) him to be able to use it
    a bow
    and
    arrows

*and to his grandmother he said,*
    and
    his grandmother
    (then) he told her

*"Make me a bow and arrows,*
    make me (it/them)
    a bow
    and
    arrows

*(so) I want to hunt deer.*
    (so) I want to hunt it
    a deer

*I am already tired of rabbit-meat and fish-meat."*
    already
    I am tired of it
    rabbit-meat
    and
    fish-meat

*Then he walked wandering, and killed a deer.*
    then· he walked wandering
    (so) he killed it
    a deer

kkīy, wəlitəhαso monimkʷehso;

    kkīy

    wəlitəhαso

    monimkʷehso

kamαč wəkapamitəhαmαl wkʷenəssal.

    kamαč

    wəkapamitəhαmαl

    wkʷenəssal

mina kiwohset, n·wənihlαn awehsohsal.

    mina

    kiwohset

    n·wənihlαn

    awehsohsal

pečohset, wəpetəwamαl awehsohsal.

    pečohset

    wəpetəwamαl

    awehsohsal

wətihlαn ohkəməssal, "awen owa?"

    wətihlαn

    ohkəməssal

    awen

    owa

monimkʷehso wanαkikətaho nαkα wəpəməkehtehsin; etoči-wəlitəhαsit.

    monimkʷehso

    wanαkikətaho

    nαkα

    wəpəməkehtehsin

    etoči-wəlitəhαsit

*Kee, Woodchuck was happy;*
> kee
> she was happy
> Woodchuck

*she was very proud of her grandson.*
> very
> she was proud of him
> her grandson

*Again when he walked wandering, then he killed a bear.*
> again
> when he walked wandering
> then· he killed it
> a bear

*When he arrived (walking), he brought the bear on his back.*
> when he arrived (walking)
> he brought it on his back
> the bear

*(Then) he said to his grandmother, "Who is this?"*
> (then) he said to her
> his grandmother
> who
> this

*Woodchuck jumped up from sitting and struck up a dance; she was so happy.*
> Woodchuck
> she jumped up from sitting
> and
> (then) she struck up a dance
> she was so happy

wətihlɑn, "nkʷenəss, kči-awaass nehlat, awehsohs!

    wətihlɑn

    nkʷenəss

    kči-awaass

    nehlat

    awehsohs

nɑkɑ sípi nihkʷɑp kolɑwəsinena—mselət pəmi—koli·č-mɑwihpipəna.

    nɑkɑ sípi

    nihkʷɑp

    kolɑwəsinena

    mselət

    pəmi

    koli·č-mɑwihpipəna

kamɑč nkʷenəss kati-kinəhánəto,

    kamɑč

    nkʷenəss

    kati-kinəhánəto

nəkinitəhamɑ:

    nəkinitəhamɑ

nekəma·č ólihalɑ eləmɑwəsit nohsəssənawa,

    nekəma·č

    ólihalɑ

    eləmɑwəsit

    nohsəssənawa

wəsɑm milikən nehsɑnɑkʷahk ketonaləkohətit nihkáni,

    wəsɑm

    milikən

    nehsɑnɑkʷahk

    ketonaləkohətit

    nihkáni

*(Then) she said to him, "My grandchild, it's a great animal that you killed, a bear!*
    (then) she told him
    my grandchild
    great (big) animal
    (that) you killed
    bear

*So finally now we live well—there is lots of grease—we will eat well together.*
    and finally
    now
    (then) we live well
    there is lots of it
    grease
    we ·WILL ·eat well together

*My grandchild is going to be very great in power,*
    very
    my grandchild
    he is going to be great in power

*I think greatly of him:*
    I think greatly of him

*He will do good for our descendants as he goes on living,*
    he ·WILL
    he is/does good for them
    as he goes on living
    our descendants

*because there are all kinds of danger seeking after them in the future,*
    because
    there is a variety of it, all kinds of it
    what is dangerous
    which hunt, seek after them
    in the future

milikəwa awaassa ketonaləkohətičəhi.

milikəwa

awaassa

ketonaləkohətičəhi

nɑkɑ·č·ahč sipəwal, wəkisi-wəlihtonal·əč,

nɑkɑ·č·ahč

sipəwal

wəkisi-wəlihtonal·əč

weči- ɑta -atoči-nsɑnɑkʷatonohk."

weči- ɑta -atoči-nsɑnɑkʷatonohk

kəloskɑpe wətihlɑn ohkəməssal,

kəloskɑpe

wətihlɑn

ohkəməssal

"nətahčəwelətamən kətakehkimin elihtɑsik akʷitən,

nətahčəwelətamən

kətakehkimin

elihtɑsik

akʷitən

weči·č-katonalok ssipsak."

weči·č-katonalok

ssipsak

nə·monimkʷehso wətihlɑn,

nə·monimkʷehso

wətihlɑn

"kehəl'·eht kətakehkiməl, nkʷenəss."

kehəl[a]·eht

kətakehkiməl

nkʷenəss

*(there are) all kinds of animals seeking after them.*
>     there is a variety of them
>     animals
>     (that) hunt, seek after them

*And also the rivers, he will be able to fix them,*
>     and ·WILL ·also
>     rivers
>     he can fix them ·WILL

*so that they are not so dangerous."*
>     so that- not -so much-they are not dangerous

*(Then) Gluskabe said to his grandmother,*
>     Gluskabe
>     (then) he said to her
>     his grandmother

*"I want you to teach me how a canoe is built,*
>     I want (it)
>     (for) you (to) teach me (it)
>     how it is made
>     canoe

*so that I will hunt ducks."*
>     so that- ·WILL -I hunt them
>     ducks

*Then Woodchuck said to him,*
>     then· Woodchuck
>     (then) she said to him

*"For sure I (will) teach you, my grandchild."*
>     for sure ·EHT
>     I teach you
>     my grandchild

n·wətahtolinα.
n·wətahtolinα

mαlam·te wəkisihtonα akʷitən.
mαlam·te
wəkisihtonα
akʷitən

kkīy, wəlitəhαso kəloskαpe.
kkīy
wəlitəhαso
kəloskαpe

nə·tte wəposin—
nə·tte
wəposin

wətahsipsohkαn; aməstəhα sipsa.
wətahsipsohkαn
aməstəhα
sipsa

mαlam saláhki peči-kəsəlαmsə́nihke.
mαlam
saláhki
peči-kəsəlαmsə́nihke

nətahtekəne kisi-amilípəye,
nətahtekəne
kisi-amilípəye

wəsαmələmsən.
wəsαmələmsən

wəkiwohsαn kpi, wəkatonkαn.
wəkiwohsαn
kpi
wəkatonkαn

*Then they built a canoe.*
    then· they built a canoe

*Finally they finished the canoe.*
    eventually ·INTENS
    they finished making it
    canoe

*Kee, Gluskabe was happy.*
    kee
    he was happy
    Gluskabe

*Right away he set off by boat—*
    then·INTENS
    (then) he set off by boat

*(then) he duck-hunted; he got a lot of ducks.*
    (then) he duck-hunted
    he got a lot of them
    ducks

*Eventually at one point a lot of wind came up.*
    eventually
    at one point
    a lot of wind came up

*He couldn't really paddle out into the water,*
    not (despite effort)
    he could not paddle out into the water

*it was too windy.*
    it was too windy

*(So) he walked wandering in the woods, (and) he hunted.*
    (so) he walked wandering
    in the woods
    (then) he hunted / (for) him to hunt

elitəhɑsit, "kamač·eht nákahokat eli-katónka."
> elitəhɑsit
> kamač·eht
> nákahokat
> eli-katónka

wəpətəkohsɑn, wəmačin wikəwɑmək.
> wəpətəkohsɑn
> wəmačin
> wikəwɑmək

*He thought, "It seems very slow going how I'm hunting."*
    what/how he thought

    very ˙EHT

    it is slow, slow going

    as I hunt, how I hunt

*(Then) he walked back; (then) he started off to his house.*
    (then) he walked back

    (then) he started off

    to his house

## NOTES

PAGE

56    *nətatlohkakan*: See the introduction for the differences between *atlohkakan* 'legendary story' and *ačəməwakan* '(ordinary) story'. In Penobscot, the word *atlohkakan* when used as a NI-word refers to a legendary story. When used as a NA-word, as in the first line of this first story, *nətatlohkakan kəloskape* 'my story (is) Gluskabe', it appears to refer to the main character/hero of the story.

60    *"awen owa?"*: In Wabanaki languages, a person asking about an unknown animal generally does not ask "What is this?" but instead, "Who is this?" Passamaquoddy, Maliseet, and Mi'kmaw speakers confirm the same for their languages.

68    *wikəwamək*: While the 1918 version is inconsistent on this point, we consistently translate *wikəwam* as 'house' rather than 'wigwam', since Penobscot *wikəwam*, like the English word "house," names any kind of residence, unlike the much narrower English use of the word "wigwam."

2

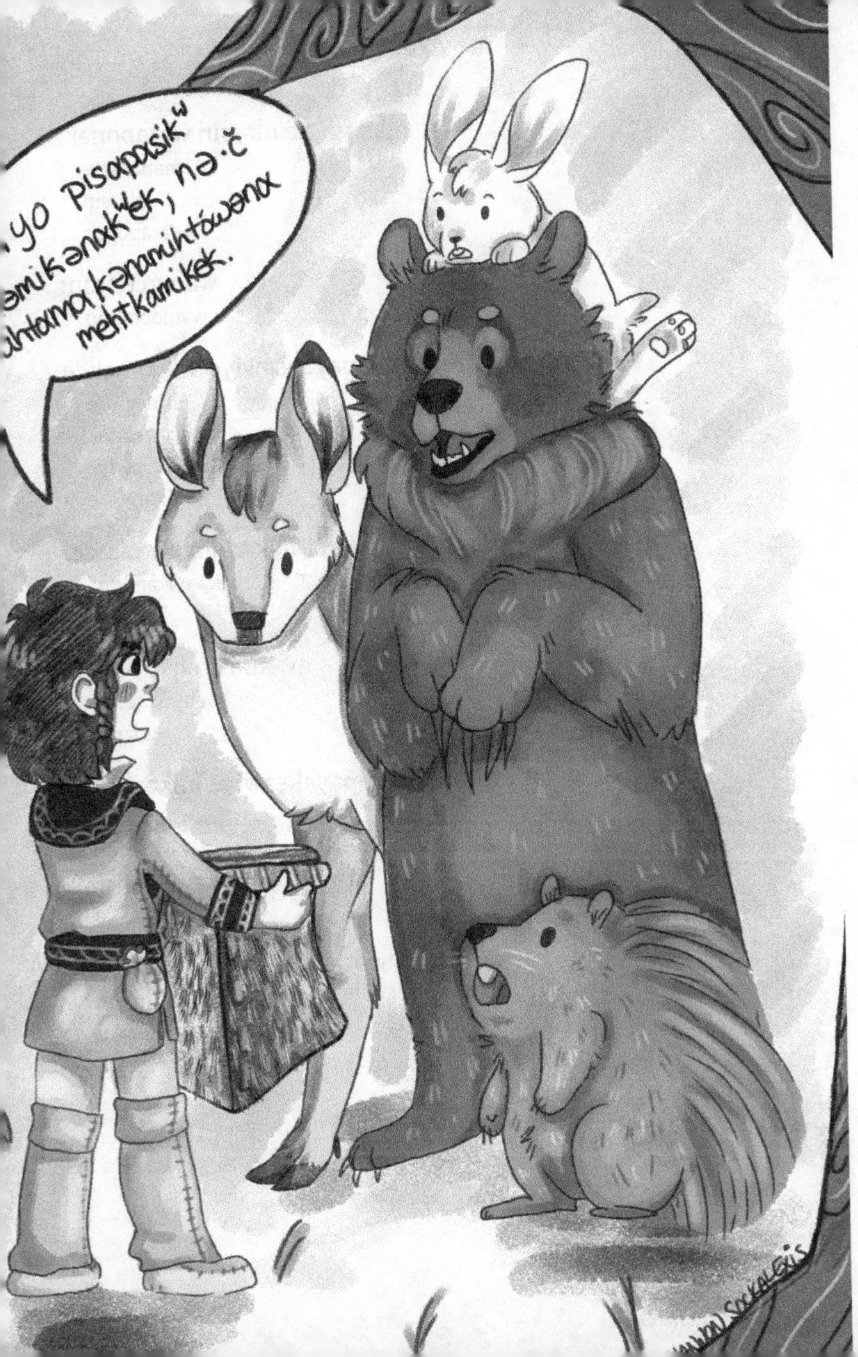
yo pisapasikʷ
əmikənakʷek, nə·č
htama kənamihtówəna
mehtkamikek.
SOCKALEXIS

nis

manəni·tte oləssin wətaponək,
  manəni·tte
  oləssin
  wətaponək

wəmačenton:
  wəmačenton

ali-nspinto ehčəwelətak pəyehsəwiye amikənakʷe
  ali-nspinto
  ehčəwelətak
  pəyehsəwiye
  amikənakʷe

weči-nəkəmihɑt awaassa.
  weči-nəkəmihɑt
  awaassa

monimkʷehso olapin
  monimkʷehso
  olapin

nɑkɑ wətəlihton nolkayi-pəyehsəwiye mikənakʷe.
  nɑkɑ
  wətəlihton
  nolkayi-pəyehsəwiye
  (a)mikənakʷe

kisihtɑkʷ, wətəlahkewɑn wkʷenəssal.
  kisihtɑkʷ
  wətəlahkewɑn
  wkʷenəssal

*Right away he lay down on his bed(ding),*
    right away ·INTENS
    (then) he lay down
    on his bed(ding)

*(then) he started to sing:*
    (then) he started to sing

*he sang, wording how he wanted an amignagweh made of hair*
    he sang wording/saying/meaning
    that he wanted it
    made of hair
    amignagweh

*in order to easily get animals.*
    in order for him to easily get them
    animals

*(Then) Woodchuck sat down*
    Woodchuck
    (then) she sat down

*and she made a deer-hair amignagweh.*
    and
    (then) she made it
    made of deer-hair
    amignagweh

*When she finished it, she threw it to her grandchild.*
    when she finished it
    she threw him it
    her grandchild

nətahtαmα čanínto kəloskαpe.

    nətahtαmα

    čanínto

    kəloskαpe

nə·mina mosi-pəyehsəwiye kətak wətəlihton monimkʷehso.

    nə·mina

    mosi-pəyehsəwiye

    kətak

    wətəlihton

    monimkʷehso

mina wətəlahkewαn; pesəkʷən elintαkʷ.

    mina

    wətəlahkewαn

    pesəkʷən

    elintαkʷ

n·etoči-manewatαkʷ monimkʷehso apəyehsomal,

    n·etoči-manewatαkʷ

    monimkʷehso

    apəyehsomal

wətəlihton kətak mikənakʷe monimkʷehsəwi-pəyehsəwiye.

    wətəlihton

    kətak

    (a)mikənakʷe

    monimkʷehsəwi-pəyehsəwiye

nαkα sípi olitəhαsin kəloskαpe;

    nαkα sípi

    olitəhαsin

    kəloskαpe

*Gluskabe did not stop singing at all.*
> not at all
> he did not pause in singing
> Gluskabe

*Then again of moose hair Woodchuck made another one.*
> then· again
> made of moose hair
> other
> (then) she made it
> Woodchuck

*Again she threw it to him; he sang just the same.*
> again
> she threw him it
> it was just the same
> how he sang

*Then when she pulled out her hair,*
> then· at the point/when she pulled them (group) out
> Woodchuck
> her hairs

*(then) she made another amignagweh of woodchuck hair.*
> (then) she made it
> other
> amignagweh
> made of woodchuck hair

*And finally then Gluskabe was happy;*
> and finally
> (then) he was happy
> Gluskabe

epəkʷahč alamiso.
epəkʷahč
alamiso

n·wəmačin kpi,
n·wəmačin
kpi

nɑkɑ wəkɑkɑlomɑn awaassa.
nɑkɑ
wəkɑkɑlomɑn
awaassa

wətihlɑn, "nawətɑpɑsikʷ awaassətok,
wətihlɑn
nawətɑpɑsikʷ
awaassətok

kati-mehtkamike, kənəkkɑnepɑ·č."
kati-mehtkamike
kənəkkɑnepɑ·č

nə·kehəla awaassak wəsɑkhɑpɑsinɑ ehkihkikičik.
nə·kehəla
awaassak
wəsɑkhɑpɑsinɑ
ehkihkikičik

*he even gave thanks.*
    even
    he says/expresses thanks/gratitude

*Then he started off into the woods,*
    then· he started off
    in the woods

*and he called out to the animals.*
    and
    (then) he called out to them
    animals

*(Then) he told them, "Come here (walking), animals,*
    (then) he told them
    (group) come here (walking)!
    animals!

*the world is going to end, you will all die."*
    it is going to be the end of the world
    you all die·WILL

*Then sure enough all kinds of animals walked up onto the scene.*
    then· sure enough
    animals
    (then) they (group) came walking into view
    ones of various kinds

n·wətihlɑn, "iyo pisɑpɑsikʷ nəmikənakʷek,
n·wətihlɑn,
iyo
pisɑpɑsikʷ
nəmikənakʷek

nə·č ahtɑmɑ kənamihtówənɑ mehtkamikek."
nə·č
ahtɑmɑ
kənamihtówənɑ
mehtkamikek

nɑkɑ nə·ka pitikɑpɑsilit mikənakʷek
nɑkɑ
nə·ka
pitikɑpɑsilit
(a)mikənakʷek

amɑčewalɑn wikəwamək.
amɑčewalɑn
wikəwamək

wətihlɑn ohkəməssal, "ɑn ni, nohkəmi,
wətihlɑn
ohkəməssal
ɑn ni
nohkəmi

nəpečiphɑn awaassak,
nəpečiphɑn
awaassak

*Then he told them, "Walk into this amignagweh of mine,*
  then· he told them
  this/here
  (group) walk inside!
  in my amignagweh

*then you won't see the end of the world at all."*
  then·WILL
  not at all
  you (pl.) do not see it
  when the world ends

*And so then when they walked inside the amignagweh,*
  and
  then·KA
  when they (group) walked inside
  in the amignagweh

*(then) he took the group of them off to his house.*
  (then) he took them (group) off away
  to his house

*(Then) he told his grandmother, "Well then, my grandmother,*
  (then) he told her
  his grandmother
  well then
  my grandmother

*(so) I brought the animals,*
  (so) I brought them
  animals

nə·či nihkʷαp αta nəsaki-pahpəmi-kiwohsewən."

> nə·či
> nihkʷαp
> αta
> nəsaki-pahpəmi-kiwohsewən

n·wənotessαn monimkʷehso.

> n·wənotessαn
> monimkʷehso

elαpit, məsi ehkihkikit awaass məsi ayolətəwak mikənakʷek.

> elαpit
> məsi
> ehkihkikit
> awaass
> məsi
> ayolətəwak
> (a)mikənakʷek

wəpitikαn monimkʷehso,

> wəpitikαn
> monimkʷehso

wətihlαn wkʷenəssal, "ahtαmα kolalohkew, nkʷenəss,

> wətihlαn
> wkʷenəssal
> ahtαmα
> kolalohkew
> nkʷenəss

kʷaskʷalαmolətəwak·əč nihkάni kohsəssənawak."

> kʷaskʷalαmolətəwak·əč
> nihkάni
> kohsəssənawak

*so now I will not have a hard time walking wandering along again and again."*
　　then·WILL
　　now
　　not
　　(then) I do not have a hard time walking wandering along again and again

*Then Woodchuck walked out.*
　　then· she walked out
　　Woodchuck

*As she looked, every kind of animal was there in the amignagweh.*
　　as she looked
　　all/every
　　which is/are of various kinds
　　animal
　　all
　　they (group) were present
　　in the amignagweh

*(Then) Woodchuck went inside,*
　　(then) she went inside
　　Woodchuck

*(then) she told her grandchild, "You did not do a good thing at all, my grandchild,*
　　(then) she told him
　　her grandchild
　　not at all
　　you did not do good
　　my grandchild

*our descendants will starve to death in the future."*
　　they (group) starve ·WILL
　　in the future
　　our descendants

wətihlɑn, "kəya nkʷenəss, kəya kənihkɑlotɑkok kohsəssənawak.

> wətihlɑn
>
> kəya
>
> nkʷenəss
>
> kəya
>
> kənihkɑlotɑkok
>
> kohsəssənawak

mosahk n·alalohkehkač;

> mosahk
>
> n·alalohkehkač

kətahčəwi·tahk[ik]-alalohke

> kətahčəwi·tahk[ik]-alalohke

tɑn·əč welihaləkohətit kohsəssənawak."

> tɑn·əč
>
> welihaləkohətit
>
> kohsəssənawak

kəloskɑpe olɑmsətawɑn ohkəməssal,

> kəloskɑpe
>
> olɑmsətawɑn
>
> ohkəməssal

n·wənotessɑn nɑkɑ apihkʷətenəmən amikənakʷe.

> n·wənotessɑn
>
> nɑkɑ
>
> apihkʷətenəmən
>
> amikənakʷe

wətihlɑn awaassa, "notɑpɑsikʷ,

> wətihlɑn
>
> awaassa
>
> notɑpɑsikʷ

*(Then) she told him, "You, my grandchild, our descendants depend on you.*
    (then) she told him
    you
    my grandchild
    you
    they depend on you
    our descendants

*Don't do that;*
    don't!
    that· don't do it

*instead you must do*
    you must ·TAHK[?] do

*whatever will do good for our descendants."*
    (that) which ·WILL
    it does good for them
    our descendants

*(Then) Gluskabe believed his grandmother,*
    Gluskabe
    (then) he believed her (in hearing her)
    his grandmother

*then he walked out and he opened the amignagweh.*
    then· he walked out
    and
    (then) he opened it
    amignagweh

*(Then) he told the animals, "Walk out,*
    (then) he told them
    animals
    (group) walk out!

kis pəmihle eli-nsɑnɑkʷahk!
kis
pəmihle
eli-nsɑnɑkʷahk

mɑčɑpɑsikʷ."
mɑčɑpɑsikʷ

*the danger has already gone by!*
    already now
    it passed by
    what is dangerous, how it is dangerous

*Start off!"*
    (group) start off walking!

**NOTES**

PAGE

73    *amignagweh made of hair*: We translate this simply as *amignagweh* because there is no common English word for the square-bottomed, round-topped folded and stitched birch bark container so basic to traditional Penobscot life.

76    *epəkʷahč*: This highly common expression is tricky to translate into English but appears to be the exact equivalent of Passamaquoddy *cel*, Mi'kmaw *lpa*, and Western Abenaki *agwachi*. Namely, it seems to give the idea of 'too, also' but with the sense usually of that this extra degree or action is unexpected, surprising, or noteworthy, i.e., '(and) even . . . !'

76    *awaassətok*: The ending added to *awaass* 'animal' here is used for addressing/calling out to a group.

3

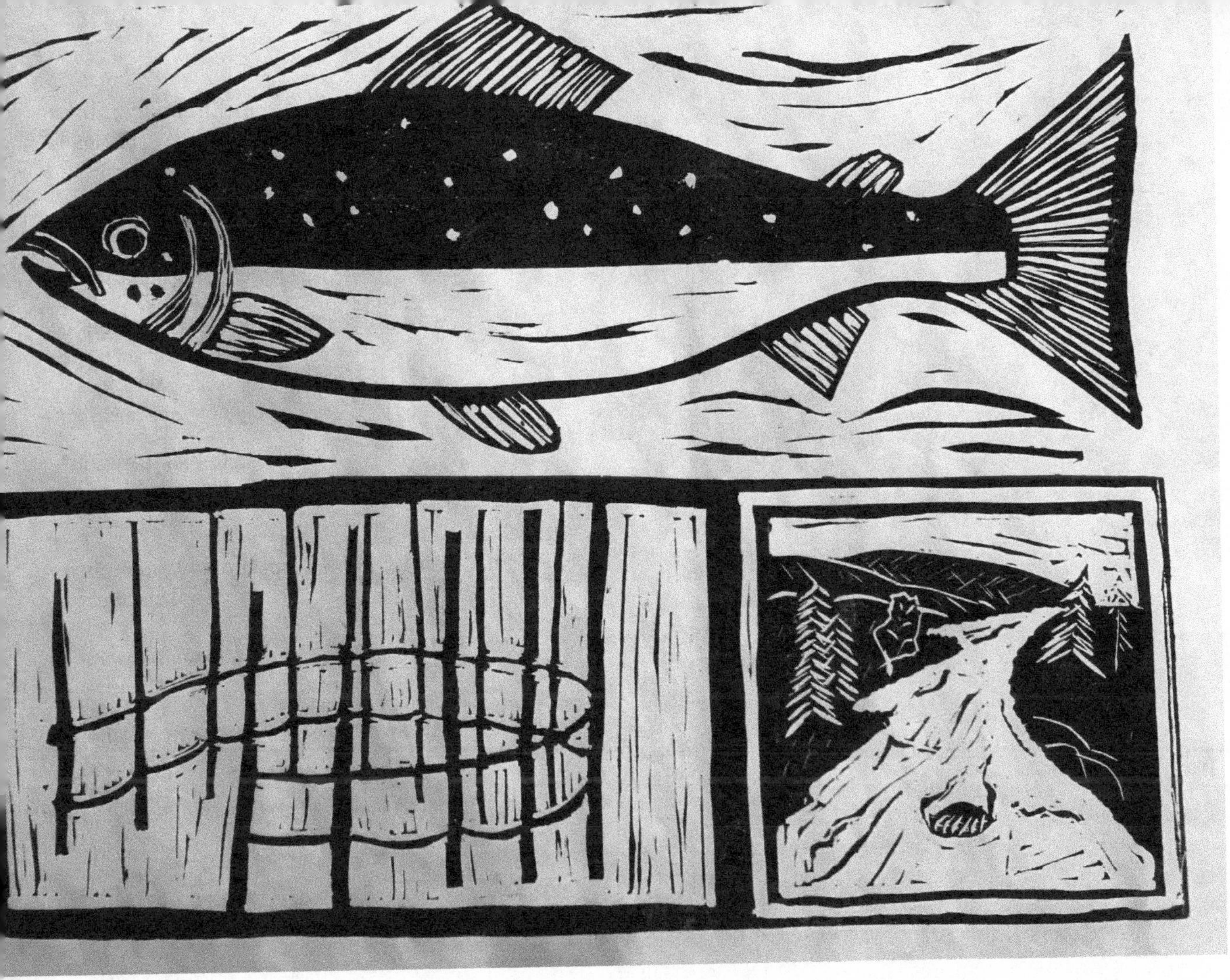

# nahs

mečími papɑmihle.
mečími
papɑmihle

nə·pečihlɑt wikəwɑmɑwɑk,
nə·pečihlɑt
wikəwɑmɑwɑk

wənamihɑn ohkəməssal etalɑmeličil.
wənamihɑn
ohkəməssal
etalɑmeličil

mɑlam·te osikitəhɑmɑl.
mɑlam·te
osikitəhɑmɑl

nətahtɑmɑ kʷina wəpəthɑwəya namehsa.
nətahtɑmɑ
kʷina
wəpəthɑwəya
namehsa

elitəhɑsit, "mewəya wičohkemoke nohkəməss,
elitəhɑsit
mewəya
wičohkemoke
nohkəməss

weči- ɑta -saki-ɑmehkʷ."
weči-
ɑta
-saki-
-ɑmehkʷ

*He was always going around.*
    always
    he went around, about

*Then when he arrived at their house,*
    then· when he arrived
    at their house

*(then) he saw his grandmother fishing.*
    (then) he saw her
    his grandmother
    where/when she was fishing

*Finally he felt sad for her.*
    eventually ·INTENS
    he felt sad for her

*She didn't really hook any fish at all.*
    not at all
    really
    she did not hook them
    fish(es)

*He thought, "It's better if I help my grandmother,*
    what/how he thought
    better
    if I help her
    my grandmother

*so that she doesn't have a hard time fishing."*
    so that
    not
    difficult hard
    (that) she does not fish

n·wətəlihton ksenɑkan kʷsakáyi sipo sɑkətehtəkʷek.

        n·wətəlihton
        ksenɑkan
        kʷsakáyi
        sipo
        sɑkətehtəkʷek

ni kisihtɑkʷ, wətasənəmən epáhsi,

        ni
        kisihtɑkʷ
        wətasənəmən
        epáhsi

weči·č- namehsak -pihthihlahətit.

        weči·č-
        namehsak
        -pihthihlahətit

n·etoči-mɑčepəyet amíli sopekok nɑkɑ apahpəmi-kɑkɑləwɑn.

        n·etoči-mɑčepəyet
        amíli
        sopekok
        nɑkɑ
        apahpəmi-kɑkɑləwɑn

wətitamən, "namehsətok,

        wətitamən
        namehsətok

kati-sinkihle sopekʷ,

        kati-sinkihle
        sopekʷ

*Then he made a weir crossing where the river had its mouth.*
    then· he made it
    fish-weir
    (going) across
    river
    where the river mouths/has its mouth

*Then when he finished it, he made an opening halfway,*
    then
    when he finished it
    he made an opening (by hand) in it
    halfway

*so that the fish would go in.*
    so that ·WILL
    fish(es)
    (that) they go in

*It's then that he paddled off out into the ocean and kept on going along calling.*
    then· when he paddled off
    away from shore/out into the water
    in the ocean
    and
    (then) he kept on going along calling

*(Then) he said, "Fishes,*
    (then) he said
    fishes!

*the ocean is going to dry up,*
    it is going to dry up
    ocean

kati-mehtkamike, məsi·č kiləwɑ kənəkkɑnepɑ.
    kati-mehtkamike
    məsi·č
    kiləwɑ
    kənəkkɑnepɑ

nə·nihkʷɑp, nəkisihton weči·č-pəmɑwəsolətəyekʷ,
    nə·nihkʷɑp
    nəkisihton
    weči·č-pəmɑwəsolətəyekʷ

məsi tɑn notawit namehsinɑkʷəsit,
    məsi
    tɑn
    notawit
    namehsinɑkʷəsit

pihthihlɑč nəsipomək.
    pihthihlɑč
    nəsipomək

məsi·č kəpəmɑwəsolətipɑ
    məsi·č
    kəpəmɑwəsolətipɑ

wəsɑm mečími·č áyo nəsipom.
    wəsɑm
    mečími·č
    áyo
    nəsipom

nihkʷɑp məsi tɑn notawit,
    nihkʷɑp
    məsi
    tɑn
    notawit

*the world is going to end, all of you will all die.*
    the world is going to end
    all ·WILL
    you (pl.)
    you all die

*So now I have made it so that you all will live,*
    then· now
    I have made it
    so that ·WILL you (pl.) (group) live

*all of the fish-kind who hear me,*
    all
    which
    one that hears me
    one that looks like fish/of the fish-kind

*let them go into my (section of) river.*
    let her/him go in
    at/in my (section of) river

*You will all live*
    all ·WILL
    you (pl.) (group) live

*because my (section of) river will always exist.*
    because
    always ·WILL
    it exists, is present
    my (section of) river

*Now all who hear me,*
    now
    all
    which
    one that hears me

pihthihlač."
    pihthihlač

ná(hə)law namehsak ehkihkičik
    ná(hə)law
    namehsak
    ehkihkičik

mɑlam psante yo ksenɑkan.
    mɑlam
    psante
    yo
    ksenɑkan

n·wəkəphamən.
    n·wəkəphamən

nə·tt' etali-mečimihasolətihətit.
    nə·tt[e]etali-mečimihasolətihətit

nəh n·wəmɑčin awikəwɑməwɑk,
    nəh
    n·wəmɑčin
    awikəwɑməwɑk

n·wətihlɑn ohkəməssal,
    n·wətihlɑn
    ohkəməssal

"ɑn ni, nohkəmi, ɑta·č nihkʷɑp kəsaki-ɑmew,
    ɑn ni
    nohkəmi
    ɑta·č
    nihkʷɑp
    kəsaki-ɑmew

*let them go in."*
    let him/her go in

*Continually all kinds of fish (went in)*
    continually/constantly/steadily
    fish(es)
    ones of all kinds

*(until) eventually this weir was full.*
    until/eventually
    it was full
    this
    weir

*Then he blocked it off.*
    then· he blocked it off

*Right there (is where) they were trapped.*
    there·INTENS (is) where they (group) were trapped there

*(Nuh) then he started off to their house,*
    [?]
    then· he started off
    to their house

*then he told his grandmother,*
    then· he told her
    his grandmother

*"Well then, my grandmother, now you won't have a hard time fishing,*
    well
    my grandmother
    not ·WILL
    now
    you do not have a hard time fishing

ípi·tte·č kənačiphɑk namehsak
>ípi·tte·č
>kənačiphɑk
>namehsak

tɑn etoči-ččəweləmat."
>tɑn
>etoči-
>ččəweləmat

nə·monimkʷehso wənači-təpənawəsin
>nə·monimkʷehso
>wənači-təpənawəsin

tɑn owa wəkisi-alalohkɑn.
>tɑn
>owa
>wəkisi-alalohkɑn

nəmɑ pečohset,
>nəmɑ
>pečohset

yo·tahk ksenɑkan wəli-psante ehkihkikihətit namehsak,
>yo·tahk
>ksenɑkan
>wəli-psante
>ehkihkikihətit
>namehsak

epəkʷahč kapahkɑwatihətəwak.
>epəkʷahč
>kapahkɑwatihətəwak

wəmačehlɑn monimkʷehso.
>wəmačehlɑn
>monimkʷehso

*you'll just go grab fish*
    only ·INTENS ·WILL
    you go grab/get them
    fish(es)

*whenever you want them."*
    whichever
    point in time
    that you want them

*Then Woodchuck went to examine*
    then· Woodchuck
    (then) she went to examine

*what this one (Gluskabe) had done.*
    which/how
    this (person)
    he had done (something/in some way)

*When she got there (walking),*
    there
    when she arrived (walking)

*here was a weir good and full of all kinds of fish,*
    here ·TAHK
    weir
    it was good and full
    (as) there are of various kinds
    fish(es)

*they were even crowding each other bodily out onto the shore.*
    even
    they (group) crowded each other bodily out onto the shore

*(Then) Woodchuck went off.*
    (then) she started off
    Woodchuck

pečihlɑt wikəwɑməwɑk, wətihlɑn, "nkʷenəss,
    pečihlɑt
    wikəwɑməwɑk
    wətihlɑn
    nkʷenəss

ahtɑmɑ kolalohkew,
    ahtɑmɑ
    kolalohkew

məsi nekkahtəhat namehsak.
    məsi
    nekkahtəhat
    namehsak

tɑn·əč wətəlawəsolətinɑ kohsəssənawak nihkȧni,
    tɑn·əč
    wətəlawəsolətinɑ
    kohsəssənawak
    nihkȧni

wəsɑm kəyona kʷaskʷayi-kehsit namehsak
    wəsɑm
    kəyona
    kʷaskʷayi-kehsit
    namehsak

tɑn kehsi-ččəweləmakʷ.
    tɑn
    kehsi-
    ččəweləmakʷ

nihkʷap·te nɑči-notahəle."
    nihkʷap·te
    nɑči-notahəle

*When she reached their house, (then) she told him, "My grandchild,*
    when she got there
    at their house
    (then) she told him
    my grandchild

*you did not do a good thing at all,*
    not at all
    you didn't do good

*when you caught all of the fish.*
    all
    when you got them all
    fish(es)

*How will our descendants live in the future,*
    which/how ·WILL
    (then) they (group) live (in some way)
    our descendants
    in the future

*since we have as many fish*
    because
    we
    those which are enough/enough of them
    fish(es)

*as we want (of them).*
    whichever/however
    as many as
    (that) we want of them

*Right now, go and let them out."*
    now· INTENS
    go to let them out!

kehəla onɑkin, itak, "kolɑme, nohkəmi,
> kehəla
> onɑkin
> itak
> kolɑme
> nohkəmi

nənɑči-pkʷətəhalɑk nihkʷɑp."
> nənɑči-pkʷətəhalɑk
> nihkʷɑp

*Sure enough (then) he got up from sitting, saying, "You're right, my grandmother,*
    sure enough
    (then) he got up from sitting
    as/(what) he said
    you are right
    my grandmother

*I am going off to open it up for them now."*
    I go in order to release them by opening (something)
    now

## NOTES

PAGE

94   *nə·tt' etali*: These are normally said very quickly and flow together: *nəttetali*.

# 4

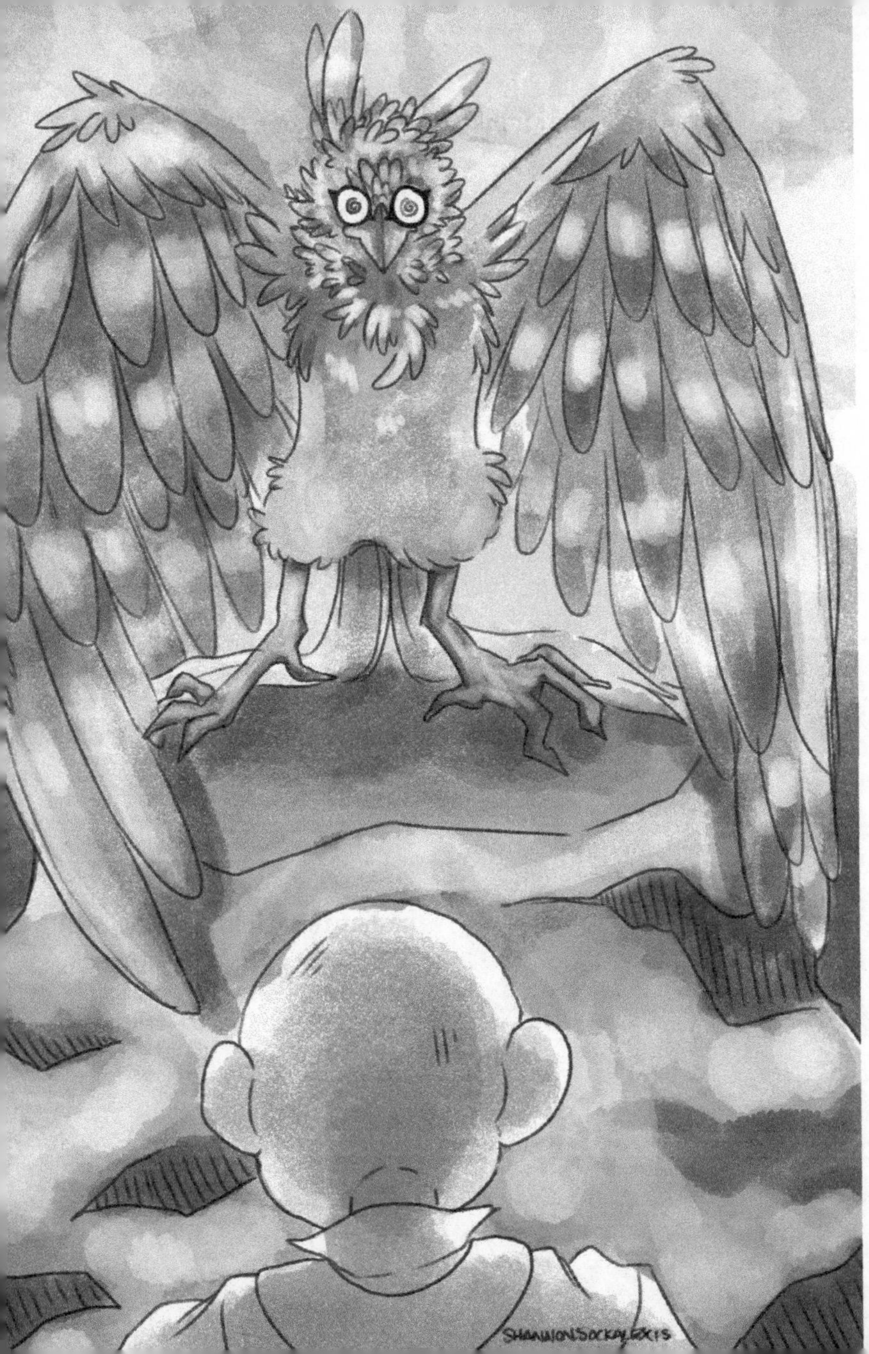

yew

n·wətamihkənəmən kəloskαpe kʷesαwahpskek,
> n·wətamihkənəmən
> kəloskαpe
> kʷesαwahpskek

očihton wətol.
> očihton
> wətol

n·wətahsipsohkαn wətolək pənahpskolakʷ.
> n·wətahsipsohkαn
> wətolək
> pənahpskolakʷ

αta kʷina wənihlαwəya ssipsa,
> αta
> kʷina
> wənihlαwəya
> ssipsa

mečími kəsəlαmsən,
> mečími
> kəsəlαmsən

saki-kisipəye.
> saki-kisipəye

mαlam·te saláhki moskawihle.
> mαlam·te
> saláhki
> moskawihle

*Then Gluskabe picked up a rocky point of land,*
    then· he lifted it up (from a lying-down position)
    Gluskabe
    what is a rocky point of land

*(and) he made his canoe from it.*
    (then) he made it from it
    his canoe

*Then he hunted ducks in his stone canoe.*
    then· he hunted ducks
    in his canoe
    stone canoe

*He didn't really kill any ducks.*
    not
    really
    he didn't kill them
    ducks

*The wind was always blowing,*
    always
    the wind was blowing

*he had a hard time being able to paddle.*
    he had a hard time being able to paddle

*Eventually at one point he got mad.*
    eventually ·INTENS
    at one point
    he got mad

elitəhasit, "tɑn ɑkima ali-təpihle,
    elitəhasit
    tɑn
    ɑkima
    ali-təpihle

etoči-mečiməlɑmsək?"
    etoči-mečiməlɑmsək

itam kəloskɑpe, "nohkəmi,
    itam
    kəloskɑpe
    nohkəmi

nəkati-kʷilawahton
    nəkati-kʷilawahton

tɑn wetəlɑmsək."
    tɑn
    wetəlɑmsək

monimkʷehso itam, "nkʷenəss, kamač nɑwatoke."
    monimkʷehso
    itam
    nkʷenəss
    kamač
    nɑwatoke

itak kəloskɑpe, "nətəlohsɑn tɑn·te pelotahk.
    itak
    kəloskɑpe
    nətəlohsɑn
    tɑn·te
    pelotahk

*He thought, "What exactly is happening,*
    what/how he thought
    which
    about/approximately
    it happens (in some way)

*the wind is so constantly blowing?"*
    the wind is so constantly blowing

*Gluskabe said, "Grandmother,*
    he said
    Gluskabe
    my grandmother

*I want to look for it*
    I want to look for it

*where the wind blows from."*
    which/where
    where the wind blows from

*Woodchuck said, "My grandchild, it is very far away."*
    Woodchuck
    she said
    my grandchild
    very
    far away

*Gluskabe said, "I am walking there however far it is.*
    what he said
    Gluskabe
    (so) I walk (to there)
    which(ever) ·INTENS
    how far it is

nəkati-namihɑ awen kisihtɑkʷ kəsəlɑmsən.

> nəkati-namihɑ
> awen
> kisihtɑkʷ
> kəsəlɑmsən

nápi·tte·č nəpečohse."

> nápi·tte·č
> nəpečohse

n·wəmɑčin: wečsək n·elohset,

> n·wəmɑčin
> wečsək
> n·elohset

ɑkkʷɑpohse aháči ɑkʷɑmələmsən,

> ɑkkʷɑpohse
> aháči
> ɑkʷɑmələmsən

mɑlam tàpawɑs kehsokənahkiwik,

> mɑlam
> tàpawɑs
> kehsokənahkiwik

kis awáhkɑč kisohse, etotələmsək.

> kis
> awáhkɑč
> kisohse
> etotələmsək

məsi manələmsənol wəpəyehsomal.

> məsi
> manələmsənol
> wəpəyehsomal

*I want to see who has made the wind.*
    I want to see him/her
    who
    the one who has made it
    wind

*I will come (back) here quickly."*
    quickly ·INTENS ·WILL
    I will arrive (walking)

*Then he started off: where the wind blows from is where he walked to,*
    then· he started off
    where the wind blows from
    there· (was) where he walked to

*The more he walked, the more the wind blew.*
    he walked so far
    more and more
    the wind blew harder

*Eventually after seven days,*
    eventually
    seven
    when it is (that) many days

*already he could barely walk, the wind blew so much.*
    already
    barely
    he could walk
    the wind blew so much

*His hair was all blown off by the wind.*
    all
    they were blown off by the wind
    his hairs

mɑlam wənamihɑl etalilək<sup>w</sup>anewilit: ktəhɑnətəwi-ssipəss.

> mɑlam
> wənamihɑl
> etalilək<sup>w</sup>anewilit
> ktəhɑnətəwi-ssipəss

mɑlam·te nəmɑ pečohset awáhkɑč

> mɑlam·te
> nəmɑ
> pečohset
> awáhkɑč

eyilit kči-ssipsal,

> eyilit
> kči-ssipsal

wətihlɑn, "nəmohsomi,

> wətihlɑn
> nəmohsomi

nətah·ap'·eht kkisihatowən ɑk<sup>w</sup>amələmsən?"

> nətah·ap[a]·eht
> kkisihatowən
> ɑk<sup>w</sup>amələmsən

nə·kči-ssipəss wətihlɑn, "nohsəss,

> nə·kči-ssipəss
> wətihlɑn
> nohsəss

*Eventually he saw him flapping his wings: a supernaturally huge bird.*
    eventually
    he saw him
    as he was moving his wings
    supernaturally huge bird

*Eventually when he arrived (walking) there barely*
    eventually ·INTENS
    there
    when he got there (walking)
    barely

*where the great big bird was,*
    where he was (at)
    great big bird

*(then) he said to him, "My grandfather,*
    (then) he said to him
    my grandfather

*couldn't you maybe make the wind blow more?"*
    not ·WOULD ·EHT
    you cannot make it
    (for) the wind to blow more

*Then the great big bird told him, "My descendant,*
    then· great big bird
    (then) he said to him
    my descendant

nə·tt'·eht kehsi-kisihatawa."
nə·tt[e]·eht
kehsi-kisihatawa

kəloskɑpe wətihlɑn, "nihkʷɑp,
kəloskɑpe
wətihlɑn
nihkʷɑp

nihkʷɑp·əpa ɑkʷɑmi-spapəyane
nihkʷɑp·əpa
ɑkʷɑmi-spapəyane

yē nəmɑ tkʷɑ́kki etali-spatənek,
yē
nəmɑ
tkʷɑ́kki
etali-spatənek

nə·pa ɑkʷɑmələmsən."
nə·pa
ɑkʷɑmələmsən

itak ssipəss, "nətahtekəne nkʷenəss,
itak
ssipəss
nətahtekəne
nkʷenəss

yo·tte epəya neke kehtoke."
yo·tte
epəya
neke
kehtoke

*that is as much as (I guess) I can do."*
    then·INTENS ·EHT
    as much as I can do to it

*(Then) Gluskabe said to him, "Now,*
    Gluskabe
    then he said to him
    now

*now if you would sit higher up*
    now ·WOULD
    if you sit more high up

*waaay over there uphill where the mountain is high,*
    waaay over there
    there
    uphill/on the hill
    where the mountain is high/where the peak is

*then the wind would blow more."*
    then·WOULD
    the wind blow more

*The bird said, "I can't, my grandchild,*
    (what) he said
    bird
    not (despite trying hard)
    my grandchild

*right here is where I've sat since the beginning."*
    here ·INTENS
    where I sit
    back then
    since before/the beginning

wətihlɑn kəloskɑpe, "nəmohsomi,
>> wətihlɑn
>> kəloskɑpe
>> nəmohsomi

nəya·č kəwičohkeməl."
>> nəya·č
>> kəwičohkeməl

ssipəss itak, "etáki·tte kisi-wičohkeməyane,
>> ssipəss
>> itak
>> etáki·tte
>> wičohkeməyane

kehəl'·eht nətəlohsɑn
>> kehəl[a]·eht
>> nətəlohsɑn

wəsɑm nətahčəwelətamən
>> wəsɑm
>> nətahčəwelətamən

məsi elkʷepəya wəli-kəsəlɑmsən."
>> məsi
>> elkʷepəya
>> wəli-kəsəlɑmsən

nə·kəloskɑpe awihkʷhəwamɑn kči-ssipsal,
>> nə·kəloskɑpe
>> awihkʷhəwamɑn
>> kči-ssipsal

wəmɑče(hə)wamɑn.
>> wəmɑče(hə)wamɑn

*(Then) Gluskabe said to him, "My grandfather,*
    (then) he said to him
    Gluskabe
    my grandfather

*I will help you."*
    I ·WILL
    I help you

*The bird said, "If you can indeed help me,*
    bird
    (what) he said
    if so/indeed ·INTENS
    if you can help me

*for sure I will walk there*
    sure ·EHT
    (then) I walk there

*because I want*
    because
    I want it

*everywhere I sit facing to have the wind blowing good."*
    all/every
    (place) where I sit facing
    (for) the wind (to) blow good

*Then Gluskabe took the great big bird up on his back,*
    Gluskabe
    (then) he took him up on his back
    great big bird

*(then) he carried him off on his back.*
    (then) he carried him off on his back

mɑlam·te etali-spahsekek,
mɑlam·te
etali-spahsekek

n·etali-paliphɑt kčawayəss,
n·etali-paliphɑt
kčawayəss

nə·kči-ssipəss təmiləkʷanehtehsin.
nə·kči-ssipəss
təmiləkʷanehtehsin

nə·kəloskɑpe oči-mɑčin.
nə·kəloskɑpe
oči-mɑčin

mɑlam·te wikəwamək pečohset,
mɑlam·te
wikəwamək
pečohset

wətihlɑn ohkəməssal, "ɑn ni,
wətihlɑn
ohkəməssal
ɑn ni

nə·č nihkʷɑp noli-ssipsohkɑn,
nə·č
nihkʷɑp
noli-ssipsohkɑn

nihkʷɑp·əč mečími wəli-awipən."
nihkʷɑp·əč
mečími
wəli-awipən

*Eventually where the ledge was high,*
    eventually ·INTENS
    where the ledge was high

*there is where he let him slip on purpose,*
    there· (is) where he let him slip
    on purpose

*then the great big bird fell and broke his wing.*
    then· great big bird
    he fell and broke his wing

*Then Gluskabe started off from there.*
    then· Gluskabe
    (then) he started off from (there)

*Eventually when he arrived (walking) at his house,*
    eventually ·INTENS
    at his house
    when he got there (walking)

*(Then) he told his grandmother, "Well then,*
    (then) he said to her
    his grandmother
    well then

*so now I will hunt ducks well,*
    so·WILL
    now
    (then) I hunt ducks well

*now the wind will always be nice and calm."*
    now ·WILL
    always
    the wind is nice and calm

kehəla·tte wəlawipən, ná(hə)law wətahsipsohkαn.

kehəla·tte

wəlawipən

ná(hə)law

wətahsipsohkαn

mečimawipən: kəspəne kehsək akʷαkʷaləsəpi

mečimawipən

kəspəne

kehsək

akʷαkʷaləsəpi

ahtαmα eləwe kisípəye.

ahtαmα

eləwe

kisípəye

wətihlαn ohkəməssal,

wətihlαn

ohkəməssal

"eləweč mina nətəlohsαn kəsəlαmsən eyit,

eləwe·č

mina

nətəlohsαn

kəsəlαmsən

eyit

wəsαmi mečimawipən."

wəsαmi

mečimawipən

*Sure enough, the wind was nice and calm, (so) he continually hunted ducks.*
> sure enough ·INTENS
> the wind was nice and calm
> continually/constantly/steadily
> (then) he hunted ducks

*The wind was constantly calm: eventually even there was so much scummy water*
> the wind was constantly calm
> eventually even
> there was so much
> scummy, slimy water

*he almost could not paddle at all.*
> not at all
> almost
> he could not paddle

*(Then) he told his grandmother,*
> (then) he told her
> his grandmother

*"It seems I will walk again to where the wind is,*
> it seems ·WILL
> again
> (then) I walk there
> wind
> where he is

*because the wind is constantly calm."*
> because
> the wind is constantly calm

mina wəmačin kči-ssipəss eyit.
 mina
 wəmačin
 kči-ssipəss
 eyit

mɑlam nəmɑ pečohset,
 mɑlam
 nəmɑ
 pečohset

nətahtɑmɑ (a)wewinɑkowəyal
 nətahtɑmɑ
 (a)wewinɑkowəyal

wəsɑm mina kisikənol wəpəyehsomal.
 wəsɑm
 mina
 kisikənol
 wəpəyehsomal

kəloskɑpe wətihlɑn kči-ssipsal, "nəmohsomi,
 kəloskɑpe
 wətihlɑn
 kči-ssipsal
 nəmohsomi

tɑn ali-təpihle etoči- mečími -awipək?"
 tɑn
 ali-təpihle
 etoči- mečími -awipək

"tɑn·əkʷa·p'·eht ali-təpihle,
 tɑn·əkʷa·p[a]·eht
 ali-təpihle

*(So) again he started off for where the great big bird was.*
    again
    (then) he started off
    great big bird
    where he is

*Eventually when he got there (walking),*
    eventually
    there
    when he got there (walking)

*he (Gluskabe) was not recognized by him (the bird) at all*
    not at all
    he did not recognize him

*because his hair had grown again.*
    because
    already
    they had grown
    his hairs

*(Then) Gluskabe said to the great big bird, "My grandfather,*
    Gluskabe
    (then) he told him
    great big bird
    my grandfather

*how does it happen that the wind is always so calm?"*
    which/how
    it happens (in some way)
    the wind is always so calm

*"Well so how it happened,*
    [see note]
    it happened (in some way)

senɑpe iyo wətali-pečohsɑn.
  senɑpe
  iyo
  wətali-pečohsɑn

apalahsɑtəpe; mɑčinɑkʷəso.
  apalahsɑtəpe
  mɑčinɑkʷəso

wətahčəwelətamən ɑkʷɑmələmsən.
  wətahčəwelətamən
  ɑkʷɑmələmsən

n·asohke nətihlɑn nətačelihton,
  n·asohke
  nətihlɑn
  nətačelihton

nə·tte tekaki-kisihatawa.
  nə·tte
  tekaki-kisihatawa

nətihləkon, 'kəmɑčewamələn etali-spatənek.'
  nətihləkon
  kəmɑčewamələn
  etali-spatənek

nə·kehəla mɑčewamit,
  nə·kehəla
  mɑčewamit

nəpənahkɑləkon, nətəmiləkʷanehtehsiməkon,
  nəpənahkɑləkon
  nətəmiləkʷanehtehsiməkon

*a man came here walking.*
> man
> here
> he arrived at . . . place (walking)

*He was bald-headed; he was ugly.*
> he was bald-headed
> he was ugly

*He wanted the wind to blow more.*
> he wanted it
> (for) the wind (to) blow more

*Then however I told him I couldn't do it,*
> then·however
> (then) I told him
> I could not do it/I was helpless about it

*that's as far as I could do.*
> that ·INTENS
> as far as I could do

*(Then) he told me, '(Then) I will carry you off on my back to where the mountain is high.'*
> (then) he told me
> (then) I carry you off (on my back)
> where the mountain is high/where the peak is

*Then sure enough when he carried me off on his back,*
> then· sure enough
> when he carried me off (on his back)

*(then) he threw me down, (then) he hit me against (the ground) so that my wing broke,*
> (then) he threw me down
> (then) he hit me (against something) breaking a wing

nihkʷαp pésəko·tte ípi nələkʷan."

    nihkʷαp

    pésəko·tte

    ípi

    nələkʷan

wətihlαn kəloskαpe, "nəmohsomi,

    wətihlαn

    kəloskαpe

    nəmohsomi

nəya·č mina kəpətəkohsaləl epəyanəpan,

    nəya·č

    mina

    kəpətəkohsaləl

    epəyanəpan

nαkα·č kolihtolən kələkʷan."

    nαkα·č

    kolihtolən

    kələkʷan

wətihlαn, "etáki·tte, nkʷenəss, ali-kisihatawane,

    wətihlαn

    etáki·tte

    nkʷenəss

    ali-kisihatawane

kamαč·əč nolitəhαsi,

    kamαč·əč

    nolitəhαsi

kis kamαč iyo nəsiwəssinən."

    kis

    kamαč

    iyo

    nəsiwəssinən

*now I have just one wing."*
>     now
>     one ·INTENS
>     only
>     my wing

*(Then) Gluskabe told him, "My grandfather,*
>     (then) he said to him
>     Gluskabe
>     my grandfather

*I will walk you back again to where you had sat,*
>     I ·WILL
>     again
>     I walk you back
>     where you had sat

*and I will fix your wing."*
>     and ·WILL
>     I make it right for you
>     your wing

*(Then) he said to him, "If indeed, my grandson, you can do that,*
>     (then) he said to him
>     if so/indeed ·INTENS
>     my grandchild
>     if you can do that

*I will be very happy,*
>     very ·WILL
>     I am happy

*already I am very tired of lying here."*
>     already
>     very
>     here
>     I am tired of lying in/on it

nə·kəloskɑpe (a)wihkʷhəwamɑn,
nə·kəloskɑpe
(a)wihkʷhəwamɑn

wətəlohsalɑn epilitəpan,
wətəlohsalɑn
epilitəpan

olihtawɑn wələkʷanal.
olihtawɑn
wələkʷanal

wətihlɑn, "nehe, nəmohsomi,
wətihlɑn
nehe
nəmohsomi

akʷečiləkʷanewi."
akʷečiləkʷanewi

nə·kehəla kči-ssipəss wətakʷečiləkʷanewin.
nə·kehəla
kči-ssipəss
wətakʷečiləkʷanewin

kəloskɑpe kipəlɑmsoke.
kəloskɑpe
kipəlɑmsoke

n·itak ssipəss, "kamɑč, nkʷenəss, kətalamihi."
n·itak
ssipəss
kamɑč
nkʷenəss
kətalamihi

*Then Gluskabe took him up on his back,*
> then· Gluskabe
> (then) he took him up on his back

*(then) he walked him to where he had sat,*
> (then) he walked him there
> where he [bird] had sat

*(then) he fixed his wing.*
> (then) he made his . . . right
> his wing

*(Then) he said to him, "Nehe, my grandfather,*
> (then) he said to him
> NEHE
> my grandfather

*try moving your wing(s)."*
> try moving your wing(s)

*Then sure enough, the great big bird tried moving his wing(s).*
> then· sure enough
> great big bird
> (then) he tried moving his wing(s)

*Gluskabe was blown over by the wind.*
> Gluskabe
> he was blown over by the wind

*Then the bird said, "I thank you very much, my grandchild."*
> then· (what) he said
> big bird
> very
> my grandchild
> you make me grateful/thankful

kəloskαpe wətihlαn, "nəmohsomi,
kəloskαpe
wətihlαn
nəmohsomi

nihkʷαp mosahk mina atoči- mečími -taliləkʷanewihkač,
nihkʷαp
mosahk
mina
atoči-
mečími
-taliləkʷanewihkač

wəsαmi mečiməlαmsək
wəsαmi
mečiməlαmsək

nətahtαmα kohsəssənawak kisi-katonkasolətiwəyak,
nətahtαmα
kohsəssənawak
kisi-katonkasolətiwəyak

etotəlαmsək tαn etoči-taliləkʷanewəyan,
etotəlαmsək
tαn
etoči-taliləkʷanewəyan

nətahtαmα kohsəssənawak kisi-ssipsohkasolətiwəyak,
nətahtαmα
kohsəssənawak
kisi-ssipsohkasolətiwəyak

wəsαm ahtαmα awen kisípəye sopekok.
wəsαm
ahtαmα
awen
kisípəye
sopekok

*(Then) Gluskabe said to him, "My grandfather,*
    Gluskabe
    (then) he said to him
    my grandfather

*now don't move your wings so constantly again,*
    now
    don't
    again
    so (much)
    always/constantly
    don't move your wings

*because when the wind blows constantly*
    because
    when the wind blows constantly

*our descendants cannot hunt for themselves at all,*
    not at all
    our descendants
    they (group) cannot hunt for themselves

*the wind blows so much whenever you move your wings,*
    the wind blows so much
    which(ever)
    point when you move your wings

*our descendants cannot hunt ducks for themselves at all,*
    not at all
    our descendants
    they (group) cannot hunt ducks for themselves

*because no one can paddle in the ocean.*
    because
    not at all
    anyone
    cannot paddle
    in the ocean

nihkʷɑp·əpa nɑnəkʷəč nkéki aliləkʷanewəyane ala nisókəni,

nihkʷɑp·əpa

nɑnəkʷəč

nkéki

aliləkʷanewəyane

ala

nisókəni

nə·kətɑtalahsimin nkéki,

nə·kətɑtalahsimin

nkéki

nə·č weči-kisi-ssipsohkasolətihətit kohsəssənawak sopekok.''

nə·č

weči-kisi-ssipsohkasolətihətit

kohsəssənawak

sopekok

itak ssipəss, ''kolɑme nkʷenəss,

itak

ssipəss

kolɑme

nkʷenəss

eləwe·tt'·eht wəsɑmi-mečimələmsən,

eləwe·tt[e]·eht

wəsɑmi-mečimələmsən

nihkʷɑp·əč ɑta atoči-mečimələmséno.''

nihkʷɑp·əč

ɑta

atoči-mečimələmséno

n·wəmɑčin wikəwɑmək kəloskɑpe.

n·wəmɑčin

wikəwɑmək

kəloskɑpe

*Now if sometimes you would move your wings all day, or for two days,*
    now ·WOULD
    some
    all day/one entire day
    if you move your wings
    or
    for two days

*then you rest for a whole day,*
    then· you rest
    all day/the whole day

*so that our descendants will be able to hunt ducks for themselves in the ocean."*
    so ·WILL
    so that they (group) can hunt ducks for themselves
    our descendants
    in the ocean

*The bird said, "You are right, my grandson,*
    (what) he said
    big bird
    you're right
    my grandchild

*I guess the wind blows too constantly.*
    it seems ·INTENS ·EHT
    the wind blows too constantly

*Now the wind will not blow so constantly."*
    now ·WILL
    not
    the wind does not blow so constantly

*Then Gluskabe started off to his house.*
    then· he started off
    to his house
    Gluskabe

nəmα pečohset, wəlitəhαso monimkʷehso.

nəmα
pečohset
wəlitəhαso
monimkʷehso

*When he got there (walking), Woodchuck was happy.*
> there
> when he got there (walking)
> she was happy
> Woodchuck

## NOTES

104   *wənihlawəya*: Verbs meaning 'kill'—rather than the more indirect 'get', 'catch', etc., as in English—are typically what are used in Penobscot (and Passamaquoddy-Maliseet) when talking about hunting success or failure.

106   *natəlohsαn*: 'Walk' sounds awkward in the English translation, but this is what is literally said, rather than a general 'go', because Penobscot speakers can (and everyday usage typically do) draw from a rich set of endings that specify which kind/means of movement is used, e.g., *-ohse* 'walk', *-pəye* 'paddle', *-αtawe* 'climb', etc.

109   *his hairs*: Penobscot generally refers to masses of strands like hair and grass as plurals. Passamaquoddy-Maliseet also does the same with seaweed (*kaskolosiyil*) and even the English terms "spaghetti" (*spaghetti-w-ol*) and "noodles" (*noodles-ol*).

110   *wənamihαl*: We refer to the Wind Bird in translation with 'he, him, his' because Gluskabe addresses him as 'my grandfather' while he addresses Woodchuck as 'my grandmother'.

110   *ktαhαnatαwi-*: Literally 'big, great, to a supernatural degree': *k(ə)t-* 'great, elder, large' plus *-ahαnəto* 'supernatural (power)'. Siebert often translated it as 'unnaturally large', but there is no evidence that it means unnatural size, only unusual, standing-out size, or size associated with power.

110   *ssipαss*: This word seems to refer originally to a certain kind of duck (according to the *Penobscot Dictionary*, the green-winged teal), and then also to ducks in general and duck-sized birds overall. (This is as opposed to *ssipsis*, which appears to refer to birds of roughly sparrow size, though the exact cutoff between these two is not known.) Many expressions referring generally to birds are also built from *ssipαss*, so for that reason and for simplicity (and also to follow the Penobscot tradition in English of calling it the Wind Bird, not the Wind Duck), we translate *ssipαss* as 'bird' here.

5

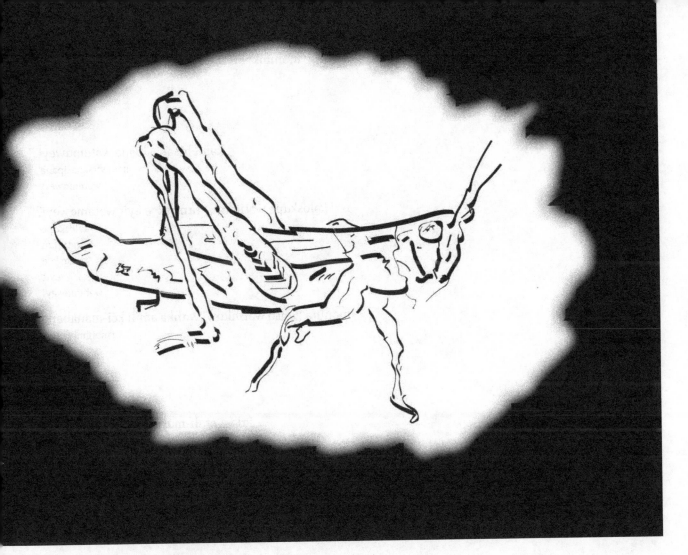

# palenəskʷ | nɑn

monimkʷehso wətihlɑn kəloskɑpal, "nkʷenəss,

> monimkʷehso
> wətihlɑn
> kəloskɑpal
> nkʷenəss

kəmehtsənasipəna wətamɑweyi."

> kəmehtsənasipəna
> wətamɑweyi

kəloskɑpe wətihlɑn, "tɑn·ɑskʷe eyit wətamɑweyi?"

> kəloskɑpe
> wətihlɑn
> tɑn·ɑskʷe
> eyit
> wətamɑweyi

monimkʷehso wətihlɑn, "wɑhka amíli kči-mənahanok,

> monimkʷehso
> wətihlɑn
> wɑhka
> amíli
> kči-mənahanok

čɑləss etali-mɑčekənɑt wətamɑweyɑl,

> čɑləss
> etali-mɑčekənɑt
> wətamɑweyɑl

*(Then) Woodchuck said to Gluskabe, "My grandchild,*
    Woodchuck
    (then) she said to him
    Gluskabe
    my grandchild

*we are out of tobacco."*
    we are out of . . .
    tobacco

*(Then) Gluskabe said to her, "Where (however) is tobacco?"*
    Gluskabe
    (then) he said to her
    where ·however
    where it is
    tobacco

*(Then) Woodchuck said to him, "Way off out on the water on a big island,*
    Woodchuck
    (then) she said to him
    way off
    out in the water
    on a big island

*(is) where Grasshopper is raising tobacco,*
    Grasshopper
    where he is raising it
    tobacco

kenok nətahtɑmɑ wəkiseləmɑwəyal.
>    kenok
>    nətahtɑmɑ
>    wəkiseləmɑwəyal

sakinɑkʷəso, nɑkɑ·ahči kinəhánəto; nsɑnɑkʷəso."
>    sakinɑkʷəso
>    nɑkɑ·ahči
>    kinəhánəto
>    nsɑnɑkʷəso

kəloskɑpe wətihlɑn ohkəməssal,
>    kəloskɑpe
>    wətihlɑn
>    ohkəməssal

"nəya·č nəkisihatawɑn wəkiseləmɑn wətamɑweyɑl."
>    nəya·č
>    nəkisihatawɑn
>    wəkiseləmɑn
>    wətamɑweyɑl

n·olihton akʷitən.
>    n·olihton
>    akʷitən

mɑlam·te kisihtɑkʷ,
>    mɑlam·te
>    kisihtɑkʷ

wəčawahpənəmən nəpik nɑkɑ wətamiltehkamən.
>    wəčawahpənəmən
>    nəpik
>    nɑkɑ
>    wətamiltehkamən

*but he does not share it at all.*
>  but
>  not at all
>  he does not share/allow it

*He is stingy, and also he has great supernatural power; he is dangerous."*
>  he is stingy
>  and ·also
>  he has great supernatural power
>  he is dangerous

*(Then) Gluskabe said to his grandmother,*
>  Gluskabe
>  (then) he said to her
>  his grandmother

*"I will be able to make him share tobacco."*
>  I ·WILL
>  I am able to make him (do it)
>  (for) him (to) allow/share it
>  (his/the) tobacco

*Then he made a canoe.*
>  then· he made it
>  canoe

*Finally when he had made it,*
>  eventually ·INTENS
>  when he had made it

*he put it in the water (by hand) and pushed it out into the water (by foot).*
>  he put it in the water (by hand)
>  in the water
>  and
>  he pushed it out into the water (by foot/body)

nə·peči-səwihle pesəkʷəta tekakɑpimək.
<br>
nə·peči-səwihle
<br>
pesəkʷəta
<br>
tekakɑpimək

nətahtekəne tepi-kəsihkɑwíhle wətol.
<br>
nətahtekəne
<br>
tepi-kəsihkɑwíhle
<br>
wətol

ni kətak wətəlihton.
<br>
ni
<br>
kətak
<br>
wətəlihton

n·ahč kisihtɑkʷ, wəčawahpənəmən.
<br>
n·ahč
<br>
kisihtɑkʷ
<br>
wəčawahpənəmən

wətepikətahin, wətamiltehkamən.
<br>
wətepikətahin
<br>
wətamiltehkamən

*Then it glided to reach one "look."*
    then· it glided to arrive at
    once/one time of
    as far as one looks (a "look")

*His canoe did not (despite his effort) go fast enough.*
    not (despite effort)
    it did not go fast enough
    his canoe

*Then he made another.*
    then
    another
    he made it

*Then also when he had made it, he put it in the water (by hand).*
    then·also
    when he had made it
    he put it in the water (by hand)

*(Then) he jumped in, (then) he pushed it out into the water (by foot).*
    (then) he jumped in
    (then) he pushed it out into the water (by foot/body)

nə·peči-səwihle nisəta tekakɑpimək.
<br>nə·peči-səwihle
<br>nisəta
<br>tekakɑpimək

mina ahtɑmɑ wətepinamowən.
<br>mina
<br>ahtɑmɑ
<br>wətepinamowən

nə·mina kətak wətəlihton.
<br>nə·mina
<br>kətak
<br>wətəlihton

nə·kisihtɑkʷ, wəčawahpənəmən.
<br>nə·kisihtɑkʷ
<br>wəčawahpənəmən

mina wətepikətahin, wətamiltehkamən.
<br>mina
<br>wətepikətahin
<br>wətamiltehkamən

nsəta tekakɑpimək peči-səwihle.
<br>nsəta
<br>tekakɑpimək
<br>peči-səwihle

nɑkɑ sípi epəkʷahč ɑpəteləmo.
<br>nɑkɑ sípi
<br>epəkʷahč
<br>ɑpəteləmo

*Then it glided to reach two "looks."*
    then· it glided to arrive at
    twice/two times
    as far as one looks (a "look")

*Again he did not at all see this as enough.*
    again
    not at all
    he did not see it as enough/it did not seem enough to him

*Then again he made another.*
    then· again
    another
    he made it

*Then when he had made it, he put it in the water (by hand).*
    then· when he had made it
    he put it in the water (by hand)

*(Then) again he jumped in, (then) he pushed it out into the water (by foot).*
    again
    (then) he jumped in
    (then) he pushed it out into the water (by foot/body)

*It glided to reach three "looks."*
    three times
    as far as one looks (a "look")
    it glided to arrive at

*And finally he even laughed.*
    and finally
    even
    he laughed

n·wətəlitəhaman čɑlsal kiwohse,

> n·wətəlitəhaman
> čɑlsal
> kiwohse

weči- nekəma -nəkihkɑnɑt wətamɑweyɑl.

> weči-
> nekəma
> -nəkihkɑnɑt
> wətamɑweyɑl

pečohset nəmɑ, kehəlɑ·tte,

> pečohset
> nəmɑ
> kehəlɑ·tte

ahtɑmɑ čɑləss áyi,

> ahtɑmɑ
> čɑləss
> áyi

məsi kehs(ə)lɑt čɑləss,

> məsi
> kehs(ə)lɑt
> čɑləss

péči·tte pemikičik wətamɑweyɑl wətahkihkɑnək [kəloskɑpe/čɑləss].

> péči·tte
> pemikičik
> wətamɑweyɑl
> wətahkihkɑnək
> kəloskɑpe/čɑləss

*Then by thinking he made Grasshopper walk wandering,*
> then· he thought him
> Grasshopper
> he walks wandering

*so that he (Gluskabe) could get all the tobacco.*
> so that
> he [emphasizing that it is Gluskabe]
> (that) he (could) get all of it
> tobacco

*When he got there (walking), sure enough,*
> when he got there (walking)
> there
> sure enough ·INTENS

*Grasshopper wasn't there at all.*
> not at all
> Grasshopper
> he was not there

*(He took) all that Grasshopper had of it (tobacco),*
> all
> how much he had
> Grasshopper

*even the ones of his/the tobacco growing in his garden [Gluskabe/Grasshopper].*
> even up to ·INTENS
> the ones that were growing (along)
> his/the tobacco
> in his [Grasshopper's] garden/planting
> Gluskabe/Grasshopper

nɑkɑ mina wətepihasin wətolək,
> nɑkɑ
> mina
> wətepihasin
> wətolək

nɑkɑ wətamiltehkamən.
> nɑkɑ
> wətamiltehkamən

nəmɑ·tte peči-səwihle wətahsitəmomək.
> nəmɑ·tte
> peči-səwihle
> wətahsitəmomək

wətihlɑn ohkəməssal, "nəpetholɑn wətamɑweyi,
> wətihlɑn
> ohkəməssal
> nəpetholɑn
> wətamɑweyi

ɑtɑ·č mina kənatawihokowina."
> ɑtɑ·č
> mina
> kənatawihokowina

wəlitəhɑso monimkʷehso.
> wəlitəhɑso
> monimkʷehso

eskʷa n·etalətonkehətit, n·wəpečipəyehlɑn čaləss,
> eskʷa
> n·etalətonkehətit
> n·wəpečipəyehlɑn
> čaləss

*And again then he got right into his canoe,*
    and
    again
    (then) he quickly got in
    into his canoe

*and he pushed it out into the water (by foot/body).*
    and
    (then) he pushed it out into the water (by foot/body)

*It glided to reach right there at his shore-strip.*
    there ·INTENS
    it glided to arrive at
    his shore-strip

*(Then) he said to his grandmother, "I bring tobacco (by boat),*
    (then) he said to her
    his grandmother
    I bring it by boat
    tobacco

*it will never be scarce for us again."*
    not ·WILL
    again
    it does not cause us scarcity/go scarce on us

*Woodchuck was happy.*
    she was happy
    Woodchuck

*While they were talking, then Grasshopper arrived paddling quickly,*
    still
    then· as they were talking
    then· he came paddling quickly up
    Grasshopper

n·wəkakaləwan, wətitamən, "kənəkka-kəmotənamin notamaweyim!"
n·wəkakaləwan
wətitamən
kənəkka-kəmotənamin
notamaweyim

nə·kəloskape wənotehlan, onaskawan čalsal.
nə·kəloskape
wənotehlan
onaskawan
čalsal

wətihlan, "kolame,
wətihlan
kolame

nənəkkana, weči·ask<sup>w</sup>e- nihkáni kohsəssənawak (·ahč nékəma) -kisawehkəhahətit."
nənəkkana
weči·ask<sup>w</sup>e-
nihkáni
kohsəssənawak
[·ahč nékəma]
-kisawehkəhahətit

wətihlan čalsal, "ahtama kolalóhke,
wətihlan
čalsal
ahtama
kolalóhke

kətali-sakeləman wətamaweyi,
kətali-sakeləman
wətamaweyi

kehsi-kisikənat,
kehsi-kisikənat

*then he called out, and he said, "You stole all of my tobacco!"*
> then· he called out
> (then) he said
> you stole (it) all from me
> my tobacco

*Then Gluskabe went out to meet Grasshopper.*
> then· Gluskabe
> (then) he went out
> (for) him (to) meet him
> Grasshopper

*(Then) he said to him, "You're right,*
> (then) he said to him
> you are right

*I took it all, so that (however) in the future our descendants [they too] can use it."*
> I took it all
> so that ·however
> in the future
> our descendants
> [·also they]
> that they can use it

*(Then) he said to Grasshopper, "You did not do a good thing at all,*
> (then) he said to him
> Grasshopper
> not at all
> you did not do a good thing

*you being stingy sharing tobacco.*
> for you to be stingy sharing it
> tobacco

*You have grown so much of it,*
> how much you raise/grow (of) it

nətah·apa kəya kkehsawehkəhαwən."
    nətah·apa
    kəya
    kkehsawehkəhαwən

itak čαləss, "kinαkʷ·əka mili skaniminal,
    itak
    čαləss
    kinαkʷ·əka
    mili
    skaniminal

weči·č-kisikənok tαn kehsi-ččəweləmok."
    weči·č-kisikənok
    tαn
    kehsi-ččəweləmok

kəloskαpe wətihlαn,
    kəloskαpe
    wətihlαn

"ahtαmα kəmiləlowənal skaniminal,
    ahtαmα
    kəmiləlowənal
    skaniminal

kenok·əči kəmilələn tαn kehsi-katawawehkəhat
    kenok·əči
    kəmilələn
    tαn
    kehsi-katawawehkəhat

tαn kʷenαwəsəyan."
    tαn
    kʷenαwəsəyan

*you would never use so much."*
    not ·WOULD
    you
    (so) you do not use so much of it

*Grasshopper said, "At least give me seeds,*
    (what) he said
    Grasshopper
    at least ·KA
    give me it/them
    seeds

*so that I will be able to grow however much I want/need."*
    so that I will be able to grow it
    which(ever)
    how much I want/need of it

*(Then) Gluskabe said to him,*
    Gluskabe
    (then) he said to him

*"I am not giving you seeds at all,*
    not at all
    I do not give you them
    seeds

*but I will give you however much you are going to use of it*
    but ·WILL
    I give you it
    which(ever)
    how much you are going to use (of) it

*for however long you live."*
    which(ever)
    how long you live

n·wətihlɑn, "nihkʷɑp,
n·wətihlɑn
nihkʷɑp

kəmilələn wətamɑweyi
kəmilələn
wətamɑweyi

tɑn kʷenɑpemat kʷenɑwəsəyan."
tɑn
kʷenɑpemat
kʷenɑwəsəyan

n·wətihlɑn, "nehe, mkətonewi."
n·wətihlɑn
nehe
mkətonewi

n·wəpisənəmawɑn wətonək wətamɑweyɑl.
n·wəpisənəmawɑn
wətonək
wətamɑweyɑl

wətihlɑn, "ɑn ni, nihkʷɑp kkisɑpesin kəya!"
wətihlɑn
ɑn ni
nihkʷɑp
kkisɑpesin
kəya

wənimiphɑn čɑlsal
wənimiphɑn
čɑlsal

nɑkɑ wəpəssikinahatawɑn wətahpskʷanse.
nɑkɑ
wəpəssikinahatawɑn
wətahpskʷanse

*Then he told him, "Now,*
  (then) he said to him
  now

*I give you tobacco*
  (then) I give you it
  tobacco

*for however long you benefit from it for however long you live."*
  which(ever)
  however long/as long as you benefit from it
  however long/as long as you live

*Then he said to him, "Nehe, open your mouth."*
  then· he said to him
  NEHE
  open your mouth!

*Then he put the tobacco inside his mouth for him.*
  then· he put it inside for him
  in his mouth
  tobacco

*(Then) he said to him, "Well then, now you have gotten your share!"*
  (then) he said to him
  well then
  now
  (so) you have gotten your share/benefit
  you

*(Then) he grabbed Grasshopper*
  (then) he grabbed him
  Grasshopper

*and he tore his coat so that it split.*
  and
  (then) he tore his . . . (so it) split
  his coat

wətihlɑn, "yok nihkʷɑp kkisihtolən kələkʷanak.
>    wətihlɑn
>    yok
>    nihkʷɑp
>    kkisihtolən
>    kələkʷanak

nihkʷɑp, mɑčetəwihla!
>    nihkʷɑp
>    mɑčetəwihla

nə·kkisɑpesin."
>    nə·kkisɑpesin

*(Then) he said to him, "So now I have made you these wings of yours.*
> (then) he said to him
> these
> now
> (so) I have made them for you
> your wings

*Now, fly off!*
> now
> fly off!

*So you have gotten your share."*
> then· you have gotten your share/benefit

## NOTES

PAGE
135    *palenəsk*ᵂ: Two words for 'five' are found in the Penobscot speech community; both are related to terms for 'five' found in various other Eastern Algonquian languages. In particular, *palenəsk*ᵂ appears to mean something like 'one side of (a pair of) the hands'.

140    *tekakɑpimək*: Literally 'as far as one looks', this form is noted in the 1918 version as "a commonly recognized unit of measure, known as a 'look'. In the open or on the water, this would mean about a league; in the woods, about two hundred yards, as the term is used by the Indians" (197). But in *Penobscot Man* (79), Speck later described it as "a familiar ancient measure of distance on water, in the forest or along the shore, and from the mountain top alike, was a 'look', called *tekakɑpimək* [*retranscribed here*], 'as far as one can see'; the 'plastic mile'. When given a trial in the wilderness its value as a measure is convincing when following directions given by a guide." The *Penobscot Dictionary* gives *tekakɑ́pimək* as 'to the limit of vision, as far as it is seen, as far as it is in sight, as far as is visible'.

145    *Then by thinking he made*: see the introduction regarding the power of thought.

154    *nə·kkisɑpesin*: The 1918 version here notes that this accounts for both the wings of grasshoppers and the brown juice that comes from their mouths, quoting unnamed community members as saying, "He only has enough for one chew, but that lasts him all the time."

6

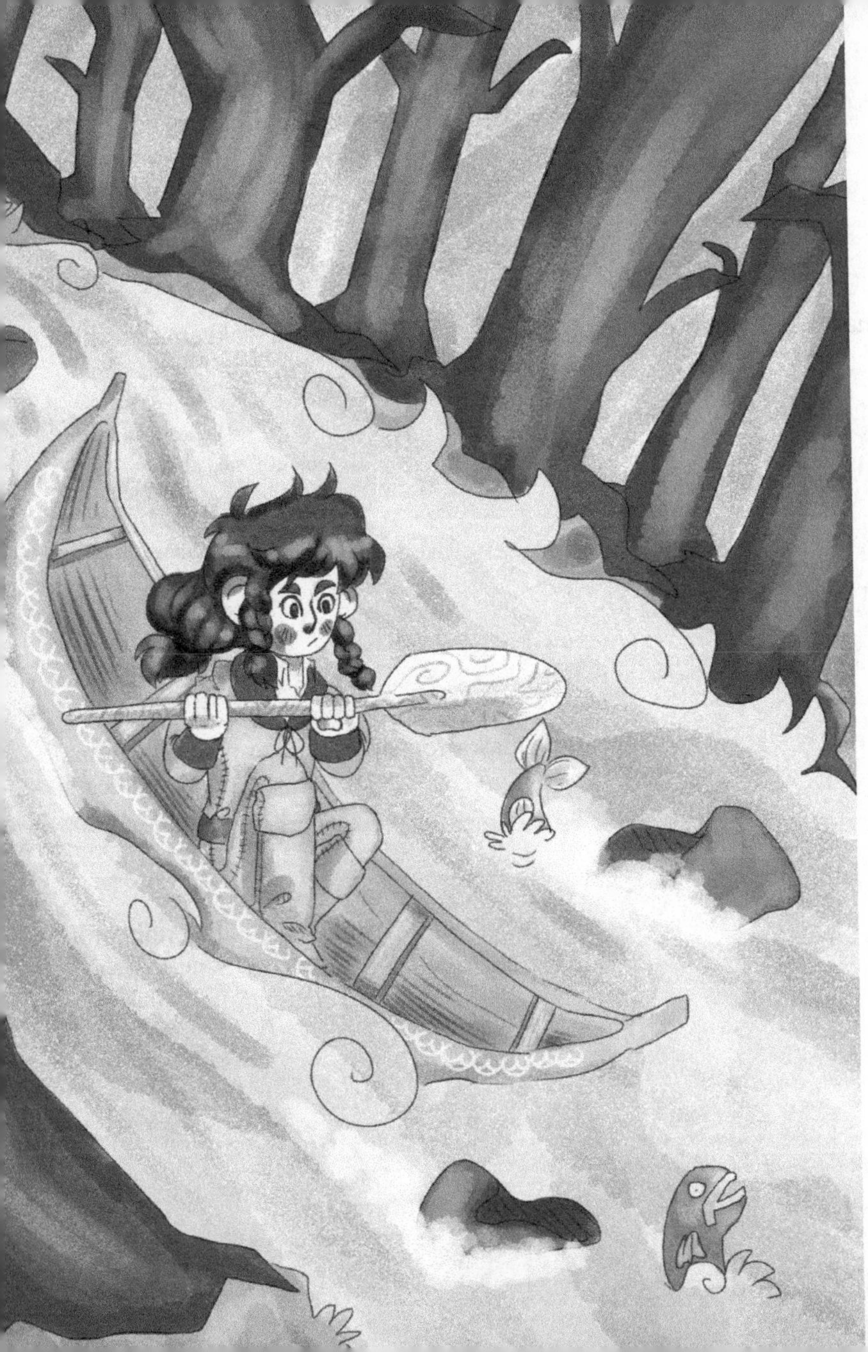

# nəkʷətɑs

kəloskɑpe wətihlɑn ohkəməssal, "nihkʷɑp, nohkəmi,

    kəloskɑpe

    wətihlɑn

    ohkəməssal

    nihkʷɑp

    nohkəmi

nəkʷilawi-wəlihton tɑn·əč kohsəssənawak weči- ɑta -sakkahətihətihkʷ

    nəkʷilawi-wəlihton

    tɑn·əč

    kohsəssənawak

    weči- ɑta -sakkahətihətihkʷ

eləmɑwəsihətit nihkáni.

    eləmɑwəsihətit

    nihkáni

nihkʷɑp nəposin,

    nihkʷɑp

    nəposin

nətəpinawihton sipəwal nɑkɑ məkʷasəpemal.

    nətəpinawihton

    sipəwal

    nɑkɑ

    məkʷasəpemal

nihkʷɑp·ahč nəsipkihla, nohkəmi,

    nihkʷɑp·ahč

    nəsipkihla

    nohkəmi

*(Then) Gluskabe told his grandmother, "Now, my grandmother,*
    Gluskabe
    (then) he told her
    his grandmother
    now
    my grandmother

*I will search for and fix up ways so that our descendants do not have a hard time*
    I will search for and fix it up
    how ·WILL
    our descendants
    so that they (group) do not have a hard time

*as they live on in the future.*
    as they live on(ward)
    in the future

*(So) now I leave by boat,*
    now
    (so) I leave by boat

*(so) I examine the rivers and lakes.*
    (so) I examine them
    rivers
    and
    lakes

*Now too I go for a long time, my grandmother,*
    now ·also
    I go (for) a long time
    my grandmother

kenok mosahk nsahihkač."

    kenok
    mosahk
    nsahihkač

n·wəposin, wəmačepəyɑn,

    n·wəposin
    wəmačepəyɑn

məsi wəpihthihlɑnal sipəwal sɑkətehtək°ekil sopekok.

    məsi
    wəpihthihlɑnal
    sipəwal
    sɑkətehtək°ekil
    sopekok

wətəpinawihtonal.

    wətəpinawihtonal

nə·tɑmɑ sakikke olihton,

    nə·tɑmɑ
    sakikke
    olihton

eləmi-pɑntək°ihkek,

    eləmi-pɑntək°ihkek

weči·č- ɑta -atoči-sakkahətihətihk° ohsəssa nihkɑ́ni.

    weči·č-
    ɑta
    -atoči-sakkahətihətihk°
    ohsəssa
    nihkɑ́ni

*but don't worry about me (facing danger)."*
>  but
>  don't
>  don't worry about me (facing danger)

*Then he set off by boat, (then) he paddled off,*
>  then he set off by boat
>  (then) he paddled off

*he entered all the rivers that open out at the ocean.*
>  all
>  he entered them
>  rivers
>  ones that open out (as rivers)
>  at the ocean

*He examined them.*
>  he examined them

*Then if it was difficult somewhere he fixed it,*
>  then· somewhere
>  if it was difficult/hard
>  (then) he fixed it

*where lots of (water)falls went onward,*
>  where lots of (water)falls went onward

*so that his descendants would not have such a hard time in the future.*
>  so that ·WILL
>  not
>  that they (group) do not have so hard a time
>  his descendants
>  in the future

**məsi·ahč péči wənikanal**
  məsi·ahč
  péči
  wənikanal

**wəkisi-mosiktehəmənal**
  wəkisi-mosiktehəmənal

**weči-wəlɑwətəssək.**
  weči-wəlɑwətəssək

**mɑlam·te pesəkʷən sipo pihthipəyet,**
  mɑlam·te
  pesəkʷən
  sipo
  pihthipəyet

**nə·ponək wətol,**
  nə·ponək
  wətol

**wəkətəkʷahton,**
  wəkətəkʷahton

**nə·tte etali-pənahpskʷihlɑk,**
  nə·tte
  etali-pənahpskʷihlɑk

*Also even all the portages*
    all ·also
    even
    portages

*he chopped them clear*
    he chopped them clear

*so that it/they would be a good path.*
    so that it/they would be a good path

*Finally when he paddled into one river,*
    eventually ·INTENS
    one/a certain one/there was one
    river
    when he paddled into

*then when he put down his canoe,*
    then· when he put it down
    his canoe

*he set it down upside down,*
    (then) he set it down upside down

*that is where it turned to stone,*
    there ·INTENS
    (is) where it turned to stone

eskʷa nihkʷαp·te.
eskʷa
nihkʷαp·te

*still even right now.*
    still
    now ·INTENS

## NOTES

PAGE

162   *wənikanal*: This term for 'portage, carry' may literally come from an old verb 'carry', in which case the French- and English-based terms may be direct translations from the Penobscot or related languages.

162   *etali-pənahpskʷihlɑk*: The 1918 version notes, "This was at the mouth of the Penobscot River, and the canoe is nowadays pointed out as rock lying on the shore near Castine" (200). Note that at the start of the fourth story, Gluskabe creates his stone canoe from a point of land, so this has gone full circle.

7

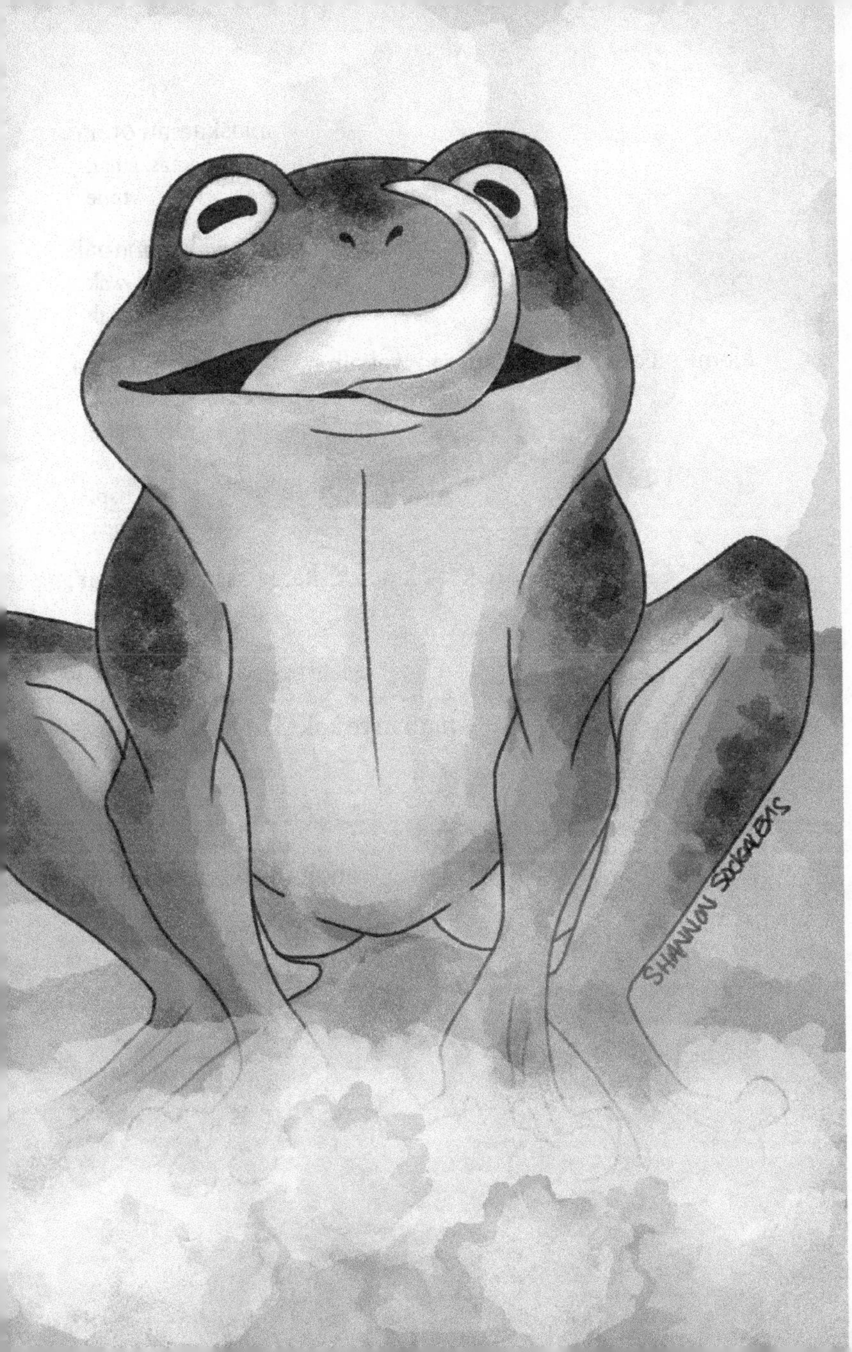

# tὰpawαs

aməskamən otene.
    aməskamən
    otene

kətəmɑkinɑkʷəsolətəwak alənɑpak.
    kətəmɑkinɑkʷəsolətəwak
    alənɑpak

eləmi-naləməwik ɑkələpemo wəkəlhamawɑn nəpi alənɑpa.
    eləmi-naləməwik
    ɑkələpemo
    wəkəlhamawɑn
    nəpi
    alənɑpa

[nəpi] nɑnəkʷəč kʷaskʷi-katawəssəmolətəwak.
    nəpi
    nɑnəkʷəč
    kʷaskʷi-katawəssəmolətəwak

mɑlam·te kəloskɑpe tali-pečohse.
    mɑlam·te
    kəloskɑpe
    tali-pečohse

wənamihɑ wətalənɑpema;
    wənamihɑ
    wətalənɑpema

*He found a village.*
   he found it
   village

*The People were looking pitiful.*
   they (group) were looking pitiful
   people/People

*Away up on the river, Uugulubemo forbid the People water.*
   away up on the river
   Uugulubemo
   he forbid them it
   water
   People

*Some died of thirst [for water].*
   water [may be error]
   some
   they (group) died of thirst

*Finally Gluskabe arrived there (walking).*
   eventually ·INTENS
   Gluskabe
   he arrived there (walking)

*He saw his people;*
   he saw them
   his people

kətəmɑkinɑkʷəsolətəwak.

kətəmɑkinɑkʷəsolətəwak

n·wətakʷečimolɑn,

n·wətakʷečimolɑn

"tɑn ali-təpihle?"

tɑn

ali-təpihle

itamohətit, "kekɑ nənəkkahtahokona ɑkələpemo,

itamohətit

kekɑ

nənəkkahtahokona

ɑkələpemo

nəkʷaskʷi-katawəssəmolətipəna,

nəkʷaskʷi-katawəssəmolətipəna

nəkəlhamɑkonena nəpi."

nəkəlhamɑkonena

nəpi

n·wətitamən kəloskɑpe,

n·wətitamən

kəloskɑpe

"nəya·č nəkisihatawɑn kəmiləkonɑ nəpi."

nəya·č

nəkisihatawɑn

kəmiləkonɑ

nəpi

n·wətəlohsɑnɑ sɑkəmɑl ɑkələpemo eyit,

n·wətəlohsɑnɑ

sɑkəmɑl

ɑkələpemo

eyit

*they were looking pitiful.*
    they (group) were looking pitiful

*Then he asked them,*
    then· he asked them

*"What happened?"*
    which
    it happened (in some way)

*They said, "Uugulubemo has almost killed us all,*
    (what) they said
    almost
    he has killed us all
    Uugulubemo

*we are dying of thirst,*
    we (group) are dying of thirst

*he has forbidden us water."*
    he forbids us it
    water

*Then Gluskabe said,*
    then· he said
    Gluskabe

*"I will be able to make him give you water."*
    I ·WILL
    I make him (do it)
    (for) him (to) give you (pl.) it
    water

*Then they went (walking) with the chief (Gluskabe) to where Uugulubemo was,*
    then· they walked there (with him)
    chief
    Uugulubemo
    where he was

n·wətihlɑn, "kekʷ mehsi-kətəmɑkihat kohsəssənawak?

    n·wətihlɑn
    kekʷ
    mehsi-kətəmɑkihat
    kohsəssənawak

n·asohke nihkʷɑp kotelətamən eli-kətəmɑkihat kohsəssənawak,

    n·asohke
    nihkʷɑp
    kotelətamən
    eli-kətəmɑkihat
    kohsəssənawak

nihkʷɑp nəya nəmilɑn nəpi,

    nihkʷɑp
    nəya
    nəmilɑn
    nəpi

nə·məsi·č kətetəpi-wəlɑpetámənɑ."

    nə·məsi·č
    kətetəpi-wəlɑpetámənɑ

wənimiphɑn nɑkɑ wətəmɑhikanephɑn:

    wənimiphɑn
    nɑkɑ
    wətəmɑhikanephɑn

weči- nihkʷɑp -təmɑhikanɑt məsi kəpalɑmak.

    weči-
    nihkʷɑp
    -təmɑhikanɑt
    məsi
    kəpalɑmak

*then he said to him, "Why are you making our descendants pitiful?*
>     then· he said to him
>     what
>     why are you making them pitiful
>     our descendants

*So however now you regret how you made our descendants pitiful,*
>     then·however
>     now
>     you regret it
>     how you make them pitiful
>     our descendants

*now I am giving them water,*
>     now
>     I
>     I give them it
>     water

*and you will all equally well benefit from it."*
>     then· all ·WILL
>     you (pl.) equally well benefit from it

*(Then) he grabbed him and he broke his spine with a yank:*
>     (then) he grabbed him
>     and
>     (then) he broke his spine (by a quick motion/grabbing)

*(that's) why every (bull)frog has a broken spine.*
>     (reason) why
>     now
>     she/he has a broken spine
>     all/every
>     (bull)frogs

mehč nətahtαmα wəkiselətamowən nəpi.

mehč

nətahtαmα

wəkiselətamowən

nəpi

kəloskαpe (a)wihkʷənəmən wətəmhikan

kəloskαpe

(a)wihkʷənəmən

wətəmhikan

nαkα sípi wətəmtəhαn—kči-apasi wikʷesk—wəkawəhαn αkələpeməwal,

nαkα sípi

wətəmtəhαn

kči-apasi

wikʷesk

wəkawəhαn

αkələpeməwal

nˑeli-kawihlαt wikʷesk, αkələpeməwal wəkʷaskʷtəhαn.

nˑeli-kawihlαt

wikʷesk

αkələpeməwal

wəkʷaskʷtəhαn

nəˑweči-kisi-təpihlαk sipo pαnawαhpskewtəkʷ,

nəˑweči-kisi-təpihlαk

sipo

pαnawαhpskewtəkʷ

nəˑməsi pskahtəkʷənol sipəwal,

nəˑməsi

pskahtəkʷənol

sipəwal

*Still he did not release the water at all.*
> still
> not at all
> he did not allow/release it
> water

*Gluskabe took his hatchet*
> Gluskabe
> he took it
> his hatchet

*and finally he chopped it down—a great big tree, a yellow birch—(then) he felled it onto Uugulubemo.*
> and finally
> he chopped it down/he severed it by hitting
> great big tree
> yellow birch
> (then) he felled it on him
> Uugulubemo

*Then as the yellow birch fell, it smashed Uugulubemo to death.*
> then· as it fell
> yellow birch
> Uugulubemo
> (then) it smashed him to death

*That is where the Penobscot River came to be from,*
> that· (is) why/from where it came to be
> river
> Penobscot River

*and then all of the branches (became) rivers,*
> then· all
> branches
> rivers

nə·məsi sakətehtəkʷal kči-sipok; wəči-kisi-təpihle kči-sipo

nə·məsi

sakətehtəkʷal

kči-sipok

wəči-kisi-təpihle

kči-sipo

nə·məsi alənɑpak etoči-katawəssəmolətihətit, nə·məsi wəčawpikətaholətinɑ,

nə·məsi

alənɑpak

etoči-katawəssəmolətihətit

nə·məsi

wəčawpikətaholətinɑ

nə·nɑnəkʷəč namehsihlawələtəwak,

nə·nɑnəkʷəč

namehsihlawələtəwak

čəkʷalsəwihlawələtəwak,

čəkʷalsəwihlawələtəwak

toləpayihlawələtəwak.

toləpayihlawələtəwak

wahkehsəwak ípi wetɑwəsolətičik.

wahkehsəwak

ípi

wetɑwəsolətičik

nihkʷɑp nə·weči-mɑčekihətit kətakik alənɑpak.

nihkʷɑp

nə·weči-mɑčekihətit

kətakik

alənɑpak

*then they all opened into the great river; the great river came from there.*
>then· all
>they open out (as river mouths)
>on the great big river
>it came from there/that
>great big river

*Then all the People were so thirsty, then they all jumped into the water,*
>then· all
>People
>they (group) were so thirsty
>then· all
>(then) they (group) jumped into the water

*(then) some turned into fish,*
>then· some
>they (group) turned into fish

*(some) turned into frogs,*
>they (group) turned into frogs

*(some) turned into turtles.*
>they (group) turned into turtles

*Only a few survived [= didn't transform].*
>a few of them
>only
>(were) the ones who (group) survived

*Now that is where the other People grew from.*
>now
>that· where they grew from
>other
>People

nihkʷɑp weči wətetakʷapihtámənɑ pɑnawɑhpskewtək.

nihkʷɑp

weči-

wətetakʷapihtámənɑ

pɑnawɑhpskewtək

nəˑweči- nihkʷɑp -ali-wisolətihətit nɑnəkʷəč namehsak,

nəˑweči-

nihkʷɑp

-ali-wisolətihətit

nɑnəkʷəč

namehsak

namehsihlɑwələtihətit wətalənɑpeməwɑka.

namehsihlɑwələtihətit

wətalənɑpeməwɑka

nihkʷɑp nəˑweči-wihkʷənəmohətit eli-wisolətihətit:

nihkʷɑp

nəˑweči-wihkʷənəmohətit

eli-wisolətihətit

ehkihkikit namehsak nɑkɑ toləpak.

ehkihkikit

namehsak

nɑkɑ

toləpak

*Now (that's) why they occupy both sides/ends of the Penobscot River.*
> now
> why/from
> they sit on both sides/ends of it
> Penobscot River

*That is why now some of them are called (as/after) fish,*
> that· (is) why
> now
> that they (group) are called . . .
> some
> fish(es)

*as their absent relatives turned into fish.*
> as they (group) became fish
> their absent/deceased people/relations/relatives

*Now that is where they took it from, how they are called:*
> now
> that· (is) where they took it from
> how they (group) are called

*all kinds of fishes and turtles.*
> which is/are of various kinds
> fish(es)
> and
> turtles

## NOTES

PAGE

168  *aləˈnɑpak:* Lyon may be using *aləˈnɑpak* here in the earlier sense of 'people, humans', rather than the later and current main use as specifically '(the) People, Indigenous people', though it is difficult to be sure, so we have chosen to translate as 'People' here.

172  *-təmɑhikanɑt:* This refers to the little crook in a frog's back.

8

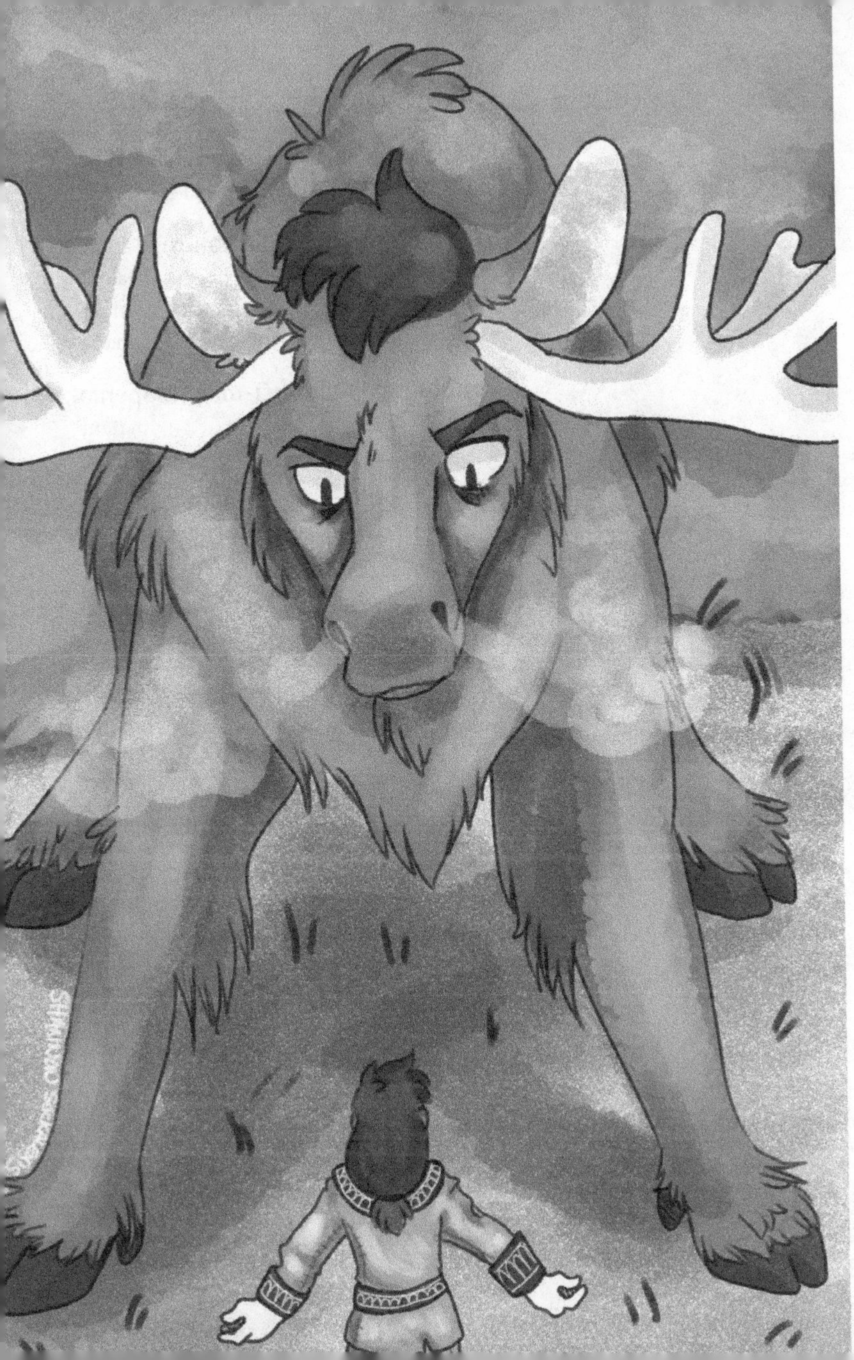

# nsɑsək

nə·kəloskɑpe oči-mɑčehlɑn.
    nə·kəloskɑpe
    oči-mɑčehlɑn

kətakihi akʷiláwəhɑn alənɑpa.
    kətakihi
    akʷiláwəhɑn
    alənɑpa

mɑlam pečihlɑt kčī-məkʷasəpemək,
    mɑlam
    pečihlɑt
    kčī-məkʷasəpemək

etali-mskawɑt alənɑpa.
    etali-mskawɑt
    alənɑpa

wətihləkon, "kamɑč nsɑnɑkʷat iyo nətotenena.
    wətihləkon
    kamɑč
    nsɑnɑkʷat
    iyo
    nətotenena

nəməsselohtəhokona ktəhɑnətəwi-mos,
    nəməsselohtəhokona
    ktəhɑnətəwi-mos

ahtɑm'·eləwe nəkisi-katonkasolətippəna."
    ahtɑm[ɑ]·eləwe
    nəkisi-katonkasolətippəna

*Then Gluskabe started off from there.*
    then· Gluskabe
    (then) he headed off from there

*(Then) he looked for other People.*
    other (ones)
    (then) he looked for them
    People

*Eventually when he got to a greeeat big lake,*
    eventually
    when he arrived
    [at] a greeeat big lake

*where he found the People.*
    where he found them
    People

*(Then) they told him, "This village of ours is very dangerous.*
    (then) they told him
    very
    it is dangerous
    this
    our town

*A supernaturally huge moose has killed a lot of us,*
    it has killed many of us
    a supernaturally huge moose

*we almost cannot hunt at all for ourselves."*
    not at all ·almost
    we (group) cannot hunt for ourselves

wətihlɑn, "nəya·č nəkʷiláwəhɑ,
  wətihlɑn
  nəya·č
  nəkʷiláwəhɑ

nəya·č kənihtamólənɑ."
  nəya·č
  kənihtamólənɑ

wespɑsahkiwik oči-mɑčehlɑn akʷiláwəhɑn kči-mosol.
  wespɑsahkiwik
  oči-mɑčehlɑn
  akʷiláwəhɑn
  kči-mosol

mɑlam aməskamən awəssənoti,etaləssinəlit.
  mɑlam
  aməskamən
  awəssənoti
  etaləssinəlit

n·as·te wəkalapənɑn, n·wənohsohkawɑn.
  n·as·te
  wəkalapənɑn
  n·wənohsohkawɑn

eləmiphəkʷet mosol,
  eləmiphəkʷet
  mosol

saláhki elɑpit nihkáni elkʷehlɑt,
  saláhki
  elɑpit
  nihkáni
  elkʷehlɑt

*(Then) he told them, "I will look for him,*
    (then) he told them
    I ·WILL
    I look for him

*I will kill him for you."*
    I ·WILL
    I kill him for you (pl.)

*The next morning, (then) he started off from there to look for the great moose.*
    the next morning
    (then) he went off from there
    (for) him to look for him
    great moose

*Eventually he found the yard, where he was bedding down.*
    eventually
    he found it
    moose-/deer-yard
    where he [the moose] was lying/bedding down

*Right then too he spooked him (by hand), then he followed him.*
    then·also ·INTENS
    he spooked him (by hand)
    then· he followed him

*As he chased the moose onward,*
    as he chased it
    moose

*at one point as he looked ahead where he was facing as he was going,*
    at one point
    as he looked
    in front
    where he was facing as he was going

wənamihton wikəwɑmsis, sətikkɑnsis.

wənamihton

wikəwɑmsis

sətikkɑnsis

n·as·te wəsɑkhi-notessɑn phenəm.

n·as·te

wəsɑkhi-notessɑn

phenəm

elɑpit kəloskɑpe, pohkəčinskʷehso.

elɑpit

kəloskɑpe

pohkəčinskʷehso

manəni·tte pəmihle.

manəni·tte

pəmihle

ahtɑmɑ wətɑsitemɑwəyal keti-pahpiməkoht.

ahtɑmɑ

wətɑsitemɑwəyal

keti-pahpiməkoht

pesəkʷən elihlɑt.

pesəkʷən

elihlɑt

pohkəčinskʷehso moskʷelətam.

pohkəčinskʷehso

moskʷelətam

itak, "kamɑč kkati-pɑlikʷewi.

itak

kamɑč

kkati-pɑlikʷewi

*he saw a little house, a little evergreen-bough house.*
> he saw it
> a little house
> a little evergreen-bough shelter

*Right then too a woman walked out into view.*
> then also ·INTENS
> (then) she walked out into view
> woman

*As Gluskabe looked, it was Jug-Woman.*
> as he looked
> Gluskabe
> (it was) Jug-Woman

*Right away he went along.*
> right away ·INTENS
> he went along

*He didn't answer her at all as she wanted to joke with him.*
> not at all
> he did not answer her
> as she wanted to joke with him

*He kept going just the same.*
> it was just the same
> (how) he went

*Jug-Woman got angry.*
> Jug-Woman
> she got angry

*She said, "You want to be all proud-faced.*
> (what) she said
> very
> you want to be proud-faced

nihkʷɑpˑɑskʷe kətəli-namihtonˑəč."

nihkʷɑpˑɑskʷe
kətəli-namihtonˑəč

nˑetoči-nohsohkawɑt kəloskɑpal.

nˑetoči-nohsohkawɑt
kəloskɑpal

eləmihlɑt, eləmihlɑt;

eləmihlɑt
eləmihlɑt

tɑmɑ pɑnihlɑt nawɑpaməkʷek, ahtɑmɑ wənamihɑwəyal;

tɑmɑ pɑnihlɑt
nawɑpaməkʷek
ahtɑmɑ
wənamihɑwəyal

mina tɑmɑ pɑnihlɑt, ahtɑmɑ wənamihɑwəyal.

mina
tɑmɑ pɑnihlɑt
ahtɑmɑ
wənamihɑwəyal

itak, "kamɑč kɑkɑwihle senɑpe."

itak
kamɑč
kɑkɑwihle
senɑpe

[n]ˑɑskʷe kəloskɑpe, pečihlɑt sipok, sɑkətehtəkok,

[n]ˑɑskʷe
kəloskɑpe
pečihlɑt
sipok
sɑkətehtəkok

*Now, however, you will see."*
    now ·however
    you see it (so) ·WILL

*That's when she followed Gluskabe.*
    that· (is) the point where she followed him
    Gluskabe

*On and on she went;*
    on she went
    on she went

*when she came out somewhere at a viewing-place, she didn't see him at all;*
    wherever she came to an opening
    viewing-place
    not at all
    she did not see him

*again when she came out somewhere (else), she didn't see him at all.*
    again
    wherever she came to an opening
    not at all
    she did not see him

*She said, "The man goes very fast."*
    (what) she said
    very
    he goes fast
    man

*[Then] however Gluskabe, when he got to the river, at the river mouth,*
    then· however
    Gluskabe
    when he got there
    at the river
    at the river mouth

elɑpit akɑ́mi kʷesɑwahpskek,
>elɑpit
>akɑ́mi
>kʷesɑwahpskek

n·wənamihɑn eləmihlɑličil mosol.
>n·wənamihɑn
>eləmihlɑličil
>mosol

n·wəkʷəssakɑkətahin, n·as·te wətemisal wətatəmihkɑkon.
>n·wəkʷəssakɑkətahin
>n·as·te
>wətemisal
>wətatəmihkɑkon

n·wətihlɑn, "iyo kəya api;
>n·wətihlɑn
>iyo
>kəya
>api

skohɑle pohkəčinskʷehso."
>skohɑle
>pohkəčinskʷehso

nə·kehəla aləmoss wətapin,
>nə·kehəla
>aləmoss
>wətapin

n·wətaskohɑlɑn pohkəčinskʷehsəwal.
>n·wətaskohɑlɑn
>pohkəčinskʷehsəwal

*as he looked across to the other side where there was a rocky point,*
>as he looked
>across to the other side
>where there is a rocky point

*then he saw the moose going away.*
>then· he saw him
>as he (the moose) was going away
>moose

*Then he jumped across, and right then too his dog caught up with him.*
>then· he jumped across
>then·also ·INTENS
>his dog
>(then) he caught up with him

*Then he said to him, "You sit here;*
>then· he said to him
>here
>you
>sit

*watch for Jug-Woman."*
>watch for her
>Jug-Woman

*Then sure enough the dog sat down,*
>then· sure enough
>dog
>(then) he sat down

*and he watched for Jug-Woman.*
>then· he watched for her
>Jug-Woman

nə·wa pohkəčinskʷehso metɑpehlɑt sipok,
  nə·wa
  pohkəčinskʷehso
  metɑpehlɑt
  sipok

wənamihton kʷesɑwahpskek,
  wənamihton
  kʷesɑwahpskek

n·as·te wəkʷəssakɑkətahin pekəssik.
  n·as·te
  wəkʷəssakɑkətahin
  pekəssik

itak, "ččih, ččo kətəli-namihton."
  itak
  ččih
  ččo
  kətəli-namihton

n·elɑpit, wənamihɑn kči-aləmossal.
  n·elɑpit
  wənamihɑn
  kči-aləmossal

n·etali-naskɑtəhɑsit, osəwehlɑn.
  n·etali-naskɑtəhɑsit
  osəwehlɑn

*Then when this Jug-Woman went down to the shore on the river,*
> then· this
> Jug-Woman
> when she went down to the shore
> at the river

*(then) she saw the rocky point,*
> (then) she saw it
> where there is a rocky point

*right then too she jumped across where he hit.*
> then·also ·INTENS
> (then) she jumped across
> where he hit [= where he landed]

*She said, "Cheeh, you (will) see it for sure."*
> (what) she said
> cheeh
> for sure
> you see it (so)

*Then as she looked, she saw a great big dog.*
> then· as she looked
> (then) she saw it
> great big dog

*That was where she got discouraged, (and then) she headed back.*
> that· (is) where she got discouraged
> (then) she headed back

mɑlam yewokənahkiwik, wətatəmihkawɑn mosol, nˑasˑte wənihlɑn.

mɑlam
yewokənahkiwik
wətatəmihkawɑn
mosol
nˑasˑte
wənihlɑn

apihkʷečilɑn, nˑwətəlahkewɑn wətemisal mosolakəsəyal,

apihkʷečilɑn
nˑwətəlahkewɑn
wətemisal
mosolakəsəyal

nsəta tekakɑpimək wətəli-nəkalɑl wətemisal.

nsəta
tekakɑpimək
wətəli-nəkalɑl
wətemisal

nəˑpetahket wəlakəsəyal,

nəˑpetahket
wəlakəsəyal

nˑaləmoss wəmitsin.

nˑaləmoss
wəmitsin

nəˑttʼ eləpektek nəpik nɑkɑ tali-kətahle,

nəˑtt[e] eləpektek
nəpik
nɑkɑ
tali-kətahle

*Eventually on the fourth day, he overtook the moose, and right then too he killed him.*
    eventually
    on the fourth day
    (then) he overtook him
    moose
    then·also ·INTENS
    (then) he killed him

*(Then) he gutted him out, then he threw his dog the moose-guts.*
    (then) he gutted him out
    (then)· he threw him them
    his dog
    moose-guts

*He left his dog three "looks" (behind).*
    three times
    as far as one looks
    he left him there
    his dog

*Then when he had thrown the guts to reach (to there),*
    then· when he threw them to reach/arrive
    (its/his) guts

*then the dog ate.*
    then· dog
    (then) it ate

*Right there they sat in the water, and (they) were sinking there,*
    there·INTENS (is) where they sat in the water
    in the water
    and
    (then) they were sinking there

nə·tt' etali-pənahpskʷihlɑk wɑpahpəskʷ.
      nə·tt[e] etali-pənahpskʷihlɑk
            wɑpahpəskʷ

eskʷa·tte nihkʷɑp wewinɑkʷatol.
            eskʷa·tte
            nihkʷɑp
            wewinɑkʷatol

nihkʷɑp ali-wihtɑso mosihkəči.
            nihkʷɑp
            ali-wihtɑso
            mosihkəči

nə·tt' etali-pənahpskʷihlɑt aləmoss,
      nə·tt[e] etali-pənahpskʷihlɑt
            aləmoss

eskʷa·tte nihkʷɑp wətapin.
            eskʷa·tte
            nihkʷɑp
            wətapin

wəmɑčin kəloskɑpe pə́təki.
            wəmɑčin
            kəloskɑpe
            pə́təki

kisi-psanlɑt wətahtawɑkkʷasotəyal wəyohs mosiye, wəpətəkohsɑn.
            kisi-psanlɑt
            wətahtawɑkkʷasotəyal
            wəyohs
            mosiye
            wəpətəkohsɑn

*right there is where they turned to stone, white stone.*
    there·INTENS (is) where they turned to stone
    white stone

*Still now they are recognizable on sight.*
    still ·INTENS
    now
    they are recognizable on sight

*Now it is called Moose-Rump.*
    now
    it is called
    Moose-Rump

*Right there is where the dog turned to stone,*
    there·INTENS (is) where it turned to stone
    dog

*still now he sits there.*
    still ·INTENS
    now
    he sits there

*(Then) Gluskabe headed off, back.*
    (then) he headed off
    Gluskabe
    back

*When he had filled his cooking kettle with meat—moose meat—(then) he headed back walking.*
    when he had filled it
    his cooking kettle
    (with) meat
    moose meat
    (then) he walked back

mɑlam pečohse kči-məkʷasəpemək; nˑetalɑkkʷasit.

    mɑlam

    pečohse

    kči-məkʷasəpemək

    nˑetalɑkkʷasit

kisɑkkʷasit, wəmitsin.

    kisɑkkʷasit

    wəmitsin

kisihpit, wəkətəkʷahkɑn wətahtawɑkkʷasotəyal pənahpskʷiyɑl,

    kisihpit

    wəkətəkʷahkɑn

    wətahtawɑkkʷasotəyal

    pənahpskʷiyɑl

nˑwəkətəkʷahlɑn, nɑkɑ wətali-nəkalɑn.

    nˑwəkətəkʷahlɑn

    nɑkɑ

    wətali-nəkalɑn

nihkʷɑp eskʷaˑtte wəkətəkʷapin,

    nihkʷɑp

    eskʷaˑtte

    wəkətəkʷapin

na nihkʷɑp wačo ali-wiso kkiniyo.

    na

    nihkʷɑp

    wačo

    ali-wiso

    kkiniyo

nəˑka wəpətəkihlɑn.

    nəˑka

    wəpətəkihlɑn

*Eventually he arrived (walking) at the great lake; that is where he cooked for himself.*
> eventually
> he arrived (walking)
> at the great lake
> then/there· (is) where/when he cooked for himself

*When he had cooked for himself, (then) he ate.*
> when he had cooked for himself
> (then) he ate

*When he had eaten, (then) he flipped over his cooking kettle of stone,*
> when he had eaten
> (then) he (sharply) flipped it over
> his cooking kettle
> of stone

*then he turned it over, and he left it there.*
> then· he turned it over
> and
> (then) he left it there

*Now still it sits overturned,*
> now
> still ·INTENS
> (so/there) it sits turned over

*that mountain now (is) called Kineo.*
> that
> now
> mountain
> it is called
> Kineo

*So then he headed back.*
> then·KA
> (then) he went back

wətihlɑn alənɑpa, ohsəssa, "ɑn ni,
> wətihlɑn
> alənɑpa
> ohsəssa
> ɑn ni

kkisi-ntamólənɑ kči-awaass,
> kkisi-ntamólənɑ
> kči-awaass

ɑta·č mina kotamihokowiwɑ."
> ɑta·č
> mina
> kotamihokowiwɑ

kamɑč wəlitəhɑsolətəwak alənɑpak.
> kamɑč
> wəlitəhɑsolətəwak
> alənɑpak

wətihlɑnɑ kəloskɑpal, "kamɑč kolihalipəna,
> wətihlɑnɑ
> kəloskɑpal
> kamɑč
> kolihalipəna

tepəne·pa·na nənəkkahtəhokona,
> tepəne·pa
> ·na
> nənəkkahtəhokona

*(Then) he told the People, his descendants, "Well then,*
    (then) he said to them
    People
    his descendants
    well then

*I have killed the great animal for you,*
    I have killed it for you (pl.)
    great animal

*it will not bother you again."*
    not ·WILL
    again
    it (will) not bother you (pl.)

*The People were very happy.*
    very
    they (group) were happy
    People

*(Then) they told Gluskabe, "You have done us a very good thing,*
    (then) they told him
    Gluskabe
    very
    you did us well

*in a little while that (animal) might have killed us all,*
    soon ·WOULD
    that one
    he (would) kill us all

kətalamisəwɑmələpəna mɑwáyi."
kətalamisəwɑmələpəna
mɑwáyi

*we are thankful to you together."*
　　we are thankful to you
　　together as a group

## NOTES

182　*kči-mɘkʷasɘpemɘk*: Given that the 1918 version transcription has Lyon saying *kči-* 'a greeeat big . . .' and not ordinary *kči-* 'great; elder/mature', this vividly underlines that the lake, otherwise not explicitly named, is a particularly big one. Both the 1918 version and Speck's original notes identify the lake as Moosehead Lake.

188　*sɘkɘtehtɘkok*: The 1918 version notes that this is on the Penobscot River, near Castine.

192　*pekɘssik*: Andrew Dana offers two tellings of this story: one briefer, personally handwritten version in the Frank T. Siebert Papers collection at the American Philosophical Society, and another, more in-depth version dictated to and transcribed by Siebert and included in the *Penobscot Legends* manuscript (*kɘloskɑpe nɑkɑ mos*). Where Gluskabe landed is identified in both versions as a ledge at Castine Point, known as Dice Head. Fannie Hardy Eckstorm, *Indian Place Names of the Penobscot Valley*, 200, specifically notes that it is near the current-day lighthouse. Both Dana's versions and the 1918 version (203) also note that Gluskabe's snowshoe left a track in the stone there, at place therefore called *matɘkɘmassɘk* 'at the bad/ragged old snowshoe'. James Francis reports that at this place a crosshatched design of quartz can be seen in the stone, one that resembles snowshoe webbing. Speck's original notes (here with Penobscot forms retranscribed) contain further details: "Where *kɘloskɑpe* and *pohkɑčinskʷehso* struck are two imprints in the rock. One of these is of the ordinary snowshoe shape, *kɘloskɑpe*'s snowshoe print, the other is a round one, *pohkɑčinskʷehso*'s. This place is still called *matɘkɘmass* 'Old Snowshoe,' and may be seen at Castine Head, Me. The impressions are rapidly disintegrating as the rock is soft."

192　*ččih*: The 1918 version notes, "Extending her finger at him at arm's length—a common sign of emphasis" (203). This word and gesture may be related to *ččasči*, discussed in story 12.

196　*mosihkɑči*: Both the 1918 Lyon version and the Andrew Dana handwritten version agree that this is present-day Cape Rosier. Dana's version, dictated to Siebert in *Penobscot Legends*, however, then has Gluskabe throwing the moose-guts into the sea to become islands (named in a footnote as the current-day Fox Islands, namely, Vinalhaven, North Haven, and Isle au Haut), rather than becoming white stone right there. A further footnote in that text (*kɘloskɑpe nɑkɑ mos*) helps explain the literal meaning of *mosihkɑči* 'Moose-Rump' from the fact that one of the promontories at Cape Rosier at low tide resembles a moose lying down. Eckstorm, *Old John Neptune*, 201, also provides a form clearly including the *-k* ending marking it as a location: *Moos-i-katch-ik*, i.e., *mosihkɑčik* 'at the Moose-Rump'. If Speck missed the final *-k*, which he sometimes did, this instead might be Lyon's original form here. Note though that Speck gives the other key location here, *matɘkɘmass* 'Bad/Ragged Old Snowshoe', also without this ending, so this may in fact be Lyon's usage in citing these placenames.

198　*pɘnahpskʷiyɑl*: The 1918 version free translation follows this with 'and left it there turned into stone' (204), but it is not clear from the Penobscot text itself whether the kettle was already made of stone (like his stone canoe in the first story), or (like the guts and the dog here) turned to stone at this point.

198　*kkiniyo*: The 1918 version notes that speakers say that the mountain was named that because the first people who saw it after its transformation declared "*kī nī yo!*" = 'oh, [see] here!'. Speck does not make it clear if this is meant as a solid tradition or a simple speculation (or even just an explanation of the current English pronunciation): note that Andrew Dana's different account suggests that it was named for *kkino*, an affectionate term for the firstborn boy of the family (based on *wskinohs* 'young man'), after the main character in another story said to have taken place there. Interestingly, Eckstorm, *Indian Place Names of the Penobscot Valley*, 200–201, reports that the kettle became current-day Kokadjo, or Little Spencer Mountain, also near Moosehead: "Kokadjo" appears to be literally *kkohkɑčo* 'pot/kettle-mountain', matching this version of the story.

9

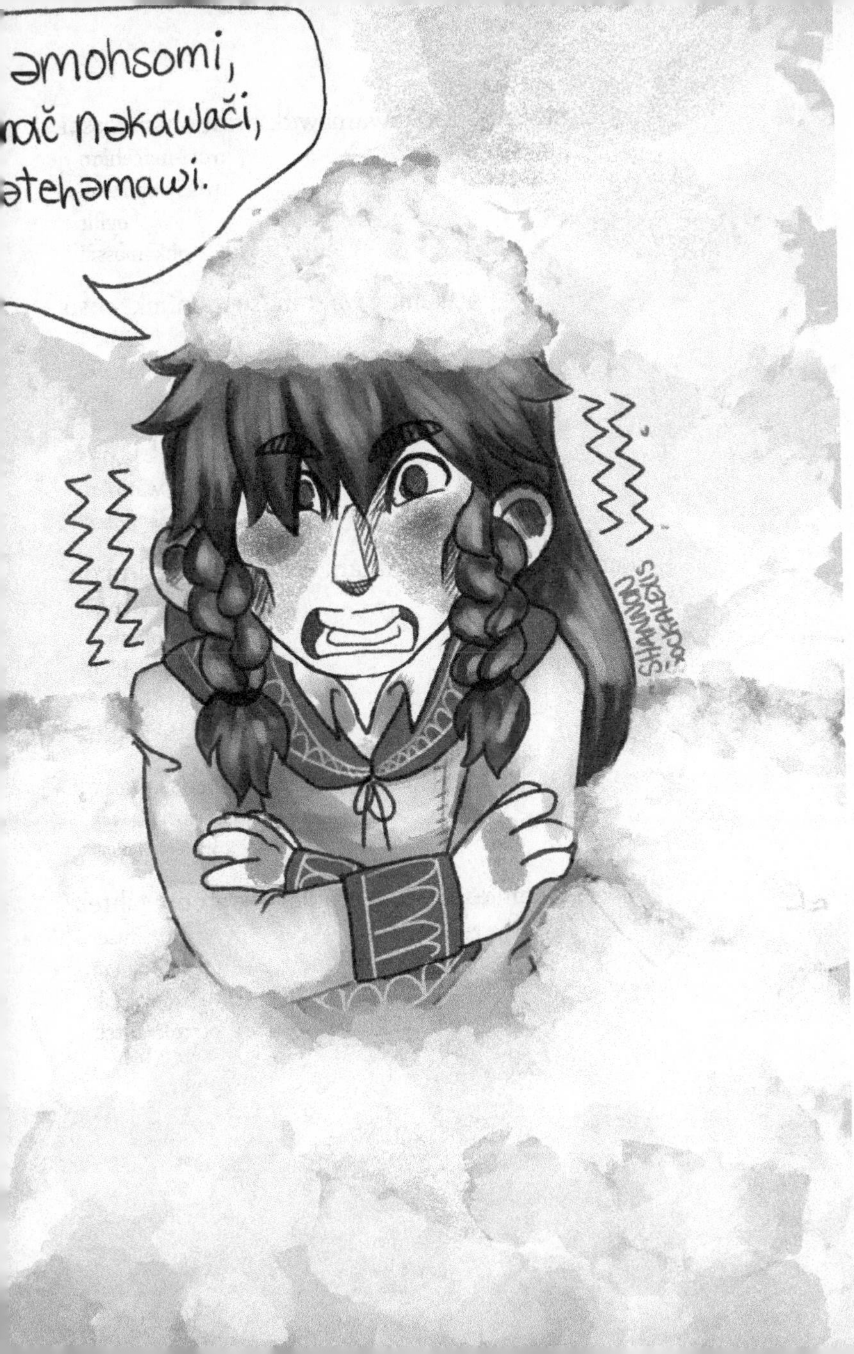
əmohsomi,
ač nəkawači,
ətehəmawi.

# nóli

n·oči-mačehlαn wikəwaməwαk eyilit ohkəməssal.

    n·oči-mačehlαn

    wikəwaməwαk

    eyilit

    ohkəməssal

kamαč wəlitəhαso monimkʷehso.

    kamαč

    wəlitəhαso

    monimkʷehso

wətihlαl, "nkʷenəss,

    wətihlαl

    nkʷenəss

kamαč nolitəhαs pečihlan: kamαč kisi-saki-ppon.

    kamαč

    nolitəhαs

    pečihlan

    kamαč

    kisi-saki-ppon

saki-kisαwəsolətəwak kohsəssənawak.

    saki-kisαwəsolətəwak

    kohsəssənawak

msel kamαč kʷaskʷalαmolətičik etotαkʷahtek,

    msel

    kamαč

    kʷaskʷalαmolətičik

    etotαkʷahtek

*Then he headed off from there to their house where his grandmother was.*

   then· he headed off from there
   to their house
   where she was
   his grandmother

*Woodchuck was very happy.*

   very
   she was happy
   Woodchuck

*She said to him, "My grandchild,*

   she said to him
   my grandchild

*I am very happy that you have come: it has been a very hard winter.*

   very
   I am happy
   that you have come
   very
   it has been a hard winter

*Our descendants have had a hard time living.*

   they (group) have had a hard time living
   our descendants

*Very many have starved to death, the snow is so deep,*

   they are many
   very
   those (group) who starved to death
   the snow is so deep

ahtɑmɑ apasəyak namihɑwəyak: məsi wanəhokhatəwak.

    ahtɑmɑ
    apasəyak
    namihɑwəyak
    məsi
    wanəhokhatəwak

n·wətihlɑn kəloskɑpe ohkəməssal,

    n·wətihlɑn
    kəloskɑpe
    ohkəməssal

"tɑn·ɑskʷe na eyit pəpon?"

    tɑn·ɑskʷe
    na
    eyit
    pəpon

wətihlɑn, "nkʷenəss,

    wətihlɑn
    nkʷenəss

kamɑč nɑwatoke,

    kamɑč
    nɑwatoke

nətah·ap' awen otɑwəsiwən alohsete: kʷaskʷačo·pa."

    nətah·ap[a] awen
    otɑwəsiwən
    alohsete
    kʷaskʷačo·pa

*the trees are not seen at all: they are all covered in snow.*
    not at all
    trees
    they are not seen
    all
    they (group) are covered in snow

*Then Gluskabe said to his grandmother,*
    then· he said to her
    Gluskabe
    his grandmother

*"Where (however) is the Winter?"*
    where ·however
    that
    where it is
    Winter

*(Then) she said to him, "My grandchild,*
    (then) she said to him
    my grandchild

*(it is) very far away,*
    very
    far away

*no one would survive it if they walked there: they would freeze to death."*
    not ·WOULD anyone
    she/he (would) not survive it
    if she/he walked there
    she/he freeze to death ·WOULD

itak kəloskαpe, "nəya nətakʷeči-alohsαn: nəkati-namihα pəpon.

> itak
> kəloskαpe
> nəya
> nətakʷeči-alohsαn
> nəkati-namihα
> pəpon

nihkʷαp nətahčəwelətamən kətəlhαkəmewin,

> nihkʷαp
> nətahčəwelətamən
> kətəlhαkəmewin

nətahčəweləmαk nisαkəmakəsəwak makαlipəwewayiyαk,

> nətahčəweləmαk
> nisαkəmakəsəwak
> makαlipəwewayiyαk

nisαkəmakəsəwak·ahč nolkewayiyαk, nisαkəmakəsəwak·ahč mosewayiyαk."

> nisαkəmakəsəwak
> ·ahč
> nolkewayiyαk
> nisαkəmakəsəwak
> ·ahč
> mosewayiyαk

n·wəmαčehlαn: ēləmihlαt . . .

> n·wəmαčehlαn
> ēləmihlαt

mαlam wəmehtkawα nisαkəmakəsəwa mosewayiyαk.

> mαlam
> wəmehtkawα
> nisαkəmakəsəwa
> mosewayiyαk

*Gluskabe said, "I (will) try to walk there: I want to see Winter.*
   (what) he said
   Gluskabe
   I
   (so) I try to walk there
   I want to see him
   Winter

*Now I want you to make me snowshoes,*
   now
   I want it
   (for) you to make me snowshoes

*I want two pairs of snowshoes of caribou pelt,*
   I want them
   two pairs of snowshoes
   of caribou pelt

*also two pairs of snowshoes of deer pelt, (and) also two pairs of snowshoes of moose pelt."*
   two pairs of snowshoes
   ·also
   of deer pelt
   two pairs of snowshoes
   ·also
   of moose pelt

*Then he went off: ooon he went . . .*
   then· he started off
   ooon he went

*eventually he wore out two pairs of moose-pelt snowshoes.*
   eventually
   he wore them out
   two pairs of snowshoes
   of moose pelt

pesək\*ən elohset; mɑlam mina wəmehtkawɑ nolkewayiyɑk.

> pesək\*ən
> elohset
> mɑlam
> mina
> wəmehtkawɑ
> nolkewayiyɑk

pesək\*ən elohset, mɑlam aháči aləmi-tke,

> pesək\*ən
> elohset
> mɑlam
> aháči
> aləmi-tke

mɑlam wəmehtkawɑ nək\*ətɑkəmakəsəwa makɑlipəwayiye,

> mɑlam
> wəmehtkawɑ
> nək\*ətɑkəmakəsəwa
> makɑlipəwayiye

məssala·tte nək\*ətɑkəmakəsəwa wətɑkəma.

> məssala·tte
> nək\*ətɑkəmakəsəwa
> wətɑkəma

n·ahč kis·ahč kamɑč kawačo,

> n·ahč
> kis·ahč
> kamɑč
> kawačo

mina wənahslɑn kətakihi.

> mina
> wənahslɑn
> kətakihi

*He walked on just the same; eventually again he wore out the deer-pelt ones.*
    it was just the same
    how he walked
    eventually/until
    again
    he wore them out
    of deer pelt

*He walked on just the same; eventually it was getting colder and colder,*
    it was just the same
    how he walked
    eventually/until
    more and more
    it was getting colder

*eventually he wore out one pair of snowshoes of the caribou-pelt,*
    eventually
    he wore them out
    one pair (of snowshoes) of them
    of caribou pelt

*(leaving only) the one very last pair of his snowshoes.*
    last ·INTENS
    one pair (of snowshoes) of them
    his snowshoes

*Then also, already also, he was very cold,*
    then·also
    already ·also
    very
    he was cold

*(so) again he put on the others.*
    again
    (so) he put them on
    the others (snowshoes)

eləmihlɑt, aháči aləmi-tke.
> eləmihlɑt
> aháči
> aləmi-tke

mɑlam·te kekɑ wəmehtkawɑ wətɑkəma; wəssaki-kawačo (kis).
> mɑlam·te
> kekɑ
> wəmehtkawɑ
> wətɑkəma
> wəssaki-kawačo
> (kis)

kis·ahč wənamihton wikəwɑm ehtek; eməkʷ·te pečohse klɑkanək,
> kis·ahč
> wənamihton
> wikəwɑm
> ehtek
> eməkʷ·te
> pečohse
> klɑkanək

n·as·te wəmehtkawɑn wətɑkəma.
> n·as·te
> wəmehtkawɑn
> wətɑkəma

wəpitikɑn; pkʷamikamikʷ.
> wəpitikɑn
> pkʷamikamikʷ

kisi-pitiket, nə·klɑkan kəpətehtehsən,
> kisi-pitiket
> nə·klɑkan
> kəpətehtehsən

*As he went onward, it was getting colder and colder.*
    as he went onward
    more and more
    it was getting colder

*Finally he had almost worn out his snowshoes; he was bitterly cold (already).*
    eventually ·INTENS
    almost
    he wore them out
    his snowshoes
    he was bitterly cold
    (already)

*Already too he saw a house sitting there; he barely reached the door (walking),*
    already ·also
    he saw it
    house
    where it sat
    barely ·INTENS
    he got there (walking)
    to the door

*right then too he wore out his snowshoes.*
    then·also ·INTENS
    (then) he wore them out
    his snowshoes

*(Then) he went into it; (it was) an ice-house.*
    (then) he entered it
    ice-house

*When he had gone in, then the door slammed shut,*
    when he had gone inside
    then· door
    it slammed shut

ahtɑmɑ wəkisi-notessewən
> ahtɑmɑ
> wəkisi-notessewən

kəloskɑpe itak, "kkʷey, nəmohsomi!"
> kəloskɑpe
> itak
> kkʷey
> nəmohsomi

manəni·tte wətamahskəlohtɑkol mlohsəssisal pkʷaməyal:
> manəni·tte
> wətamahskəlohtɑkol
> mlohsəssisal
> pkʷaməyal

itak wa mlohsəssis, "kkʷey, nəmohsomi!"
> itak
> wa
> mlohsəssis
> kkʷey
> nəmohsomi

kəloskɑpe etoči-kawačit, wətihlɑn, "nəmohsomi,
> kəloskɑpe
> etoči-kawačit
> wətihlɑn
> nəmohsomi

*(so) he could not walk outside at all.*
    not at all
    (then) he could not walk outside

*Gluskabe said, "Hello, my grandfather!"*
    Gluskabe
    (what) he said
    hello
    my grandfather!

*Right away the little old man of ice imitated him:*
    right away
    he mocked/imitated him
    little old man
    (of) ice

*The little old man said, "Hello, my grandfather!"*
    (what) he said
    this
    little old man
    hello
    my grandfather!

*Gluskabe was so cold, so he said to him, "My grandfather,*
    Gluskabe
    he was so cold
    (so) he said to him
    my grandfather!

kamač nəkawači; pkʷətehəmawi."

> kamač
> nəkawači
> pkʷətehəmawi

mlohsəssis wətamahskəlohtawαn, "nəmohsomi,

> mlohsəssis
> wətamahskəlohtawαn
> nəmohsomi

kamač nəkawači; pkʷətehəmawi."

> kamač
> nəkawači
> pkʷətehəmawi

nə·kəloskαpe itam, "nəmohsomi,

> nə·kəloskαpe
> itam
> nəmohsomi

pkʷətehəmawi; kekα nəkʷaskʷači."

> pkʷətehəmawi
> kekα
> nəkʷaskʷači

mlohsəssis wətamahskəlohtawαn αkʷαmatoke,

> mlohsəssis
> wətamahskəlohtawαn
> αkʷαmatoke

epəkʷahč awihkʷinawαn: "nəmohsomi,

> epəkʷahč
> awihkʷinawαn
> nəmohsomi

*I am very cold; open the door for me."*
>     very
>     I am cold
>     open the door for me

*(Then) the little old man imitated him, "My grandfather,*
>     little old man
>     (then) he mocked/imitated him
>     my grandfather!

*I am very cold; open the door for me."*
>     very
>     I am cold
>     open the door for me

*Then Gluskabe said, "My grandfather,*
>     then· Gluskabe
>     he said
>     my grandfather!

*open the door for me; I am almost frozen to death."*
>     open the door for me
>     almost
>     I am frozen to death

*(Then) the little old man imitated him more than ever,*
>     little old man
>     (then) he mocked/imitated him
>     more than ever

*(and) he even saw him as funny: "My grandfather,*
>     even
>     (then) he saw him as funny
>     my grandfather!

pkʷətehəmawi; kekɑ nəkʷaskʷači."

    pkʷətehəmawi

    kekɑ

    nəkʷaskʷači

nə·wəkʷaskʷačin kəloskɑpe.

    nə·wəkʷaskʷačin

    kəloskɑpe

mlohsəssis wənotahkɑlɑn.

    mlohsəssis

    wənotahkɑlɑn

nə·tt' eləssik kəloskɑpe.

    nə·tt[e] eləssik

    kəloskɑpe

mɑlam sikʷan, nə·mina apəmɑwəsihlɑn,

    mɑlam

    sikʷan

    nə·mina

    apəmɑwəsihlɑn

itak tohkihlɑt, "ččehe, nə·tt'·eht nəya nəkawinessa."

    itak

    tohkihlɑt

    ččehe

    nə·tt[e]·eht

    nəya

    nəkawinessa

elɑpit, ahtɑmɑ tɑmɑ wikəwɑm ttewi

    elɑpit

    ahtɑmɑ

    tɑmɑ

    wikəwɑm

    ttewi

*open the door for me; I am almost frozen to death."*
    open the door for me
    almost
    I am frozen to death

*Then Gluskabe froze to death.*
    then· he froze to death
    Gluskabe

*(Then) the little old man threw him outside.*
    little old man
    (then) he threw him outside

*Right there (was where) Gluskabe lay.*
    there·INTENS (was) where he lay
    Gluskabe

*Eventually it was spring, then he came to life again,*
    eventually
    it was spring
    then· again
    (then) he came to life

*he said when he woke up, "Cheheh, so I guess I must have been asleep."*
    (what) he said
    when he woke up
    CHEHEH
    then·INTENS ·EHT
    I
    (so) I must have been asleep

*As he looked, there was no house anywhere at all.*
    as he looked
    not at all
    anywhere
    house
    it was not there

oči-mačehlαn; awikəwaməwαk wətəlihlαn.
oči-mačehlαn
awikəwaməwαk
wətəlihlαn

*(So) he went from there; (then) he went home.*
    (then) he went from there
    to their house
    (then) he went there

## NOTES

PAGE

216   *nəmohsomi*: Gluskabe addresses the old man as 'my grandfather' to show respect for him as an elder.

216   *"kkʷey, nəmohsomi!"*: Speck's original notes here indicate that all of the old man's imitations of Gluskabe's greeting and requests to enter are done with "deep voice" mocking; the same again is noted for Gluskabe's mocking in return in story 12.

222   *awikəwaməwak*: In Penobscot and Passamaquoddy-Maliseet, speakers tend to use 'our house' rather than 'my house' and 'their house' rather than 'his/her house' when the person spoken of does not live there alone. So while English might say "Gluskabe went to his house," Penobscot speakers seem to usually say "Gluskabe went to their house" = his and Woodchuck's.

# 10

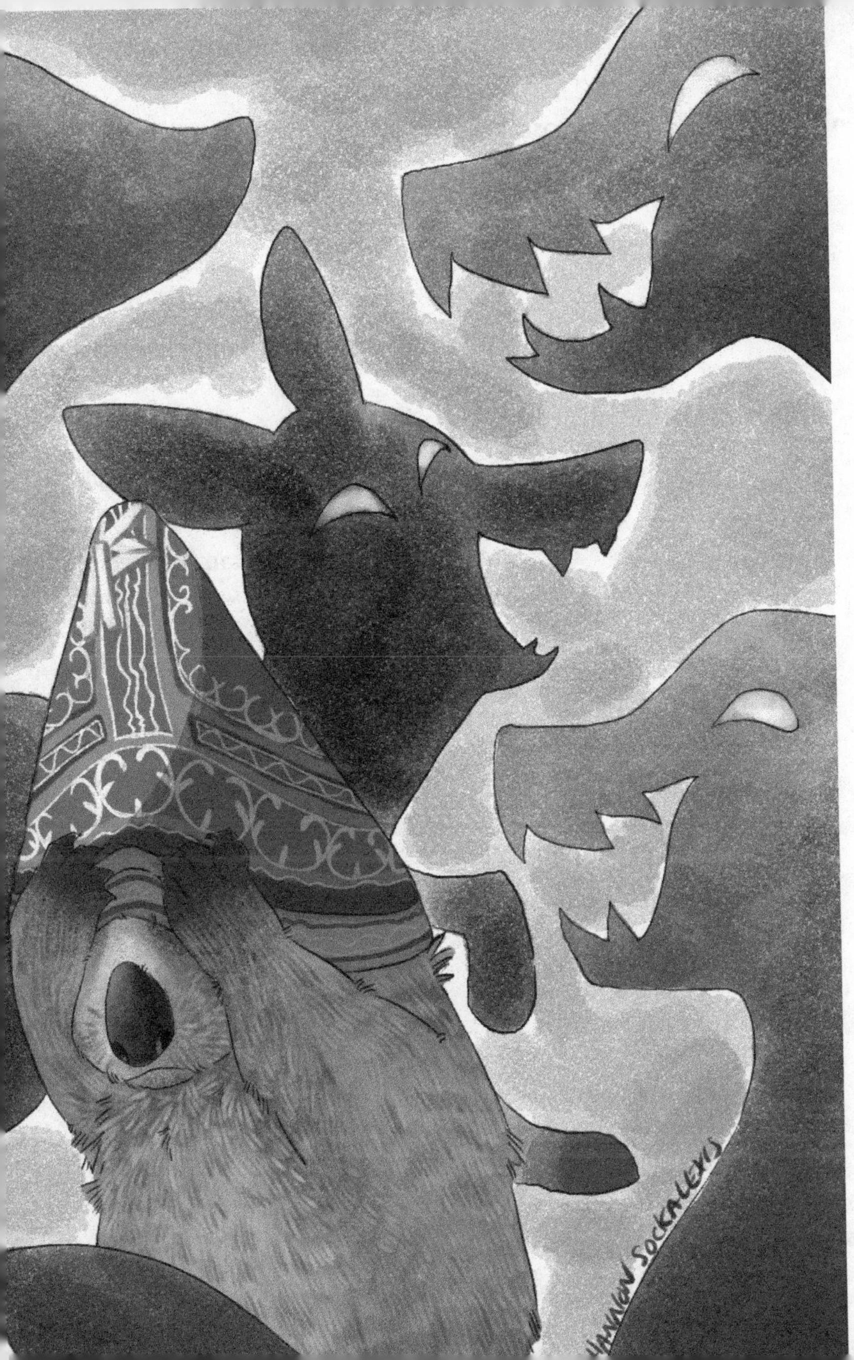
SOCKALEXIS

# mətala

kʷenihlɑt kəloskɑpe, kʷɑkʷsəssak wənəpahkatawɑnɑ monimkʷehsəwal.

kʷenihlɑt
kəloskɑpe
kʷɑkʷsəssak
wənəpahkatawɑnɑ
monimkʷehsəwal

mečími kʷɑkʷsəss wətəlihlɑn wikilit monimkʷehsəwal

mečími
kʷɑkʷsəss
wətəlihlɑn
wikilit
monimkʷehsəwal

nɑkɑ wətihlɑn, "nohkəmi, nəpečihla:

nɑkɑ
wətihlɑn
nohkəmi
nəpečihla

kkʷenəss kəloskɑpe."

kkʷenəss
kəloskɑpe

sɑkhɑpilite monimkʷehsəwal, wəsəkilɑn wsisəkok.

sɑkhɑpilite
monimkʷehsəwal
wəsəkilɑn
wsisəkok

nə·č monimkʷehso wəkinilawehlɑn.

nə·č
monimkʷehso
wəkinilawehlɑn

*While Gluskabe was gone, (then) the foxes tricked Woodchuck.*
>  while he was gone
>  Gluskabe
>  foxes
>  (then) they tricked her
>  Woodchuck

*Always a fox went to where Woodchuck lived*
>  always
>  fox
>  it went there
>  where she lived
>  Woodchuck

*and said to her, "My grandmother, I have arrived:*
>  and
>  (then) he said to her
>  my grandmother!
>  I have arrived

*your grandchild Gluskabe."*
>  your grandchild
>  Gluskabe

*If/when Woodchuck stuck her head out to look, (then) he peed on her in her eyes.*
>  if/when she stuck her head out to look
>  Woodchuck
>  (then) he peed on her
>  in her eyes

*Then Woodchuck would get furious.*
>  then·WILL
>  Woodchuck
>  (then) she got greatly angry

nə·č kʷɑkʷsəss wəmɑče-kʷakʷəmahlɑn,
> nə·č
> kʷɑkʷsəss
> wəmɑče-kʷakʷəmahlɑn

nɑkɑ wətɑpəteləmohkɑsin,
> nɑkɑ
> wətɑpəteləmohkɑsin

mečími nə·kʷɑkʷsəssak eli-nəpahkatawahətit monimkʷehsəwal.
> mečími
> nə·kʷɑkʷsəssak
> eli-nəpahkatawahətit
> monimkʷehsəwal

mɑlam eləwe nkɑpo monimkʷehso,
> mɑlam
> eləwe
> nkɑpo
> monimkʷehso

ahtɑmɑ kisi-msáwihɑ: mečími sɑkhɑpihaso,
> ahtɑmɑ
> kisi-msáwihɑ
> mečími
> sɑkhɑpihaso

etoči-kʷilomɑt wkʷenəssal kəloskɑpal.
> etoči-kʷilomɑt
> wkʷenəssal
> kəloskɑpal

mɑlam·te saláhki nkɑpo,
> mɑlam·te
> saláhki
> nkɑpo

*Then the fox would run off,*
    then·WILL
    fox
    (then) he ran off

*and he would laugh to himself.*
    and
    (then) he laughed to himself

*Always that was how the foxes tricked Woodchuck.*
    always
    that (was)· foxes
    how they tricked her
    Woodchuck

*Eventually Woodchuck was almost blind,*
    eventually
    almost
    she was blind
    Woodchuck

*she could not be made to hesitate at all: she always stuck her head quickly out to look,*
    not at all
    she could not be made to hesitate
    always
    she stuck her head quickly out to look

*she missed her grandchild Gluskabe so much.*
    she missed him so much
    her grandchild
    Gluskabe

*Eventually at one point she was blind,*
    eventually ·INTENS
    at one point
    she was blind

nə·či naskɑtəhɑmɑt wəpečihlɑlin kəloskɑpal wkʷenəssal.

    nə·či
    naskɑtəhɑmɑt
    wəpečihlɑlin
    kəloskɑpal
    wkʷenəssal

pečihlɑt kəloskɑpe wətihlɑn, "nohkəmi,

    pečihlɑt
    kəloskɑpe
    wətihlɑn
    nohkəmi

nəpečihla, pkʷətehəmawi."

    nəpečihla
    pkʷətehəmawi

nə·monimkʷehso wətihlɑn, "kkeləpi-mɑčin, kʷɑkʷsəss,

    nə·monimkʷehso
    wətihlɑn
    kkeləpi-mɑčin
    kʷɑkʷsəss

kekɑ kənihlipɑ, kehsi-səkiləyekʷ."

    kekɑ
    kənihlipɑ
    kehsi-səkiləyekʷ

kəloskɑpe wəkətəmɑksətawɑl ohkəməssal,

    kəloskɑpe
    wəkətəmɑksətawɑl
    ohkəməssal

*that's when she would get discouraged about Gluskabe, her grandchild, coming.*
    then·WILL
    that she was discouraged about him
    (for) him (to) come
    Gluskabe
    her grandchild

*When Gluskabe arrived (then) he said to her, "My grandmother,*
    when he arrived
    Gluskabe
    (then) he said to her
    my grandmother!

*I have arrived, open the door for me."*
    I have arrived
    open the door for me

*Then Woodchuck said to him, "You hurry up and leave, fox,*
    then· Woodchuck
    (then) she said to him
    you hurry up and leave
    fox

*you've all almost killed me, how much you've all peed on me."*
    almost
    you (pl.) kill me
    how much you pee on me

*Gluskabe felt pity hearing his grandmother,*
    Gluskabe
    he felt pity hearing her
    his grandmother

wətihlɑn, "nohkəmi, ɑta·ka nəya kʷɑkʷsəss!"

    wətihlɑn
    nohkəmi
    ɑta·ka
    nəya
    kʷɑkʷsəss

nə·monimkʷehso wətihlɑn,

    nə·monimkʷehso
    wətihlɑn

"nətahtɑmɑ mina kkisi-nəpahkatawippɑ."

    nətahtɑmɑ
    mina
    kkisi-nəpahkatawippɑ

kəloskɑpe wətihlɑn, "nəta nəya kʷɑkʷsəss, nohkəmi: ipa wəčkawihptinewi."

    kəloskɑpe
    wətihlɑn
    nəta/ɑta
    nəya
    kʷɑkʷsəss
    nohkəmi
    ipa
    wəčkawihptinewi

nə·kehəla wənotehptinewin monimkʷehso.

    nə·kehəla
    wənotehptinewin
    monimkʷehso

*(so) he said to her, "My grandmother, I am not a fox!"*
  (then) he said to her
  my grandmother!
  not ·KA
  I
  fox

*Then Woodchuck said to him,*
  then· Woodchuck
  (then) she said to him

*"You can't trick me again at all."*
  not at all
  again
  you (pl.) do not trick me

*(Then) Gluskabe said to her, "I am not a fox, my grandmother: just put your paw over this way."*
  Gluskabe
  (then) he said to her
  not
  I
  fox
  my grandmother!
  just
  put your paw/hand over this way

*Then sure enough, Woodchuck put her paw out.*
  then· sure enough
  (then) she put her paw/hand out
  Woodchuck

nə·kəloskɑpe (a)wihkʷənəmawɑn wpətin.

> nə·kəloskɑpe
> (a)wihkʷənəmawɑn
> wpətin

kkīy! wəlitəhɑso.

> kkīy
> wəlitəhɑso

etoči-wəlitəhɑsit, epəkʷahč sehskatemo.

> etoči-wəlitəhɑsit
> epəkʷahč
> sehskatemo

itak, "kamɑč nolitəhɑs pečihlan: kekɑ kʷɑkʷsəssak nənihləkok,

> itak
> kamɑč
> nolitəhɑs
> pečihlan
> kekɑ
> kʷɑkʷsəssak
> nənihləkok

epəkʷahč nihkʷɑp ahtɑmɑ kənamiholo, nkʷenəss,

> epəkʷahč
> nihkʷɑp
> ahtɑmɑ
> kənamiholo
> nkʷenəss

ɑta·č mina kənamiholo, wəsɑm nənihkɑpi."

> ɑta·č
> mina
> kənamiholo
> wəsɑm
> nənihkɑpi

*Then Gluskabe took her paw.*
    then· Gluskabe
    (then) he took it (of her)
    her paw/hand

*Kee! She was happy.*
    kee
    she was happy

*She was so happy, she even cried.*
    she was so happy
    even
    she cried

*She said, "I am very happy that you have come: the foxes have almost killed me,*
    (what) she said
    very
    I am happy
    that you have come
    almost
    foxes
    they kill me

*now I even can't see you at all, my grandchild,*
    even
    now
    not at all
    I don't see you
    my grandchild

*I won't see you again, because I am blind."*
    not ·WILL
    again
    I (don't) see you
    because
    I am blind

kəloskɑpe wətihlɑn ohkəməssal, "ehkʷi- ni -ita,

        kəloskɑpe

        wətihlɑn

        ohkəməssal

        ehkʷi- ni -ita

mina·tte·č kənamihi; nəya·č kətahsihpiləl; mina·tte·č kənamihi."

        mina·tte·č

        kənamihi

        nəya·č

        kətahsihpiləl

        mina·tte·č

        kənamihi

nə·kəloskɑpe wətahsihpilɑn; napinɑkʷat wəkikəhɑn.

        nə·kəloskɑpe

        wətahsihpilɑn

        napinɑkʷat

        wəkikəhɑn

kkīhīī, wəlitəhɑso monimkʷehso.

        kkīhīī

        wəlitəhɑso

        monimkʷehso

nə·kəloskɑpe wətihlɑn ohkəməssal,

        nə·kəloskɑpe

        wətihlɑn

        ohkəməssal

*(Then) Gluskabe said to his grandmother, "Stop saying that,*
    Gluskabe
    (then) he said to her
    his grandmother
    stop saying that

*you will see me again; I will treat you with medicine; you will see me again."*
    again ·INTENS ·WILL
    you see me
    I ·WILL
    I treat you with medicine
    again ·INTENS ·WILL
    you see me

*Then Gluskabe treated her with medicine; soon he cured her.*
    then· Gluskabe
    (then) he treated her with medicine
    soon
    (then) he cured her

*Keehee, Woodchuck was happy.*
    keehee
    she was happy
    Woodchuck

*Then Gluskabe said to his grandmother,*
    then· Gluskabe
    (then) he said to her
    his grandmother

"nihkʷɑp mečími kənamihi askámi."
> nihkʷɑp
> mečími
> kənamihi
> askámi

nə·kəloskɑpe wəkatonalɑn kʷɑkʷsəssa.
> nə·kəloskɑpe
> wəkatonalɑn
> kʷɑkʷsəssa

mɑlam wənəkkahtəhɑ; pesəkəwal wətahkʷəčihtəhɑn,
> mɑlam
> wənəkkahtəhɑ
> pesəkəwal
> wətahkʷəčihtəhɑn

wəmɑčephɑn awikəwɑməwɑk, wətəlahkewɑn ohkəməssal.
> wəmɑčephɑn
> awikəwɑməwɑk
> wətəlahkewɑn
> ohkəməssal

wətihlɑn, "ɑn ni, kəpečiptolən kʷɑkʷsəss,
> wətihlɑn
> ɑn ni
> kəpečiptolən
> kʷɑkʷsəss

nihkʷɑp kətɑpenkɑtɑssin kehsi-wəsikihosk kʷɑkʷsəssak."
> nihkʷɑp
> kətɑpenkɑtɑssin
> kehsi-wəsikihosk
> kʷɑkʷsəssak

*"Now you (will) always see me forever."*
    now
    always
    you see me
    forever

*Then Gluskabe went after the foxes.*
    then· Gluskabe
    (then) he hunted/went after them
    foxes

*Eventually he killed them all; (then) he spared one of them,*
    eventually
    he killed them all
    one
    (then) he spared him

*(then) he took him home, (then) he threw him to his grandmother.*
    (then) he took him
    to their house
    (then) he threw him to her
    his grandmother

*(Then) he said to her, "Well then, I bring you a fox,*
    (then) he said to her
    well then
    I bring you it
    fox

*now you (can) pay yourself (back) for how much the foxes have abused you."*
    now
    (then) you pay yourself for it
    how much they abused you
    foxes

wənači-katonaton ipisəyal monimkʷehso,

wənači-katonaton

ipisəyal

monimkʷehso

nɑkɑ wəkəlahkʷepilɑn kʷɑkʷsəssal, nɑkɑ wətasemhɑn.

nɑkɑ

wəkəlahkʷepilɑn

kʷɑkʷsəssal

nɑkɑ

wətasemhɑn

mɑlam kʷɑkʷsəss sehsi-awikotəme,

mɑlam

kʷɑkʷsəss

sehsi-awikotəme

wətihlɑn, "nohkəmi, notelətamən kehsi-wəsikiholek,

wətihlɑn

nohkəmi

notelətamən

kehsi-wəsikiholek

ɑta·č mina kətəliholowən.

ɑta·č

mina

kətəliholowən

kətəmɑksətawi; tepat ehkʷtahi."

kətəmɑksətawi

tepat

ehkʷtahi

nə·monimkʷehso wətehkʷtəhɑn.

nə·monimkʷehso

wətehkʷtəhɑn

*(Then) Woodchuck went to gather switches,*
>   (then) she went to gather them
>   switches
>   Woodchuck

*and she tied the fox to a tree, and she whipped him.*
>   and
>   (then) she tied him to a tree
>   fox
>   and
>   (then) she whipped him

*Eventually the fox begged crying,*
>   eventually
>   fox
>   he begged crying

*(then) he said to her, "My grandmother, I regret how much we abused you,*
>   (then) he said to her
>   my grandmother!
>   I regret it
>   how much we abused you

*I will not do it to you again.*
>   not ·WILL
>   again
>   I (will) not do it to you

*Hear me with pity; so stop beating me."*
>   hear me with pity
>   so
>   stop beating me

*Then Woodchuck stopped beating him.*
>   then· Woodchuck
>   (then) she stopped beating him

wətihlɑn, "ɑn ni, kolɑmsətol."
wətihlɑn
ɑn ni
kolɑmsətol

n·wətɑpkʷihalɑn.
n·wətɑpkʷihalɑn

wətihlɑn, "nihkʷɑp, eləmɑwəsəyan,
wətihlɑn
nihkʷɑp
eləmɑwəsəyan

mosahk mina wininawahkač winehsohsis
mosahk
mina
wininawahkač
winehsohsis

tali-nəkʷihčinite tɑmɑ."
tali-nəkʷihčinite
tɑmɑ

nə·kəloskɑpe wətihlɑn kʷɑkʷsəssal,
nə·kəloskɑpe
wətihlɑn
kʷɑkʷsəssal

"mosahk amočke pehsotkamohkač wikəwɑm apihtɑsike."
mosahk
amočke
pehsotkamohkač
wikəwɑm
apihtɑsike

*(Then) she said to him, "Well then, I believe you."*
    (then) she said to him
    well then
    I believe you (in hearing you)

*Then she untied him.*
    then· she untied him

*(Then) she said to him, "Now, as you go on living,*
    (then) she said to him
    now
    as you go on living

*don't ever again look down on a little old woman*
    don't
    again
    don't look down on her
    little old woman

*if she is living alone somewhere."*
    if she is living alone there
    somewhere

*Then Gluskabe said to the fox,*
    then· Gluskabe
    (then) he said to him
    fox

*"Don't even come close to a house if it is occupied."*
    don't
    (not) even
    don't come close to it
    house
    if it is occupied

nə·weči- nihkʷαp kʷαkʷsəss -ahkʷαləmit.

nə·weči-

nihkʷαp

kʷαkʷsəss

-ahkʷαləmit

*That is why now the fox is shy.*
then· why
now
fox
she/he is shy

## NOTES

PAGE

232  *wačkawihptinewi*: In Penobscot, animal paws are spoken of using the same words as for human hands and feet. So here and below, 'paw' is the same expression as for human 'hand'. Carol Dana notes hearing a Passamaquoddy-Maliseet speaker say the equivalent word *ckuwiptinèw* to their grandchildren to help them wash up.

236  *kkīhīī*: This appears to be an especially drawn-out form of *kkiy*, the general Penobscot expression of excitement, interest, happiness, etc.

11

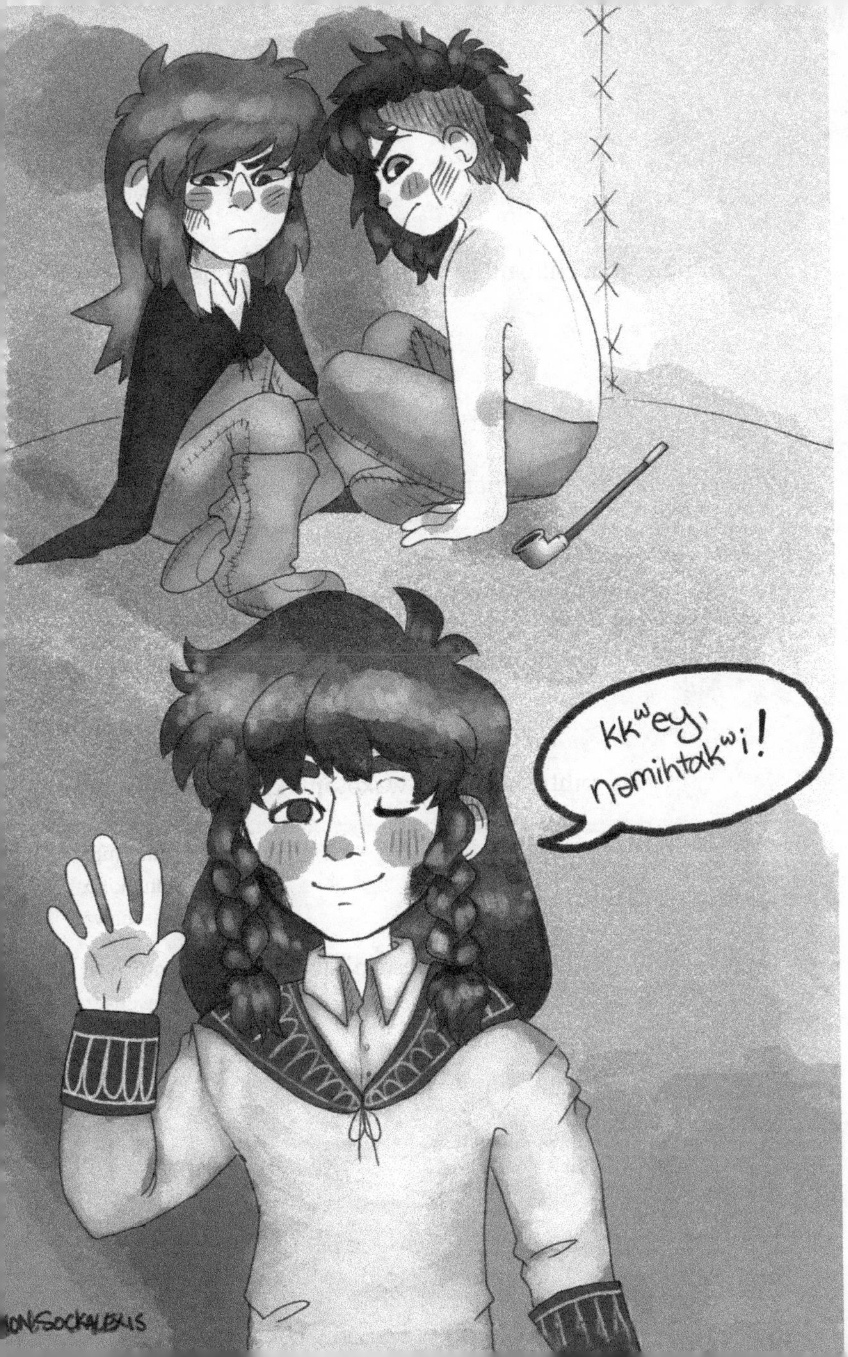
kkʷey, nəmihtakʷi!
...ON SOCKALEXIS

# nəkʷətɑnkaw

nihkʷɑp wətihlɑn ohkəməssal,
   nihkʷɑp
   wətihlɑn
   ohkəməssal

"mina nəmačehla, nihkʷɑp·əkahk nətah·apa nəsipkohsew."
   mina
   nəmačehla
   nihkʷɑp·əkahk
   nətah·apa
   nəsipkohsew

wətihlɑn ohkəməssal, "nətahčəwi-alohkewɑk kohsəssənawak,
   wətihlɑn
   ohkəməssal
   nətahčəwi-alohkewɑk
   kohsəssənawak

nəkati-nači-otehkkawɑ pəpon.
   nəkati-nači-otehkkawɑ
   pəpon

pihta mačamto: wəkətəmɑkihɑ kohsəssənawa,
   pihta
   mačamto
   wəkətəmɑkihɑ
   kohsəssənawa

wesɑmi-awehket eləhɑnətəwit."
   wesɑmi-awehket
   eləhɑnətəwit

*So now he said to his grandmother,*
> now
> (then) he said to her
> his grandmother

*"I'm starting off again; this time there's no way I will be gone a long time."*
> again
> I start off
> now ·KAHK
> not ·WOULD
> I (would) not walk for a long time

*(Then) he said to his grandmother, "I have to work for our descendants,*
> (then) he said to her
> his grandmother
> I have to work for them
> our descendants

*I am going to go visit Winter.*
> I am going to go visit him
> Winter

*He is very mean: he makes our descendants pitiful,*
> very
> he is mean/cruel
> he makes them pitiful
> our descendants

*(as) he overuses how supernaturally powerful he is."*
> as he uses it too much
> how supernaturally powerful he is

wətihlɑn ohkəməssal, "tɑn·ɑskʷe eyit nipən?"

    wətihlɑn

    ohkəməssal

    tɑn·ɑskʷe

    eyit

    nipən

wətihlɑn, "sɑwanawok: kamɑč saki-nenawelətɑso;

    wətihlɑn

    sɑwanawok

    kamɑč

    saki-nenawelətɑso

mečími wənenawelәmawɑl spətáhi ahč nipáyi."

    mečími

    wənenawelәmawɑl

    spətáhi

    ahč

    nipáyi

wətihlɑn ohkəməssal, "nətahčəwi-alihlɑn.

    wətihlɑn

    ohkəməssal

    nətahčəwi-alihlɑn

alɑpehsəmawi wəlokehsal nɑkɑ kətatəphoton."

    alɑpehsəmawi

    wəlokehsal

    nɑkɑ

    kətatəphoton

nə·kehəla ná(hə)law wətəlɑpehsikɑn monimkʷehso,

    nə·kehəla

    ná(hə)law

    wətəlɑpehsikɑn

    monimkʷehso

*(Then) he said to his grandmother, "Where (however) is Summer?"*
    (then) he said to her
    his grandmother
    where ·however
    where she/he is
    Summer

*(Then) she said to him, "In the south: it is guarded very hard;*
    (then) she said to him
    in the south
    very
    it is guarded hard

*they are always guarding him during the day and also at night."*
    always
    they guard him
    during the day
    also
    at night

*(Then) he said to his grandmother, "I have to go there.*
    (then) he said to her
    his grandmother
    I have to go there/to it

*Cut rawhide strings up for me and roll them up (into a ball)."*
    cut them up for me
    rawhide strings
    and
    (then) you roll them up (into a ball)

*Then sure enough, Woodchuck steadily cut up cords,*
    then· sure enough
    continually/constantly/steadily
    (then) she cut up cords
    Woodchuck

mɑlam tɑ̀pawɑs kehsahpskal wəlokehsal.
>
> mɑlam
> tɑ̀pawɑs
> kehsahpskal
> wəlokehsal

"nɑkɑ nisɑkəmakəsəwak alihtawi."
>
> nɑkɑ
> nisɑkəmakəsəwak
> alihtawi

nə·kehəla monimkʷehso wətəlhɑkəmɑn.
>
> nə·kehəla
> monimkʷehso
> wətəlhɑkəmɑn

n·wəmɑčehlɑn kəloskɑpe; wətihlɑn ohkəməssal,
>
> n·wəmɑčehlɑn
> kəloskɑpe
> wətihlɑn
> ohkəməssal

"mosahk nsahihkɑč! nápi·tte·č nəpečihla."
>
> mosahk
> nsahihkɑč
> nápi·tte·č
> nəpečihla

monimkʷehso wkʷenəssal wətihlɑl,
>
> monimkʷehso
> wkʷenəssal
> wətihlɑl

*until (there were) seven balls of rawhide cords.*
> until
> seven
> (amount of) balls/round things
> rawhide cords

*"And make for me two pairs of snowshoes."*
> and
> two pairs of snowshoes
> make them for me

*Then sure enough, Woodchuck made snowshoes.*
> then· sure enough
> Woodchuck
> (then) she made snowshoes

*Then Gluskabe started off; (then) he told his grandmother,*
> then· he started off
> Gluskabe
> (then) he told her
> his grandmother

*"Don't worry about me! I will come (back) soon."*
> don't
> don't worry about me
> soon/quickly ·INTENS ·WILL
> I will come

*Woodchuck told her grandchild,*
> Woodchuck
> her grandchild
> she told him

"nəmɑ pečihláne, weči·č -wewinawat kəmihtɑkʷəss nəkʷətɑlakikʷe."

nəmɑ
pečihláne
weči·č -wewinawat
kəmihtɑkʷəss
nəkʷətɑlakikʷe.

wəmɑčehlɑn; eləmihlɑt.

wəmɑčehlɑn
eləmihlɑt

mɑlam·te saláhki mɑče-pahpɑkʷɑkʷahte.

mɑlam·te
saláhki
mɑče-pahpɑkʷɑkʷahte

pesəkʷən elihlɑt: mɑlam·te [mam]tahkamike.

pesəkʷən
elihlɑt
mɑlam·te
[mam]tahkamike

n·as·te wəmehtkawɑn wətɑkəma; nə·kətakihi wətekholɑn wətɑkəma,

n·as·te
wəmehtkawɑn
wətɑkəma
nə·kətakihi
wətekholɑn
wətɑkəma

*"When you get there, what you will recognize your father from is (that) he has one eye."*
    there
    when you arrive there
    what you will recognize him from
    your father
    he is one-eyed

*(Then) he started off; on he went.*
    (then) he started off
    on he went

*Finally at one point the snow (on the ground) started to get thin.*
    eventually ·INTENS
    at one point
    the snow (on the ground) started to get thin

*He went on the same: finally the ground was bare.*
    it was just the same
    how he went
    eventually ·INTENS
    it was bare exposed ground

*Right then too he wore out his snowshoes; then he hung up his other snowshoes,*
    then·also ·INTENS
    (then) he wore them out
    his snowshoes
    then· others
    (then) he hung them
    his snowshoes

nɑkɑ wəmanənəmən wsisəkʷ nɑkɑ wətahsapkʷɑn apikʷehsakok,

> nɑkɑ
> wəmanənəmən
> wsisəkʷ
> nɑkɑ
> wətahsapkʷɑn
> apikʷehsakok

nɑkɑ wətihlɑn kəčəkikilahsəwal, "kənenawɑpatamən nsisəkʷ."

> nɑkɑ
> wətihlɑn
> kəčəkikilahsəwal
> kənenawɑpatamən
> nsisəkʷ

wəmɑčehlɑn [ma]mčəsitáhi; eləmihlɑt.

> wəmɑčehlɑn
> [ma]mčəsitáhi
> eləmihlɑt

mālam·te, saláhki wənotamən ketəwəkɑmək.

> mālam·te
> saláhki
> wənotamən
> ketəwəkɑmək

n·wənamihton otene.

> n·wənamihton
> otene

*and he took his eye out and he cached it in a hollow tree,*
    and
    he took it out
    his eye
    and
    he cached it (in a tree)
    in a hollow tree

*and he said to Chickadee, "(So) you keep a watch on my eye."*
    and
    (then) he said to him/her
    Chickadee
    (so) you keep a watch on it
    my eye

*(Then) he headed off with feet exposed; on he went.*
    (then) he headed off
    with feet exposed
    on he went

*Fiiinally, at one point he heard the sound of dancing.*
    eventually ·INTENS
    at one point
    he heard it
    as one is heard dancing

*Then he saw a village.*
    then· he saw it
    village

nəmɑ pečihlɑt, wətali-wəčihčihəwɑn wəmihtɑkʷsal wikəwɑmək.

nəmɑ
pečihlɑt
wətali-wəčihčihəwɑn
wəmihtɑkʷsal
wikəwɑmək

wətihlɑn, "kkʷey, nəmihtɑkʷi!"

wətihlɑn
kkʷey
nəmihtɑkʷi

itak, "kkʷey, nənemɑn, kəpetotehkkawi: nolitəhɑs."

itak
kkʷey
nənemɑn
kəpetotehkkawi
nolitəhɑs

nə·kenok awičəya ɑta kʷina apehkʷihlɑməkowəya.

nə·kenok
awičəya
ɑta
kʷina
apehkʷihlɑməkowəya

*When he got there, he was a guest of his father there at his house.*
    there
    when he arrived
    (then) he was there as a guest of
    his father
    at his house

*(Then) he said to him, "Hello, my father!"*
    (then) he said to him
    hello
    my father!

*He said, "Hello, my son, you've come to visit me: I am happy."*
    (what) he said
    hello
    my son
    you come to visit me
    I am happy

*So however his brothers did not really welcome him.*
    then· but/however
    his brothers
    not
    really
    they did not welcome him

manəni·tte (a)wewinawɑ wəkatonaləko.

     manəni·tte
     (a)wewinawɑ
     wəkatonaləko

nə·pesəko wətali-pitsənɑlɑn ktəhɑnətəwi-pənahpskʷahsənal.

     nə·pesəko
     wətali-pitsənɑlɑn
     ktəhɑnətəwi-pənahpskʷahsənal

wəpəskʷəlehpɑn, nɑkɑ wətihlɑn kəloskɑpal, "nehe, wətama!"

     wəpəskʷəlehpɑn
     nɑkɑ
     wətihlɑn
     kəloskɑpal
     nehe
     wətama

nə·kehəla, kəloskɑpe awihkʷənɑn otamɑkanal,

     nə·kehəla
     kəloskɑpe
     awihkʷənɑn
     otamɑkanal

n·wəmamhonasahəlɑn nisəta.

     n·wəmamhonasahəlɑn
     nisəta

*Right away he recognized they were after him.*
    right away ·INTENS
    he recognized them
    they were after him

*Then one was filling a supernaturally huge stone pipe.*
    then· one
    (then) he was filling it
    supernaturally huge stone pipe

*(Then) he lit it, and he said to Gluskabe, "Come on, smoke!"*
    (then) he lit it
    and
    (then) he said to him
    Gluskabe
    NEHE
    smoke

*Then sure enough, Gluskabe took his pipe,*
    then· sure enough
    Gluskabe
    (then) he took it
    his pipe

*then he inhaled it deeply twice.*
    then· he inhaled it deeply
    twice

eli-asahəlɑt, n·wəsihkihalɑn wətamɑkanal.

    eli-asahəlɑt
    n·wəsihkihalɑn
    wətamɑkanal

nə·mina wihkʷipəkətehpɑt, n·wəsəkʷskɑmkihasin wətamɑkan.

    nə·mina
    wihkʷipəkətehpɑt
    n·wəsəkʷskɑmkihasin
    wətamɑkan

wətitamən, "ahkkʷátale,

    wətitamən
    ahkkʷátale

poskəlisəsso kotamɑkan, ničəye,

    poskəlisəsso
    kotamɑkan
    ničəye

ččena nəya nəpitsənɑn."

    ččena
    nəya
    nəpitsənɑn

*As he inhaled it, then he emptied the pipe.*
    as he inhaled it
    then· he emptied it
    the pipe

*Then again when he took a puff from it, then the pipe shattered into a mass of pieces.*
    then· again
    when he took a puff from it
    then· it shattered into a mass of pieces
    pipe

*(Then) he said, "Ahkwadaleh,*
    (then) he said
    ahkwadaleh

*your pipe is a fragile little one, my brother,*
    it is a fragile/soft little one
    your pipe
    my brother

*so let me fill up a pipe."*
    let me
    I
    (then) I fill up a pipe

nə·nekəma otamɑkanal wəpitsənalɑn.

> nə·nekəma
> otamɑkanal
> wəpitsənalɑn

piwsəssəwal, kenok wɑpikaniyɑl.

> piwsəssəwal
> kenok
> wɑpikaniyɑl

wəpəskʷəlehpɑn, nɑkɑ wəmilɑn wičəyal:

> wəpəskʷəlehpɑn
> nɑkɑ
> wəmilɑn
> wičəyal

"ččena owa akʷeči-wətamehkhɑne!"

> ččena
> owa
> akʷeči-wətamehkhɑne

manəni·tte kataweləməwal wičəyal,

> manəni·tte
> kataweləməwal
> wičəyal

awihkʷitəhamɑl otamɑkanal, etoči-piwsəssilit.

> awihkʷitəhamɑl
> otamɑkanal
> etoči-piwsəssilit

*Then he filled up his own pipe.*
    then· he
    his pipe
    (then) he filled it

*It was small, but (made) of ivory.*
    it is small
    but
    it is of white-bone

*(Then) he lit it and gave it to his brother:*
    (then) he lit it
    and
    (then) he gave it to him
    his brother

*"Let's try to smoke this one!"*
    let's
    this
    let's try to smoke it

*Right away his brother wanted to laugh,*
    right away ·INTENS
    he wanted to laugh
    his brother

*he thought his pipe was funny, it was so small.*
    he thought it (was) funny
    his pipe
    it was so small

elitəhɑsit, "wa·kahk·əč pesəkʷəta wihkʷipəkətehpoke, nəsihkihalɑ·č."

elitəhɑsit
wa·kahk·əč
pesəkʷəta
wihkʷipəkətehpoke
nəsihkihalɑ·č

nə·kehəla (a)wihkʷipəkətenalɑl; otamɑn.

nə·kehəla
(a)wihkʷipəkətenalɑl
otamɑn

mɑlam pahtaso.

mɑlam
pahtaso

n·wətihlɑn kətakil wičəyal, "nehe, kəy'·ahč wətama,

n·wətihlɑn
kətakil
wičəyal
nehe
kəy[a]·ahč
wətama

kamɑč wəlahsənal otamɑkɑnal kətohkanimisəna."

kamɑč
wəlahsənal
otamɑkɑnal
kətohkanimisəna

*He thought, "As for this one, if I take a puff from it once, I will empty it."*
    what/how he thought
    this ·KAHK ·WILL
    once
    if I take a puff from it
    I empty it ·WILL

*Then sure enough, he took a puff from it; (and) he smoked.*
    then· sure enough
    he took a puff from it
    (then) he smoked

*Eventually he got sick on the smoke.*
    eventually
    he got sick on smoke

*Then he said to his other brother, "Come on, you smoke too.*
    then· he said to him
    other
    his brother
    NEHE
    you ·also
    smoke

*Our younger brother's pipe has a nice flavor."*
    very
    it has a nice flavor
    his pipe
    our younger brother

nə(h·ə)nn'·ahč nekəma otamɑn.
    nə(h·ə)nn[a]·ahč
    nekəma
    otamɑn

mɑlam pahtaso.
    mɑlam
    pahtaso

mina kətak otamɑn.
    mina
    kətak
    otamɑn

ənn'·ahč pahtaso.
    ənn[a]·ahč
    pahtaso

mɑlam·te məsi kehsilit awičəya nəkihkɑ-pahtasolətəwak.
    mɑlam·te
    məsi
    kehsilit
    awičəya
    nəkihkɑ-pahtasolətəwak

nə·mlohsəss wətihlɑn, "kamɑč ktəhánəto kətohkanimisəwɑ;
    nə·mlohsəss
    wətihlɑn
    kamɑč
    ktəhánəto
    kətohkanimisəwɑ

ehkʷi-katonalohk: mehč·ətte kəsehkɑkowɑ·č."
    ehkʷi-katonalohk
    mehč·ətte
    kəsehkɑkowɑ·č

*Then that one, too, he smoked.*
  then·that ·also
  he
  (then) he smoked

*Eventually he got sick on the smoke.*
  eventually
  he got sick on smoke

*(Then) another one smoked.*
  again
  other
  (then) he smokes

*That one too got sick on the smoke.*
  that one ·also
  he got sick on smoke

*Finally every one of his brothers all got sick on the smoke.*
  eventually ·INTENS
  all
  how many they were
  his brothers
  they (group) all got completely sick on smoke

*Then the old man said to them, "Your younger brother has great supernatural power;*
  then· old man
  (then) he said to them
  very
  he has great supernatural power
  your younger brother

*stop going after him: he will still defeat you."*
  stop going after him
  still ·INTENS
  he defeat you (pl.) ·WILL

mehčˑətte wəkatonalɑwɑl wətohkanimisəwɑl,
mehčˑətte
wəkatonalɑwɑl
wətohkanimisəwɑl

wəsɑm wəčəskawɑlɑwɑl.
wəsɑm
wəčəskawɑlɑwɑl

nəˑmina wətihlɑnɑ wətohkanimisəwɑl,
nəˑmina
wətihlɑnɑ
wətohkanimisəwɑl

"ɑmatihətine; wɑlatehəmhatine!"
ɑmatihətine
wɑlatehəmhatine

amoskənɑnɑ wɑlatehəmɑkanal; pənahpskʷiye.
amoskənɑnɑ
wɑlatehəmɑkanal
pənahpskʷiye

kīnəhɑnətəwinɑkʷəso.
kīnəhɑnətəwinɑkʷəso

*They still went after their younger brother,*
    still ·INTENS
    they went after him
    their younger brother

*because they were jealous of him.*
    because
    they were jealous of him

*Then again they told their younger brother,*
    then· again
    (then) they said to him
    their younger brother

*"Let's play against each other; let's play bowl-and-dice!"*
    let's (group) play against each other
    let's (group) play bowl-and-dice

*(Then) they brought out a bowl-and-dice game; it was made of stone.*
    (then) they brought it out
    bowl-and-dice game
    (it was) of stone

*It looked supernaturally enoooormous.*
    it looked supernaturally/powerfully enooormous

itak kəloskɑpe, "nehe, ɑmatihətine,
> itak
> kəloskɑpe
> nehe
> ɑmatihətine

wəsɑm nəya kamɑč nəwikɑmke."
> wəsɑm
> nəya
> kamɑč
> nəwikɑmke

n·wətɑmatihətinɑ.
> n·wətɑmatihətinɑ

ntamka·tte kehčayiwit awihkʷənɑn wɑlatal,
> ntamka·tte
> kehčayiwit
> awihkʷənɑn
> wɑlatal

wətəltehsimɑn; mɑlam aməstehəmənal akitamɑkanal.
> wətəltehsimɑn
> mɑlam
> aməstehəmənal
> akitamɑkanal

nə·kəloskɑpe awihkʷənɑn wɑlatal,
> nə·kəloskɑpe
> awihkʷənɑn
> wɑlatal

*Gluskabe said, "Come on, let's play against each other,*
  (what) he said
  Gluskabe
  NEHE
  let's (group) play against each other

*because I very much like playing."*
  because
  I
  very
  I like to play (game)

*Then they played against each other.*
  then· they (group) played against each other

*(Then) the eldest one took the bowl,*
  first ·INTENS
  the eldest one
  (then) he took it
  bowl

*(then) he hit it (against something); eventually he got a lot of counters.*
  (then) he hit it (against something)
  eventually
  he got a lot of them
  counters

*Then Gluskabe took the bowl,*
  then· Gluskabe
  (then) he took it
  bowl

pesək<sup>w</sup>əta·tte elahket, wəsək<sup>w</sup>skɑmkihtehsimɑl.

pesək<sup>w</sup>əta·tte
elahket
wəsək<sup>w</sup>skɑmkihtehsimɑl

wəmemlaweləmin kəloskɑpe,

wəmemlaweləmin
kəloskɑpe

itak, "ahkk<sup>w</sup>átale, poskəlisəsso kəwɑlatena.

itak
ahkk<sup>w</sup>átale
poskəlisəsso
kəwɑlatena

ččena owa nəya nəwɑlate ak<sup>w</sup>ečskohalɑne."

ččena
owa
nəya
nəwɑlate
ak<sup>w</sup>ečskohalɑne

n·wəmoskənan awɑlatal: piwsəssəwal wɑpikaniyɑl.

n·wəmoskənan
awɑlatal
piwsəssəwal
wɑpikaniyɑl

nə(h·ə)nna katawelǝmo kehčayiwit wičəyal.

nə(h·ə)nna
katawelǝmo
kehčayiwit
wičəyal

nə·kəloskɑpe wətəltehsiman awɑlatal.

nə·kəloskɑpe
wətəltehsiman
awɑlatal

*as he threw it just once, he hit it (against something), shattering it into a mass of pieces.*
> once ·INTENS
> as he threw it
> he hit it (against something) such that it shattered into a mass of pieces

*(Then) Gluskabe laughed deeply.*
> (then) he laughed deeply
> Gluskabe

*He said, "Ahkwadaleh, our bowl is a fragile little one.*
> (what) he said
> ahkwadaleh
> it is a fragile/soft little one
> our bowl

*Let's try this bowl of mine."*
> let's
> this
> me
> my bowl
> let's try it

*Then he brought out his bowl: (it was) small, (it was) of ivory.*
> then· he brought it out
> his bowl
> it was small
> of white-bone

*Then that eldest brother of his, he wanted to laugh.*
> then·that
> he wanted to laugh
> the eldest one
> his brother

*Then Gluskabe hit his bowl (against something).*
> then· Gluskabe
> (then) he hit it (against something)
> his bowl

mɑlam aməstehəmənal akitamɑkanal.
> mɑlam
> aməstehəmənal
> akitamɑkanal

nə(h·ə)nna kehčayiwit wičəyal (a)wihkʷənɑn wɑlatal.
> nə(h·ə)nna
> kehčayiwit
> wičəyal
> (a)wihkʷənɑn
> wɑlatal

elitəhɑsit, "wa·kahk pesəkʷəta alahkáne, nəsəkʷsktehsimɑ."
> elitəhɑsit
> wa·kahk
> pesəkʷəta
> alahkáne
> nəsəkʷsktehsimɑ

nə·keti-alahket, wətɑlawənɑl.
> nə·keti-alahket
> wətɑlawənɑl

ípitte tali-wasahsihásəwa wkasəya.
> ípi·tte
> tali-wasahsihásəwa
> wkasəya

n·etali-sehkalot, wətihlɑn,
> n·etali-sehkalot
> wətihlɑn

*Eventually he got a lot of counters.*
    eventually
    he got a lot of them
    counters

*Then that eldest brother of his, he took the bowl.*
    then·that
    the eldest one
    his brother
    (then) he took it
    bowl

*He thought, "This one, if I throw it once, I will hit it (against something) into pieces."*
    what/how he thought
    this ·KAHK
    once
    if I throw it
    I hit it (against something) into pieces

*Then as he was going to throw it, he (tried but) could not lift it.*
    then· as he was going to throw it
    he tried but could not lift it

*His fingernails just slipped on it.*
    only ·INTENS
    they slipped on it there
    his fingernails

*Then as he was defeated there, (then) he said to him,*
    then· as he was defeated there
    (then) he said to him

"nətahtekəne ičəye pəkʷánɑ wɑlate. kəsehkawi."
nətahtekəne
[n]ičəye
pəkʷánɑ
wɑlate
kəsehkawi

*"The bowl cannot be lifted, my brother. You beat me."*

not (despite effort)

my brother

it is (not) successfully lifted

bowl

you beat me

## NOTES

PAGE

254 *wətekholan watakəma*: Regarding hanging up the snowshoes, Speck adds, "on a tree."

256 *wsisək*ʷ: It is interesting that his father is to be known by having one eye, and now Gluskabe too has one eye.

258 *nəmihtak*ʷi: Some relationship words have special forms for addressing the person directly: *nəmihtak*ʷi 'my father!'; *nohkəmi* 'my grandmother!'; etc., and Passamaquoddy-Maliseet has both *nuhkomi* and *uhkomi* for this. The 1918 version suggests *mihtak*ʷi, which may parallel Passamaquoddy-Maliseet *uhkomi* 'grandma!' in dropping *n(ə)*- (compare *(n)ičaye* 'my [fellow] brother!' later in this story), but this also may simply be Speck not hearing the weak *nə*- in *nəmihtak*ʷi before -*m*-.

258 *nanemən*: The 1918 version suggests *neman*; see the above discussion of *nəmihtak*ʷi.

262 *n·wəsihkihalan*: The 1918 version notes that the word translated 'emptied' here means Gluskabe (in two puffs) smoked it all to ashes. The element *sihk*- (whose sound may reflect its meaning/feeling, as is common in Wabanaki languages) is used referring to evaporating a liquid dry or smoking tobacco to bare ashes, so it may refer not so much to completely emptying it out as to just removing the main/useful substance.

262 *ahkk*ʷátale: Difficult to translate, this word can be used as an expression of surprise or a response to something that is too much, over the top. The common expression "Kadaleh" in contemporary Penobscot English comes from this.

264 *wapikaniyəl*: Literally 'made of white bone', but according to the 1918 version, specifically 'ivory', i.e., walrus tusk, etc. Note that the bow and arrow Woodchuck makes for Gluskabe are also described as being *wapikaniye*, as is a rolling skull in a later Lyon story. Likewise, a *wapsk*ʷ, literally 'white-bear' (i.e., a polar bear), and also *wapi-awehsohs* 'white bear' figure heavily in his later stories too. It may also be significant that *wapapi* 'wampum' is literally 'white-cord'.

266 *·kahk*: This is a common expression, used after the first word in a phrase, to mean 'as for . . . (as opposed to the others)'.

266 *kəy·ahč*: *kəya* 'you' and *·ahč* 'also, too' are typically run together in pronunciation as *kəyahč*.

266 *kətohkanimisəna*: This suggests that Gluskabe is the *mətehsən*, the youngest child of the family, who in many stories has power.

270 *walatehəmhatine*: The 1918 version notes, "This is the well-known dish and dice game. It is played with six dice and fifty-two counting sticks. The dice are shaken in the dish, five or six of one face counting for the thrower. The counting is very complex." In Speck, *Penobscot Man*, 174, however, he refers to "the counters, consisting of one crooked stick, four flat ones and fifty-six thin round sticks." Siebert noted that one elder told him that Speck got the rules wrong.

270 *pənahpsk*ʷiye: Once again, something not normally made of stone is here made of stone.

12

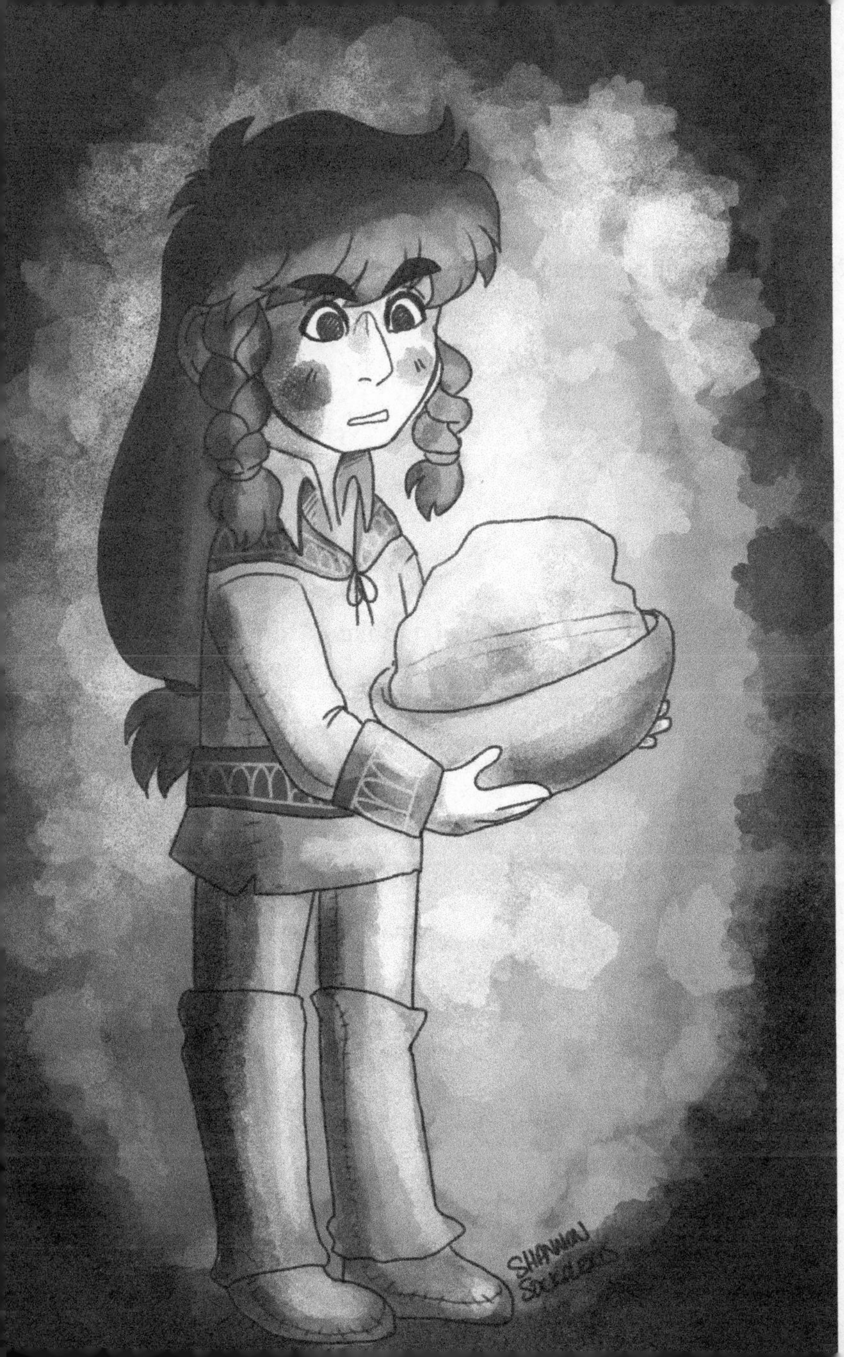

# nisαnkaw

wətəlohsɑn etaləkamək; wənɑči-witəkɑn.

    wətəlohsɑn

    etaləkaмək

    wənɑči-witəkɑn

nəmɑ pečohset, wənamihɑn pəmɑwəsəwínəwa, pepɑmi-kikimətonkahətičik.

    nəmɑ

    pečohset

    wənamihɑn

    pəmɑwəsəwínəwa

    pepɑmi-kikimətonkahətičik

n·ahč nekəma wətahsičohsɑn.

    n·ahč

    nekəma

    wətahsičohsɑn

wətakʷečotəmohkɑn, "tɑn mina ali-təpihle,

    wətakʷečotəmohkɑn

    tɑn

    mina

    ali-təpihle

kekʷəss alihtɑkʷat?"

    kekʷəss

    alihtɑkʷat

manəni·tte pesəkəwal wətihləkol,

    manəni·tte

    pesəkəwal

    wətihləkol

*(Then) he walked to where there was a dance; then he went to join in the dance.*
   (then) he walked to there
   where there was a dance
   (then) he went to join in the dance

*When he got there (walking), (then) he saw people there, going around secretly talking.*
   there
   when he got there (walking)
   (then) he saw them
   people
   (ones that/as they) were (group) going around secretly talking

*Then he too walked up close by.*
   then also
   he
   (then) he walked up close by

*(Then) he asked, "What has happened,*
   (then) he asked
   how/what
   again
   it happened (in some way)

*what's the news?"*
   what
   it is heard (in/to be some way)

*Right away one (of them) told him,*
   right away ·INTENS
   one
   he told him

"ččəsči, kəya·p'·eht elikəyan! kəwewelətamən eltɑkʷahk!"

ččəsči
kəya·p[a]·eht
elikəyan
kəwewelətamən
eltɑkʷahk

nə(h·ə)nna·ahč nekəma kəloskɑpe wətihlɑl,

nə(h·ə)nna·ahč
nekəma
kəloskɑpe
wətihlɑl

"kəya·k'·ahč ččəsči!"—wəmanihtanenɑn,

kəya·k[a]·ahč
ččəsči
wəmanihtanenɑn

n·wəpitikɑn etaləkamək; n·(a)witəkɑn.

n·wəpitikɑn
etaləkamək
n·(a)witəkɑn

(a)wiwənəkehtawawɑl nipənal; tepapo kči-pkənačok.

(a)wiwənəkehtawawɑl
nipənal
tepapo
kči-pkənačok

*"Chuschee, the likes of you! You know what's going on!"*
    CHUSCHEE
    you ·WOULD ·EHT
    how you are (in appearance/form)
    you know it
    how it sounds

*Then that Gluskabe too, he himself said to him,*
    then·that ·also
    he
    Gluskabe
    he said to him

*"YOU chuschee too!"—(then) he twisted his nose off (with his fingers),*
    you ·KA ·also
    CHUSCHEE
    (then) he twisted his nose off (with his fingers)

*then he went in to where there was dancing; then he joined in the dancing.*
    then· he went in
    where there was dancing
    then· he joined in the dancing

*They were dancing around Summer; it was sitting inside a great bark container.*
    they were dancing around it
    Summer
    it was sitting inside
    great bark container

nə·yo peməkahətit nisəwak nákskʷak; wəlikəwak.

nə·yo
peməkahətit
nisəwak
nákskʷak
wəlikəwak

wəkəlolɑn; nətahtɑmɑ wətɑsiteməkowəya; epəkʷahč awihkʷinɑko.

wəkəlolɑn
nətahtɑmɑ
wətɑsiteməkowəya
epəkʷahč
awihkʷinɑko

amoskʷilawəhoko: epəkʷahč wəsɑmihpskʷanenɑn,

amoskʷilawəhoko
epəkʷahč
wəsɑmihpskʷanenɑn

n·eləmi-wiwənəkahətit pesəkʷəta, kis mɑče-piləwinɑkʷəsəwak.

n·eləmi-wiwənəkahətit
pesəkʷəta
kis
mɑče-piləwinɑkʷəsəwak

mehsəma mina wiwənəkahətihkʷ, wətɑlawəkɑnɑ.

mehsəma
mina
wiwənəkahətihkʷ
wətɑlawəkɑnɑ

elɑpolətihətit alənɑpak, wənamihɑnɑ nisəwa máskkak epičik,

elɑpolətihətit
alənɑpak
wənamihɑnɑ
nisəwa
máskkak
epičik

286 ~ nisɑnkaw

*Then here were dancing two young women; they were beautiful.*
> then· here
> there they were dancing (along)
> two
> young women
> they are beautiful

*(Then) he spoke to them; they didn't answer him at all; they even saw him as funny.*
> (then) he spoke to them
> not at all
> they did not answer him
> even
> they saw him as funny

*They made him angry: (so then) he even touched them on the back,*
> they made him angry
> even
> (then) he touched them on the back

*then as they danced off in a circle one time, already they started to look different.*
> then· as they danced away in a circle
> one time
> already
> they started to look strange

*Before they danced around the circle again, they (tried but) could not dance.*
> not yet
> again
> when they had not danced around in a circle
> (then) they (tried but) could not dance

*As the People looked, (then) they saw two toads sitting there,*
> as they (group) looked
> People
> (then) they saw them
> two
> toads
> (them) sitting there

n·wənotahkαnα.

n·wənotahkαnα

mαlhitəhαsolətəwak eli-maskkayihlahətit nάkskʷak,

mαlhitəhαsolətəwak
eli-maskkayihlahətit
nάkskʷak

kenok pesəkʷən eləkahətit, wəsαm mečími ččəwi-wiwənəkehtawα nipən,

kenok
pesəkʷən
eləkahətit
wəsαm
mečími
ččəwi-wiwənəkehtawα
nipən

weči·č- αta awen -kisi-sαmənαhkʷ.

weči·č-
αta
awen
-kisi-sαmənαhkʷ

kəloskαpe elitəhαsit, "pəsəkάhtahasič wikəwαm."

kəloskαpe
elitəhαsit
pəsəkάhtahasič
wikəwαm

n·wəkisi-nimiphαn nipənal kʷeni-pəsəkahtek.

n·wəkisi-nimiphαn
nipənal
kʷeni-pəsəkahtek

wənotekətahin, amαče-kʷakʷəmahlαn.

wənotekətahin
amαče-kʷakʷəmahlαn

*then they threw them outside.*
    then· they threw them outside

*They were amazed at how the young women had turned into toads,*
    they (group) were amazed
    how they had turned into toads
    young women

*but they danced on the same, because Summer always had to be danced around,*
    but
    it was just the same
    how they danced
    because
    always
    it had to be danced around
    Summer

*so that no one will be able to touch it.*
    so that ·WILL
    not
    anyone
    that they cannot touch it

*Gluskabe thought, "Let the house go dark."*
    Gluskabe
    what/how he thought
    let it turn dark (suddenly)
    house

*Then he was able to grab Summer while it was dark.*
    then· he was able to grab it
    Summer
    while it was dark

*(Then) he jumped outside, (and) he started running.*
    (then) he jumped outside
    (then) he started running

saláhki·tte yok etaləkačik wənotawawɑl nipənal mekʷeličil.

saláhki·tte

yok

etaləkačik

wənotawawɑl

nipənal

mekʷeličil

nə·tepənawihahətit, čilənɑso.

nə·tepənawihahətit

čilənɑso

manəni·tte kɑkɑləwahətəwak,

manəni·tte

kɑkɑləwahətəwak

"awen wəkisi-čilənɑl nipənal."

awen

wəkisi-čilənɑl

nipənal

itamohətit, "na piləwi-alənɑpe n·elalohket."

itamohətit

na

piləwi-alənɑpe

n·elalohket

n·wənotekətaholətinɑ; n·wənohsohkawɑnɑ kəloskɑpal.

n·wənotekətaholətinɑ

n·wənohsohkawɑnɑ

kəloskɑpal

saláhki·tte kəloskɑpe eləmihlɑt,

saláhki·tte

kəloskɑpe

eləmihlɑt

*Suddenly these ones who were dancing heard Summer groaning.*
  suddenly ·INTENS
  these
  ones that were dancing
  they heard it
  Summer
  as it groaned

*Then when they inspected it, it was marked by hand.*
  then· when they inspected it
  it was marked by hand

*Right away they called out,*
  right away ·INTENS
  they (group) called out

*"Someone has marked Summer with their hand."*
  someone
  she/he has marked it with his/her hand
  Summer

*They said, "That stranger is the one who has done that."*
  (what) they said
  that
  stranger
  that· (is the) one who did it

*Then they jumped outside; then they followed Gluskabe.*
  then· they (group) jumped outside
  then· they followed him
  Gluskabe

*Suddenly, as Gluskabe was going onward,*
  suddenly ·INTENS
  Gluskabe
  as he went onward

wənotawα nohsohkαkohči(či)hi kči-mkasessa.

wənotawα

nohsohkαkohči(či)hi

kči-mkasessa

n·wətahsitapiton wətəpək pesək<sup>w</sup>ən petək<sup>w</sup>ahpskek wəlokehs.

n·wətahsitapiton

wətəpək

pesək<sup>w</sup>ən

petək<sup>w</sup>ahpskek

wəlokehs

pesək<sup>w</sup>ən elihlαt; mαlam·te pesəkəwal kči-mkasessal wətatəmihkαkol, nə·wənimiphokon wətəpək.

pesək<sup>w</sup>ən

elihlαt

mαlam·te

pesəkəwal

kči-mkasessal

wətatəmihkαkol

nə·wənimiphokon

wətəpək

nə·mkasess wəmαwipton petək<sup>w</sup>ahpskek wəlokehs, nαkα ak<sup>w</sup>ələpitəwihlαn.

nə·mkasess

wəmαwipton

petək<sup>w</sup>ahpskek

wəlokehs

nαkα

ak<sup>w</sup>ələpitəwihlαn

*he heard great big crows following him.*
    he heard them
    ones that followed him
    great big crows

*Then he tied one ball of rawhide cord close on his head.*
    then· he tied it close
    on his head
    one
    what is a round ball
    rawhide cord

*He went on just the same; finally one great big crow overtook him, and grabbed him on his head.*
    just the same
    how he went
    eventually ·INTENS
    one
    great big crow
    he overtook him
    then· he grabbed him
    on the head

*Then the crow caught the rawhide ball exactly, and he turned around flying back.*
    then· crow
    (then) he caught it exactly
    what is a round ball
    rawhide cord
    and
    (then) he turned around flying

alitəhɑso mkasess wətəp kəloskɑpe pemiptɑkᵂ.
alitəhɑso
mkasess
wətəp
kəloskɑpe
pemiptɑkᵂ

mɑlam·te elɑpit, wəlokehs kelənək mehči-ɑpihtahpote.
mɑlam·te
elɑpit
wəlokehs
kelənək
mehči-ɑpihtahpote

mɑlhitəhɑso mkasess.
mɑlhitəhɑso
mkasess

nə·mina wənohsohkawɑn, mina wətatəmihkawɑn.
nə·mina
wənohsohkawɑn
mina
wətatəmihkawɑn

mina wənimiphɑn wətəpək; mina osəwetəwihlɑn.
mina
wənimiphɑn
wətəpək
mina
osəwetəwihlɑn

*The crow thought it was Gluskabe's head he was carrying along.*
    he thought
    crow
    his head
    Gluskabe
    what he carried along

*Finally as he looked, the rawhide cord that he held unrolled completely.*
    eventually ·INTENS
    as he looked
    rawhide cord
    that he held
    it unrolled completely

*The crow was amazed.*
    he was amazed
    crow

*Then he chased him again, (and) overtook him again.*
    then· again
    (then) he followed him
    again
    (then) he overtook him

*(Then) again he grabbed him on the head; (then) again he flew back.*
    again
    (then) he grabbed him
    on his head
    again
    (then) he headed back flying

nə·mina ípi·tte wəlokehs kelənək; mehči-ɑpihtahpote.
nə·mina
ípi·tte
wəlokehs
kelənək
mehči-ɑpihtahpote

n·wənaskɑtəhɑsin mkasess.
n·wənaskɑtəhɑsin
mkasess

pesəkʷən elihlɑt kəloskɑpe; elɑpit, wənamihton wasɑli.
pesəkʷən
elihlɑt
kəloskɑpe
elɑpit
wənamihton
wasɑli

mɑlam·te pečihle wasɑli eyik.
mɑlam·te
pečihle
wasɑli
eyik

kis·ahč mkasessak wkʷáhli ayolətəwak,
kis· ahč
mkasessak
wkʷáhli
ayolətəwak

*Then again it was only rawhide cord that he held; it unrolled completely.*
  then· again
  only ·INTENS
  rawhide cord
  that he held
  it unrolled completely

*Then the crow was discouraged.*
  then· he was discouraged
  crow

*Gluskabe went on the same; as he looked, he saw snow.*
  it was just the same
  how he went
  Gluskabe
  as he looked
  he saw it
  snow

*Finally he arrived at where the snow was.*
  eventually ·INTENS
  he arrived
  snow
  where it was

*Already too the crows were nearby,*
  already ·also
  crows
  near(by)
  they (group) were there

kenok namihtohətit wasɑli, wənaskɑtəhɑsolətinɑ, n·wəpətəkitəwihalətinɑ.

kenok
namihtohətit
wasɑli
wənaskɑtəhɑsolətinɑ
n·wəpətəkitəwihalətinɑ

kəloskɑpe wənamihɑn wətɑkəma ekhočinəličihi.

kəloskɑpe
wənamihɑn
wətɑkəma
ekhočinəličihi

pečihlɑt, wənahslɑn wətɑkəma,

pečihlɑt
wənahslɑn
wətɑkəma

nə·wək^wilawahton wsisək^w; ahtɑmɑ wəməskamowən.

nə·wək^wilawahton
wsisək^w
ahtɑmɑ
wəməskamowən

nə·kəčəkikilahsəwal wətihlɑn, "tɑn nsisək^w?"

nə·kəčəkikilahsəwal
wətihlɑn
tɑn
nsisək^w

*but when they saw the snow, (then) they got discouraged, and then flew back again.*
> but
> when they saw it
> snow
> (then) they (group) got discouraged
> then· they (group) headed back flying

*(Then) Gluskabe saw his snowshoes hanging up.*
> Gluskabe
> (then) he saw them
> his snowshoes
> ones that are hanging up

*When he got there, (then) he put on his snowshoes,*
> when he arrived
> (then) he put them on
> his snowshoes

*then he looked for his eye; he didn't find it at all.*
> then· he looked for it
> his eye
> not at all
> he did not find it

*Then he said to Chickadee, "Where's my eye?"*
> then· Chickadee
> (then) he said to him
> where (is)
> my eye

wətihləkon, "tihtəkəli wətələmiptone."

wətihləkon

tihtəkəli

wətələmiptone

n·wəkɑkɑlomɑn tihtəkələyal; (a)wihkʷimɑn.

n·wəkɑkɑlomɑn

tihtəkələyal

(a)wihkʷimɑn

wəpečitəwihlɑn tihtəkəli.

wəpečitəwihlɑn

tihtəkəli

n·wənimiphɑn kəloskɑpe, n·wəketənəmawɑn wsisəkʷ, nekəma wənahston.

n·wənimiphɑn

kəloskɑpe

n·wəketənəmawɑn

wsisəkʷ

nekəma

wənahston

n·wəmɑčehlɑn pəponkik; eləmihlɑt, kʷaskʷáyī

n·wəmɑčehlɑn

pəponkik

eləmihlɑt

kʷaskʷáyī

*(Then) he told him, "Great Horned Owl has taken it away."*
    (then) he said to him
    Great Horned Owl
    he has taken it away

*Then he (Gluskabe) called out to Great Horned Owl; (then) he summoned him.*
    then· he called out to him
    Great Horned Owl
    (then) he summoned him

*(Then) Great Horned Owl came flying.*
    (then) he came flying
    Great Horned Owl

*Then Gluskabe grabbed him, and then he took his eye out of him, and he put it in.*
    then· he grabbed him
    Gluskabe
    then· he took it (of him) out of him
    his eye
    he
    he put it in/on [his own head]

*Then he headed off for the winter land; as he went on, little by little (it grew colder).*
    then· he started off
    to/at the winter land
    as he went along
    little by little

malam·te wənamihton ehtek pkʷamikamikʷ.

> malam·te
> wənamihton
> ehtek
> pkʷamikamikʷ

nəma pečihlɑt, wəpitikɑn; nə·mlohsəssis epit.

> nəma
> pečihlɑt
> wəpitikɑn
> nə·mlohsəssis
> epit

wətihləkol, "kkʷēy, nkʷenəss!"—"kkʷēy, nkʷenəss!"

> wətihləkol
> kkʷēy
> nkʷenəss
> kkʷēy
> nkʷenəss

nə·kəloskɑpe amoskənɑn nipənal,

> nə·kəloskɑpe
> amoskənɑn
> nipənal

nɑkɑ aponɑn elkʷepilit mlohsəssisal.

> nɑkɑ
> aponɑn
> elkʷepilit
> mlohsəssisal

*Finally he saw the ice-house sitting there.*
    eventually ·INTENS
    he saw it
    where it sat
    ice-house

*When he got there, (then) he went in; there sat the old man.*
    there
    when he arrived
    (then) he went in
    there· little old man
    where he sat

*He (the little old man) said to him, "Hello, my grandchild!"—(Gluskabe said back) "Hello, my grandchild!"*
    he said to him
    hello
    my grandchild
    hello
    my grandchild

*Then Gluskabe brought out Summer,*
    then· Gluskabe
    (then) he brought it out
    Summer

*and he put it down where the little old man was facing.*
    and
    (then) he put it down
    in the direction he faced
    little old man

saláhkitte peči-ɑpseso mlohsəssis.

> saláhki·tte
>
> peči-ɑpseso
>
> mlohsəssis

itak, "nkʷenəss, kamɑč nətapamalsin; mewəya mɑčəyane."

> itak
>
> nkʷenəss
>
> kamɑč
>
> nətapamalsin
>
> mewəya
>
> mɑčəyane

"nkʷenəss, kamɑč nətapamalsin; mewəya mɑčəyane."

> nkʷenəss
>
> kamɑč
>
> nətapamalsin
>
> mewəya
>
> mɑčəyane

kenok kəloskɑpe pesəkʷən elapit.

> kenok
>
> kəloskɑpe
>
> pesəkʷən
>
> elapit

nə·mina mlohsəssis awihkʷətəmawɑn kəloskɑpal amɑčilin.

> nə·mina
>
> mlohsəssis
>
> awihkʷətəmawɑn
>
> kəloskɑpal
>
> amɑčilin

*Suddenly the little old man came to a sweat.*
    suddenly ·INTENS
    he came to a sweat
    little old man

*He said, "My grandchild, I feel very hot [from it]; it is better if you go."*
    (what) he said
    my grandchild
    very
    (so) I feel hot [from it]
    (it is) better
    if you leave

*(Gluskabe said back), "My grandchild, I feel very hot [from it]; it is better if you go."*
    my grandchild
    very
    (so) I feel hot [from it]
    (it is) better
    if you leave

*But Gluskabe sat there just the same.*
    but
    Gluskabe
    it was just the same
    how he sat

*Then again the little old man begged Gluskabe to leave.*
    then· again
    little old man
    (then) he begged it of him
    Gluskabe
    (for) him (to) leave

wətihlɑn, "nkʷenəss, nəˑpʼ·eht mɑčəyane: kekɑ kənihli!"

wətihlɑn
nkʷenəss
nəˑp[a]·eht
mɑčəyane
kekɑ
kənihli

"nkʷenəss, nəˑpʼ·eht mɑčəyane: kekɑ kənihli!"

nkʷenəss
nəˑp[a]·eht
mɑčəyane
kekɑ
kənihli

wətamahskəlohtawɑl kəloskɑpe.

wətamahskəlohtawɑl
kəloskɑpe

mɑlam mlohsəssis wihtan pənihle;

mɑlam
mlohsəssis
wihtan
pənihle

kəspəne wpətinal pənihlal; nkaskəmehlal.

kəspəne
wpətinal
pənihlal
nkaskəmehlal

nəˑkəloskɑpe oči-mɑčin,

nəˑkəloskɑpe
oči-mɑčin

*(Then) he said to him, "My grandchild, if only you would leave: you have almost killed me!"*
    (then) he said to him
    my grandchild
    then·WOULD ·EHT
    if you leave
    almost
    you kill me

*(Gluskabe said back,) "My grandchild, if only you would leave: you have almost killed me!"*
    my grandchild
    then·WOULD ·EHT
    if you leave
    almost
    you kill me

*Gluskabe imitated him.*
    he imitated him
    Gluskabe

*Eventually the little old man's nose fell off;*
    eventually
    little old man
    his nose
    it fell off

*eventually even his hands/arms fell off; they melted away.*
    eventually even
    his hands/arms
    they fell off
    they melted away

*Then Gluskabe headed off from there,*
    then· Gluskabe
    (then) he headed off from there

n·eli-notesset, n·as·te kipihle pkʷamikamikʷ.

n·eli-notesset
n·as·te
kipihle
pkʷamikamikʷ

*then as he walked outside, right then too the ice-house toppled over.*

    then· as he walked outside

    then·also ·INTENS

    it toppled over

    ice-house

## NOTES

PAGE

284  *ččɔsči*: The 1918 version has this footnote: "Accompanied by an insulting gesture, spreading the knuckles of the first two fingers and pointing towards him,—a most insulting exclamation and motion." The *Penobscot Dictionary* has *ččɔsči* (spelled there as *ččìsči*) classified as a vulgar interjection 'kiss my backside!' with the note, "said twice as *ččìsčí ččìsčí* shaking the hand with the index and middle fingers crooked or sometimes with the thumb protruding between these two fingers; usually done by old women as an obscene and insulting gesture."

292  *kči-mkasessa*: Related to *mkase* 'live coal, ember' (compare *mkases* 'ember, small (live) coal' and *mkasehs* 'charcoal, dead coal') is *mkasess* 'crow' here—and also *mkasew-* 'black'. Similarly related are *wɔpan* 'it is dawn' and *wɔp-* 'white', and *wisi* 'gall, bile' and *wisɑw-* 'yellow'. While *pakahkan* is now the word for 'blood', *mkʷ-/mihkʷ-* 'red', as in *mihkɔwe* '(red) squirrel', comes from an old word for 'blood' still heard in part in *alihkʷakihle* 'she/he/it bleeds' (retranscribed from *Penobscot Dictionary* form "*alihkɔwákihle*") and still used in related languages, as in Lenape *moxkw* 'blood'.

296  *wɔnamihton wasɑli*: The choice of a NI verb means that this is snow on the ground, because snow is NI as snow on the ground (as it is again in the next two lines) versus NA as snowflakes in the air. *pkʷami* 'ice' seems to show a similar alternation of NI as ground/lake ice (e.g., NI form *elɔmɑlakahk pkʷami* 'where the ice had a hole stretching away', from an Arthur Neptune story) versus NA as chunks of ice, etc. The *Penobscot Dictionary* gives it only as NA, however.

300  *wɔtɔlɔmiptone*: There is another, possibly related story about *kɔčɔkikilahso* playing with "eyeballs" but actually using spruce gumballs to trick others into believing him. We wonder too whether *tihtɔkɔli* having taken Gluskabe's eye might be why owls have super eyes.

300  *n·wɔketɔnɔmawɔn*: This expression usually refers to the taking out of someone a part/possession of the person taken from, so it is not clear if this means Gluskabe took his own eye back from Great Horned Owl or took out one of Great Horned Owl's own.

300  *pɔponkik*: Literally 'at the winter land', this is also a common term for the north.

302  "*kkʷēy, nkʷenɔss!*": Gluskabe's repetitions here (again noted by Speck as using a "deep voice") are mocking the little old man, the same way Gluskabe himself was earlier mocked by Winter and frozen to death. Note too that this means he no longer uses the respectful expression *nɔmohsomi* 'my grandfather' to address the old man, perhaps also because Winter has been so cruel to the people with his cold and deprivation.

# 13

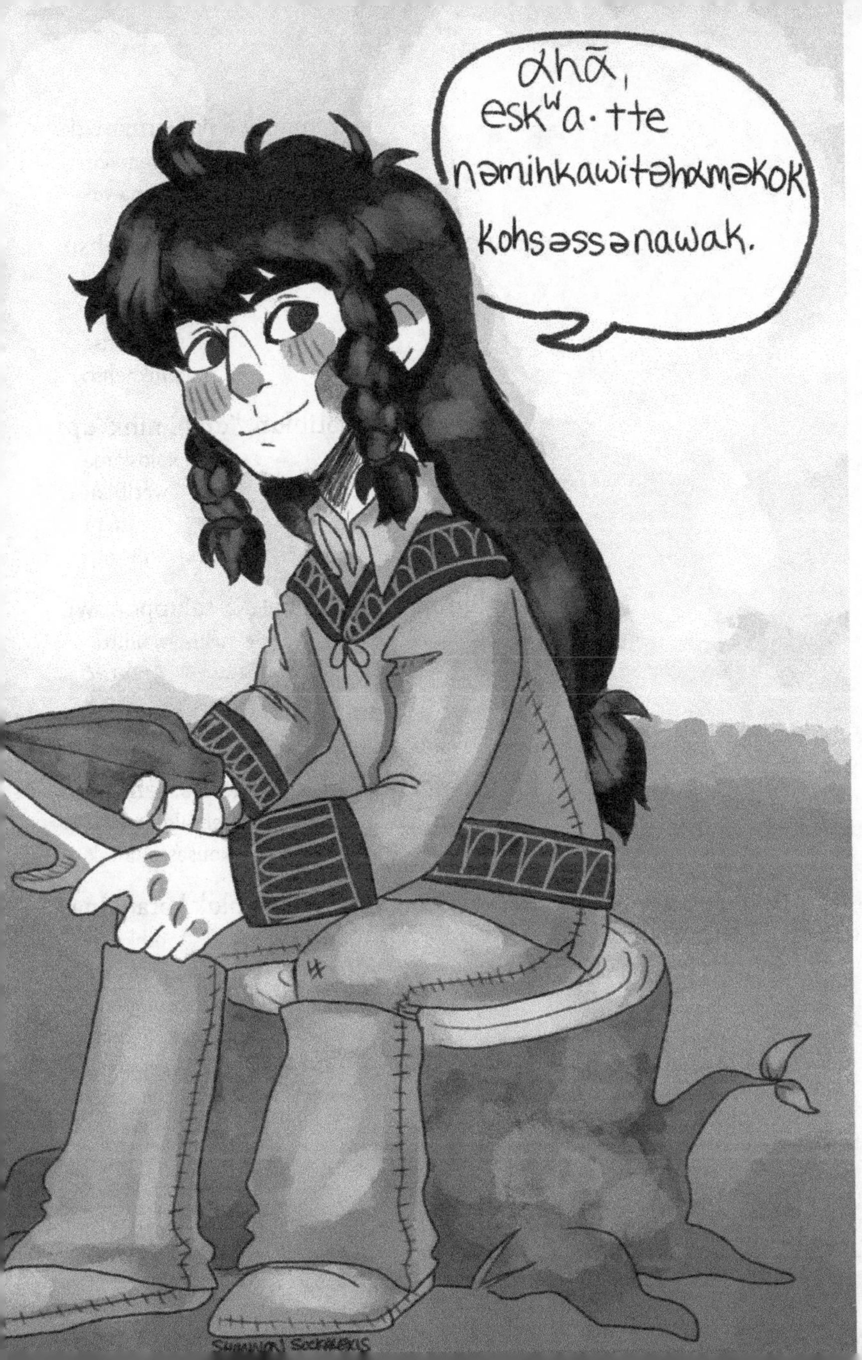
ɑhā, eskʷa·tte nəmihkawitəhɑməkok kohsəssənawak.

# nsɑnkaw

wəmačin wikəwaməwαk.

    wəmačin

    wikəwaməwαk

nəmα pečohset, wəlitəhaso monimkʷehso.

    nəmα

    pečohset

    wəlitəhaso

    monimkʷehso

kəloskαpe wətihlαn, "αn ni nihkʷαp,

    kəloskαpe

    wətihlαn

    αn ni

    nihkʷαp

nəkisi-wəlihton αta·č mina atoči-sakipponowi.

    nəkisi-wəlihton

    αta·č

    mina

    atoči-sakipponowi

nəmehtalohkewαn kohsəssənawak.

    nəmehtalohkewαn

    kohsəssənawak

nihkʷαp kəyona kəmαčewotepəna mehtakʷičihlαk kətahkina.

    nihkʷαp

    kəyona

    kəmαčewotepəna

    mehtakʷičihlαk

    kətahkina

*(Then) he headed off home.*
  (then) he headed off
  to their house

*When he got there (walking), Woodchuck was happy.*
  there
  when he arrived (walking)
  she was happy
  Woodchuck

*(Then) Gluskabe said to her, "Well then now,*
  Gluskabe
  (then) he said to her
  well then
  now

*I have fixed it so that it will never again be so hard a winter.*
  I have fixed it
  not ·WILL
  again
  (for) winter (to) not be so hard

*(So) I have finished working for our descendants.*
  (so) I have finished working for them
  our descendants

*Now we (will) move away to the end of our land.*
  now
  we
  we move away
  (to) the end of the land
  our land

nə·či wikəyakʷ, askámi.

nə·či
wikəyakʷ
askámi

mehč·ətte·č kətalohkewɑnawak kohsəssənawak:

mehč·ətte·č
kətalohkewɑnawak
kohsəssənawak

mečími·č nənotawɑk wihkʷətəmawihətite wičohketəwɑkan.

mečími·č
nənotawɑk
wihkʷətəmawihətite
wičohketəwɑkan

nə·či nihkʷɑp, nə·č nətalalohkɑn, etalihtawa ssawɑnal.

nə·či
nihkʷɑp
nə·č
nətalalohkɑn
etalihtawa
ssawɑnal

ččipatok eləmi-katək kči-awotin;

ččipatok
eləmi-katək
kči-awotin

nil·əč ewehkehətičil mikahkehətihətit kohsəssənawak."

nil·əč
ewehkehətičil
mikahkehətihətit
kohsəssənawak

*There we will live, forever.*
> there ·WILL
> where we live
> forever

*We will still work for our descendants:*
> still ·INTENS ·WILL
> we work for them
> our descendants

*I will always hear them if they ask me for help.*
> always ·WILL
> I hear them
> if they ask me for it
> help

*Then (it will be) now, then I will be working (there), making arrowheads.*
> then/there·WILL
> now
> then/there·WILL
> (then) I am working (there)
> as I am making them (there)
> arrowheads

*Maybe as the years go by, there is a great contest;*
> maybe
> as years go on
> there is a great contest

*those will be the ones our descendants use when they fight."*
> those ·WILL
> the ones that they use
> when they (group) fight
> our descendants

n·wətitamən monimkʷehso, "ɑn ni,
n·wətitamən
monimkʷehso
ɑn ni

nə·ka·č nəya nətəlihton nimɑwan pəsətamon;
nə·ka·č
nəya
nətəlihton
nimɑwan
pəsətamon

awotiməke, kohsəssənawak wənimawánəwɑl."
awotiməke
kohsəssənawak
wənimawánəwɑl

nihkʷɑp peməkisəkahk, tɑn etoči-ɑtlohkɑlot, čanalohke kəloskɑpe.
nihkʷɑp
peməkisəkahk
tɑn etoči-ɑtlohkɑlot
čanalohke
kəloskɑpe

n·wətapaskʷasin nɑkɑ wətɑpəteləmin;
n·wətapaskʷasin
nɑkɑ
wətɑpəteləmin

"wətitamən, ɑhā, eskʷa·tte nəmihkawitəhɑmɑkok kohsəssənawak."
wətitamən
ɑhā
eskʷa·tte
nəmihkawitəhɑmɑkok
kohsəssənawak

*Then Woodchuck said, "Well then,*
    (then) she said
    Woodchuck
    well then

*then I will make lunch(es) of pəsətamon;*
    then·ᴋᴀ ·ᴡɪʟʟ
    I
    (then) I make it
    (portable) lunch
    pəsətamon

*if there is a contest, (they will be) our descendants' lunches."*
    if there is a contest
    our descendants
    their lunches

*Now today, whenever he is told about in sacred stories, Gluskabe stops working for a moment.*
    now
    today
    whenever he is told about in sacred stories
    he stops/pauses in working
    Gluskabe

*Then he raises his head and laughs;*
    then· he raises his head
    and
    (then) he laughs

*(then) he says, "Yeees, our descendants still remember me."*
    (then) he says
    yeees
    still ·ɪɴᴛᴇɴs
    they remember me
    our descendants

317   *pəsətamon*: The 1918 version gives *pəsətamon* as 'crushed corn' (and the original notes as 'baked crushed corn') alongside a note explaining *nimɑwan* this way: "Hunters and warriors carried small quantities of prepared corn and smoked meat in their belts on their journeys, called 'lunches'." The *Penobscot Dictionary* gives *pə̀sətamon* as 'stew made of corn on the cob with various other ingredients such as venison, fish and bear or eel grease'.

# Technical Notes on the Newell Lyon Text

## 1 pesək<sup>w</sup>

56 *wikičik*: Following this but crossed out in the original notes and omitted from the 1918 version is the sequence *ohkəmssal nisinihətit* 'him living together (literally '[them] residing as two') with his grandmother'. This component does not seem to clearly integrate syntactically with the rest of the text here and may represent a false start, and hence perhaps its deletion. The use of a Conjunct form *wikičik* may be giving more of a presentative sense, i.e., 'there they lived'; same too possibly for the omitted *nisinihətit*.

56 *eli-ahč-amalot namehsak*: The 1918 version suggests *eli-ahč-amalot namehsa*, which fits either *eli-ahč-amalat namehsa* 'also how he [Gluskabe] catches fishes' or *eli-ahč-amalot namehsak* 'also how one catches fishes'. The latter choice fits the context better, especially with parallel impersonal-agent form *eli-katonkemək* 'how one hunts', and needs only assume that Speck missed word-final /-k/, a recurrent error of his. The stem here is derived from *ame-*, given in the *Penobscot Dictionary* as referring to fishing with hook and line, so it may mean 'fish for ... with hook and line'.

58 *wəkiwohsan*: The literal translation of *kiwohse* is 'walk wandering' (from *kiw-* 'roam, go with no specific destination' plus *-ohse* 'walk, go on foot'), but the expression very often refers to going out to hunt.

58 *nolkal*: Although the 1918 version suggests *nolka* 'deer (obv. pl.)', we restore *nolkal* based on the explicitly singular translation, plus Speck's tendency to miss final single consonants. Compare story 4, where the 1918 version suggests *wəpəyehsoma*, which is an almost certain transcription error for *wəpəyehsomal* 'his hairs', especially since the same expression is transcribed with *-al* earlier in the same text.

62 *kolawəsinena—mselət pəmi—koli·č-mawihpipəna*: The prosodic and syntactic breaks are uncertain here. Speck's original notes give *mselət* 'there is a lot of ...', which is the expected form for a NI element like *pəmi* 'grease, oil'. The 1918 version omits the /t/ in *mselət*; we assume this is merely a typographical error, rather than an indicator of bare particle *msel* 'much', which is also mainly attested as the NA singular form for 'there is a lot of ...'. The original notes and 1918 version give *pəmi* as 'fat', but usage elsewhere suggests 'grease, oil', with 'fat' itself as *wihke*. The phrase *koli·č-mawihpipəna* is originally glossed as 'we will live richly', with the element identified here as *maw-* 'together in a group', transcribed as /muw-/. This may possibly be *maw-* 'exactly, just right'—used together with *-nam* 'look at, view NI as ...' in *nətàhtama wəmawinámowən wəkáwoti* 'she ... did not fully esteem the appearance of her bed' in a *Penobscot Legends* text (*awehsohsak*), and having Passamaquoddy-Maliseet cognate *miyaw-* 'exactly, just right'—and so may suggest 'we will eat well (and) just right', which fits the original gloss somewhat better. However, speaker Roger Paul notes that in Passamaquoddy-Maliseet, *kuli·hc miyawihpòn* does not fit the context here, as it would mean 'we'll eat well in a strange way'. In addition to *kuli·hc mawihpòn* 'we'll eat together (as a group) well' (matching the Penobscot form we have gone with), he suggests that Speck's transcription could be a mishearing of *kuli·hc memihpòn* 'we'll eat good and full' in its Penobscot equivalent. This would be to *koli·č memihpipəna*; this particular collocation is commonly encountered in both languages.

62 *ólihala*: Speck's original notes give *welihalat* 'he who ...', an alternative phrasing that might gloss as 'he will be the one that does good for them'. Notice that the stem here is directly cognate to that used in Mi'kmaw *wela'lin* 'thank you', literally 'you do good for me'.

62 *nihkáni*: Not certain if *nihkáni* 'in the future' goes with the preceding or following clause. We follow the 1918 translation in associating it with the preceding clause, noting that this pattern recurs several more times in these texts.

66 *wəlitəhaso*: The 1918 version translates 'happy' as referring to Woodchuck but it may more likely apply to Gluskabe instead. Otherwise, the following *kəloskape* has to be read as preceding *na·tte* 'right away' in the same clause, which is almost never attested: *na·tte* is typically first in its clause. In contrast, *wəlitəhaso kəloskape* as 'Gluskabe was happy' both is a common word order and also fits the context well, as Gluskabe's reaction to now having a canoe.

66 *wətahsipsohkαn*: The 1918 version suggests *wətahsipsak*, which as *wətahsipsa* 'his birds/ducks' would not fit the context. Restoring a missing syllable as *wətahsipsohkαn* '(so) he hunted ducks' fits the context and original translation 'ducking', where this Subordinative form is expected in narrative clause-linking after either an *na·* 'then' (Lyon's preferred form, also found as unreduced *ni*), or its common omission, particularly since the latter is a frequent pattern in Penobscot texts. This is supported by the 1918 version transcription /udasi·ʹpsak/, where the stress is marked not on the expected third-from-end syllable but instead on the second-from-end. This is exactly where it would naturally be in *wətahsípsohk[αn]*, if Speck missed that last syllable, which could be more easily missable as an acoustically low-energy nasal vowel + nasal consonant sequence. Other versions of this story, collected by Siebert, also use the exact word *wətahsipsohkαn* at this point in the story, and it shows up several times in story 4. It is possible that the Subordinative here is actually 'for him to duck-hunt', i.e., as a chained event-sequence 'he set off by boat to duck-hunt'.

66 *nətahtekəne*: The 1918 version consistently suggests *nətahtekəni* for this element, while Siebert reports *(nət)áhtekəne*, which is also suggested in Jesuit transcriptions of Caniba, such as Rasles *m̄da [= mañida] tégné kég̑i* 'rien du tout' (563). This negative particle's exact meaning is still uncertain, though it is likely related to Passamaquoddy-Maliseet *katekon* 'not at all; not quite, not really'. This *nətahtekəni* form may be a genuine variation but is more likely a Speck mishearing, as he rather frequently conflated /i/ and /e/ in transcriptions of Penobscot and Becancour Abenaki.

66 *kisi-amilípəye*: This is the first of many examples of a very distinctive pattern of negative concord in Lyon's texts. The more commonly attested pattern would be *kisi-amilípəyewi*, but in these cases from Lyon, the full negative-concord element -*wi* is dropped, even as the original antepenultimate primary accent is maintained in its original position, as a now contrastive penultimate primary accent. This pattern is occasionally attested in Siebert's documentation after high vowels /i/ and /o/, but Lyon's texts so far show the only cases with non-high /e/ and /α/ as well. The high vowel instances are clearly related to a more general pattern: contrastive penultimate primary accent emerging from contracting high vowel-glide-high vowel sequences, e.g., especially /iwi/ (and /owo/), as in Penobscot *nipáyi* vs. W. Abenaki *nibôiwi* vs. Passamaquoddy-Maliseet *nipayìw* 'at night'. The extension here to non-high-vowel cases, however, seems to be morphosemantic/paradigmatic rather than strictly diachronic-phonological: this resembles the phonologically unmotivated but similarly paradigmatically motivated contrast of *àwan* 'fog' with *áwan* 'it is foggy' reported in Siebert, "The Suprasegmental Phonemes . . .", 734.

66 *wəkiwohsαn*: The flexible use of the Subordinative makes it difficult to determine if *wəkatonkαn* should be chained to the previous clause as '(so) he walked wandering in the woods to hunt' or if this should be '(so) he walked wandering in the woods; (and) he hunted'. We follow the latter based on the 1918 version gloss. It is also not clear if *kpi* 'in the woods' belongs to the first or second clause.

68 *wəpətəkohsαn, wəmačin*: Overall, this text has more examples than not of bare Subordinatives, namely, forms that effectively imply something like a preceding *na·* 'then' element.

## 2 nis

PAGE

72 *ali-nspinto*: The precise meaning is not clear, but this appears to be a form of the verb 'sing' using *əl-* 'way, how; (going) to', an element that often refers to the content of thought or speech, here perhaps to focus on what the content/meaning of the singing is. Speck's original notes gloss this as 'wording his song'; the 1918 version gives it as 'so singing his words'.

72 *amikənakʷe*: For unclear reasons, the first vowel in this form has been documented as /a/ (as here and in the original notes and 1918 version), /α/, or, as seen through the rest of this text until its final instance, even absent. Siebert's field notes even show a form originally suggesting

*mikənak<sup>w</sup>e*, with a different speaker (Andrew Dana) then noted as the source for emending it to *amikənak<sup>w</sup>e*. The possessed form *nəmikənak<sup>w</sup>ek* 'in my amignagweh' in the same texts suggests that the *a-* in these two cases is in fact the variant of *wə-* 'her-/his-' used before labials, but its contexts of use in this story, plus the noted independent attestation of unpossessed *amikənak<sup>w</sup>e*, make this possibility unclear. (Further complicating matters, the second and last instance of *amikənak<sup>w</sup>e* in this text is glossed as 'his bag' in Speck's original notes but as 'the bag' in the 1918 version.) Given this uncertainty, we leave original *mikənak<sup>w</sup>e* forms as they are but note them as *(a)mikənak<sup>w</sup>e* in the word breakdowns. Since Speck often mistranscribed /ɑ/ as /a/, and Siebert attests the word only once, it is possible that the final element in *(a)mikənak<sup>w</sup>e* is in fact *-ɑk<sup>w</sup>e*. This would related it to other birchbark terms like *wasɑk<sup>w</sup>e* 'streaking, marking, eye in birch bark' and two forms in Speck, *Penobscot Man*, 122, that can be reconstructed as *wəla(h)sɑk<sup>w</sup>al* 'good bark . . . (i.e., with short scar-marks)' (probably plural of a form in *-ɑk<sup>w</sup>e*) and *kahka(h)sɑk<sup>w</sup>e* 'brittle (eyelets or scars)', but otherwise there is no direct evidence supporting this.

72  *wk<sup>w</sup>enəssal*: The 1918 version form superficially suggests contracted *wk<sup>w</sup>ensal*, but Speck's original notes suggest full *wk<sup>w</sup>enəssal*, which we restore here.

74  *čanínto*: Another of Lyon's distinctive contrastively accented negative concord forms; the more commonly attested pattern would be *čaníntowi*.

74  *nə·mina mosi-pəyehsəwiye kətak*: The unusual syntax here, where the common collocation *mina kətak* 'still another' is split by *mosi-pəyehsəwiye* 'of moose hair' may be genuine, or it may be an artifact of *mosi-pəyehsəwiye* being a later/separate insertion, as the original Speck notes show.

76  *nawətɑpɑsik<sup>w</sup>*: The 1918 version suggests *newətɑpasik<sup>w</sup>*, but 'come here, in this direction' is elsewhere attested as *nawət-* in Siebert's documentation. This may be a genuine variation or a Speck mishearing.

76  *kənəkkɑnepɑ·č*: The 1918 version suggests *kənəkkɑnepa·č*, which may be a genuine form retaining the archaic *-a* rather than leveled *-ɑ* for the second-person plural.

78  *nə·ka*: The 1918 version (following Speck's original notes) gives /neˊka/, which is ambiguous between the variants *nə·ka* or *ni·ka* 'so then'. Given that Lyon much more commonly used *nə·* than *ni·* for 'then', we use the first option here and in dealing with similar ambiguities elsewhere in these texts.

78  *ɑn ni*: We follow Siebert's transcription of this common expression, in contrast to Speck's, which generally suggest *ənni*. Western Abenaki appears to attest the forms *enni* and *enna* (where "e" = /ə/) as prosodically reinforced versions of the NI and NA 'that' respectively. Given Speck's transcriptions, it may be that this Penobscot discourse element is simply a special use of this kind of prosodically reinforced deictic.

80  *kohsəssənawak*: The 1918 version here, as it does several times in these texts, suggests *kohsəssənawa* for expected *kohsəssənawak* 'our descendants'. The only known uses that *kohsəssənawa* fits are 'our (incl.) descendants (obviative pl.)' or 'our (incl.) descendant (absentative sing.)', neither of which fits this context—nor do they match the verb *k<sup>w</sup>ask<sup>w</sup>alɑmolətawak* 'they (group) starve'. Speck likely simply did not hear this often weak final /k/, or mistakenly thought the form was/should be one of those two actual possible forms with *-a*. From hereon, cases amended from *kohsəssənawa* to *kohsəssənawak* are noted; all other instances of *kohsəssənawa* are as per the 1918 version.

82  *kənihkɑlotɑkok*: The 1918 version translates *kənihkɑlotɑkok* as 'I have great confidence in you [for them]', a somewhat surprising gloss given that the endings mean 'they . . . you'. Passamaquoddy-Maliseet usage of its equivalent *nihkalutuwa-* simply means 'depend on (a person)', which fits this context and the 'they . . . you' relationship much better.

82  *·tahk[ik]*: The element between *·tahk,* which here roughly means 'instead', and *alalohke* 'do' is not clear at all. It may be a mishearing of *·əč* 'will . . .', which would simply change this to 'you will instead have to . . .', or possibly of *·tahki,* the more archaic form of *·tahk* attested in Caniba/Kennebec and Western Abenaki.

82  *kohsəssənawak*: The 1918 version again suggests *kohsəssənawa* for expected *kohsəssənawak* 'our descendants'.

# 3 nahs

88  *pečihlɑt*: The 1918 version suggests *pečihlɑč*, which appears to be a mishearing of *pečihlɑt*.

88  *osikitəhɑmɑl*: The 1918 version gives as 'he became impatient', but all other attestations of *wəsik-* with *-təhɑ-* 'heart, mind, feeling, thought' suggest mostly the sense of 'sad', which certainly fits here. Francis, Leavitt, and Apt, *Passamaquoddy-Maliseet Dictionary*, gives only '*sikitahasu* 'she/he has painful thoughts' and partially related '*sikitahatomon* 'she/he thinks it a difficult (task, chore); she/he is reluctant to do it, does not want to do it'.

88  *wəpəthɑwəya*: The 1918 version translates as 'he', referring to Gluskabe, but especially with previous translation changes, it makes more sense that this is referring to Woodchuck, since there is no other context suggesting that Gluskabe himself is trying to fish, and the next few sentences strongly indicate that it is Woodchuck who is having a hard time, such that Gluskabe feels sad for her and wants to help her.

90  *-pihthihlahətit*: The element *pihth-* (possibly *pith-*) is relatively rarely attested in other twentieth-century Penobscot sources but recurs in these texts. The *Penobscot Dictionary* has *nəpihtha* 'I stuff him' and *nəpíhthamən* 'I fill it (as a crook, gap, not container)'; Passamaquoddy-Maliseet has '*pithomon* 'she/he stuffs it [in]', *pithotuhke* 'she/he stuffs' (possibly in reference to deer, given *-otuhk-* 'deer' here), and *nuci-pithotuhket* 'taxidermist'. Western Abenaki has an extensive set of stems in *bidh-*, all pertaining to entering or filling, again showcasing Lyon's possibly more Western dialectal associations.

92  *kənəkkɑnepɑ*: The 1918 version suggests *kənəkkɑnepa*, which again may be a genuine form retaining the archaic *-a* rather than leveled *-ɑ* for the second-person plural.

92  *kəpəmɑwəsolətipɑ*: The 1918 version suggests *kəpəmɑwəsolətipa*, which again may be a correct, archaic 'you (pl.)' form.

92  *áyo*: 'NI is there, present, located at'; may also possibly be simple *ayo*.

94  *ná(hə)law*: The *Penobscot Dictionary* has *náhlaw* "1) constantly, steadily, incessantly, 2) steadfastly, persistently, with determination, resolutely; [synonym] *mìnakʷ* 'constantly, steadily'." The form is variantly transcribed in Siebert's documentation as *nálaw*, *náhlaw*, and *náhəlaw*. So far no cognates have helped resolve the exact transcription.

94  *nə·tt[e]*: The *nə·* 'there; then' here is omitted in the 1918 version transcription; sound recordings of this common collocation confirm that *nə·* is often only weakly audible before *·tte*, which otherwise never appears phrase-initially and instead only ever as a second-position clitic.

94  *nəh*: The 1918 version's original *neh* here might possibly be *nehe* 'hey [calling the listener's attention]', but it may simply be a false start, or it may be tied to the prosodically reinforced versions of *ni* 'that; there; then', which we see further hints of in Lyon's texts but which do not appear attested in Siebert's documentation. For more on this, see the discussion of *na(h·ə)nn·ahč* in story 11 (and 12). If so, the first *nəh* may in fact be the 'then', and the *n·* following it may instead be a prosodically reinforced *ənni/ənnə·* 'that (NI); there' that possibly forms a discontinuous constituent with *awikəwaməwak* 'to their house'.

96  *kapahkɑwatihətəwak*: This is a rare case of the still incompletely understood specialized nonsingular *-(o/ə)hkɑwati*, which appears to refer to individuals moving bodily in tandem with each other, with the group/extended plural ending *-hati* in its relatively uncommon use (as variant *-həti*) after stems in /-i/.

98  *kəyona*: The discontinuous constituent *kəyona . . . tɑn kehsi-ččəweləmakʷ* 'as many as we (incl.) want' is split by the phrase *kʷaskʷayi-kehsit namehsak* 'enough fish (pl.)'. The agreement mismatch between singular *-kehsit* and plural *namehsak* is similar to that seen in Passamaquoddy-Maliseet *Elinaqsit (elinaqsihtit) cossuwihik* 'There are a lot of mosquitoes'. This poorly understood kind of mismatch is seen in a small set of quantification-focusing constructions like these and may relate to other patterns of apparent number mismatch seen in these and other texts. Note, however, that the original Speck notes and 1918 version in fact suggest *namehsa*, superficially an obviative plural, which does not fit the context. It is pos-

sible that this is just a rare additive transcription error for singular *namehs*, which would match the singular *kʷaskʷayi-kehsit*. Here we amend as proximate plural *namehsak*.

100 *nənači-pkʷətəhalαk*: Lyon uses the *pkʷəte-* variant of 'open', which in other sources is most commonly found as *αpkʷəte-*. The combination of *-e* and *-halα* here is typically recorded as *-a-həlα* or *-a-halα*, but *-ə-halα* is sometimes found and is probably not actually distinct from *-a-halα*.

## 4 yew

104 *n·wətαmihkənəmən*: The 1918 version gloss is 'flipped over', but the verb here appears to actually mean 'pick it up (by hand) from a lying-down position'.

106 *ali-təpihle*: This word literally means 'it happens in . . . way', with the *al-/əl-* meaning 'in . . . way'. Combined with *tαn* 'which?' the resulting question 'in which way?' is the Penobscot construction for 'how?' English asks, "What happened?"; Penobscot asks, "How did it happen?"—possibly since what happened is an event, not a thing. The term *αkima*, which the *Penobscot Dictionary* glosses as '(1) to the degree, extent, or number; (2) to the count of, to the sum or total of; (3) the condition, the nature, quality; (4) like, kind', seems here to mean a rhetorical "just exactly [what] . . . ?" ' Compare to Passamaquoddy-Maliseet *Tan akim kil ktoleyin?* 'Just what is wrong with you?'

106 *itam kəloskαpe, "nohkəmi*: The original Speck notes transition from story 2 directly to this line to start story 4. All of story 3 and the story 4 material preceding this point are a later/separate insertion.

108 *wečsək*: The 1918 version has this 'against the wind', for which there are other terms in Penobscot, but this could reasonably be a specialized use of this expression, especially since *wetəlamsək* has been used earlier for literal 'where the wind blows from'. This *wečsək* (probably also *wetsək*) uses the older and rarer ending *-ahsən* 'wind blow', to which the more common *-əlam-[ah]sən* 'wind blow' is apparently a reinforcement. Here *-əlam-* may possibly be an old variant/relative of *-alam-* 'breath', as in *-alαmi* 'breathe'.

108 *n·elohset*: The 1918 version's *n·alohset* is most likely a transcription error for *n·elohset*. It could possibly be the very rare unchanged Conjunct *alohset*. These forms, scantily attested and poorly understood, are associated with some uncertain type of temporal immediacy. Siebert mentions this twice in annotations to *Penobscot Legends* texts, noting of *nòka pálihkʷsαt, wətamihkíkətahin owa mèkʷe* 'At the very moment when he missed slashing his throat, the Mohawk sprang to his feet' that "the simple or unchanged conjunct AI verb *pálihkʷsαt* rather than *pélihkʷsαt* is employed to emphasize a simultaneous event" (*məkʷayí-sαkəma*). Of *nìtte pàsətehsək mačé-təpihle* 'the festivity started promptly at dusk', he writes, "Following *nìtte* and some other particles an unchanged conjunct verb appears, except when a preverb is present to form a compound verb" (*awehsohsak*). It is not certain if these points apply to the form in question, in part because *ni·tte, nə·tte* 'right then/there' when used with Conjunct verbs is more frequently than not followed by either a relative root or aspectual element in a cleft-like construction ('it is then that . . .', etc.), with initial change being frequently found on the relevant initial vowel of the stem or preverb. The sequence *n·wəmačin wečsək n·elohset* may alternatively possibly parse not in this clefting way but instead as 'then he started off (to) where the wind blows from; then, as he was walking to there . . .'.

108 *αkkʷαpohse*: This correlative 'the more . . . the more . . .'. expression is perhaps not a precise translation. Literally it is 'he walked such a distance, increasingly the wind blew more'.

108 *manəlαmsənol*: The 1918 version and original notes both end this verb with /αl/, which may represent *-əl, -αl,* or *-al*. Notably both sources give a different vowel (writing /al/) in the ending of the following word, *wəpəyehsomal* 'his hairs'. It is possible that this represents a genuine leveled variant *manəlαmsənal* rather than the expected form *manəlαmsənol* 'they were blown off' (cf. *kisikənol* 'they had grown' below), from *man-* 'taken off, removed, separated' and *-əlαmsən* 'wind blow; blown by wind'. Or it could be a mishearing from Speck matching it too directly

to the following *wəpəyehsomal*. Most likely, however, is that the distinct vowel transcription represents hearing the distinct *-ol* form, and so we amend accordingly, in contrast to the unexpectedly but consistently leveled form *nipənal* discussed for story 12.

110 *pečohset*: The 1918 version suggests *pečohse*, but the collocation *nəma pecohset* 'when she/he arrived there' is extremely common in stories, and we restore it based on the use of "when" in the 1918 translation, noting again that Speck often missed single final consonants.

110 *kči-*: We are uncertain whether to translate *kči-* as 'great big' or just 'great'. The first is a bit more natural everyday speech; the second sounds more formal than *kči-* usually seems to be.

110 *nətah·ap'·eht*: The element *nəta* 'not', plus *·əpa* 'would', plus *·eht*, a marker of uncertainty, come together as *nətahapeht*. This is the first of many clear examples in Lyon's texts of the schwa assimilation effect (from *nətah·əpa* to *nətah·apa*) described in LeSourd, "Enclitic Particles in Western Abenaki," 321, for Western Abenaki.

110 *nohsəss*: The 1918 version gives *nohsəss* as 'my grandchild' here, the same gloss as Woodchuck's term for Gluskabe, *nkʷenəss*, which the Wind Bird also uses for him a few lines later. Elsewhere this word is translated as '[someone's] descendant', but the Mi'kmaw near-equivalent, *nuji'j*, is also 'my grandchild'. Rasles explicitly gives *n8ssessak* 'mes déscendants' under the heading "Déscendant" (432). The *Penobscot Dictionary* glosses *nòhsəss* as '1) my kinsmen or kinswoman, 2) my consaguineal relative, 3) my child of my nephew or niece [popular usage]', giving instead *nətankáwinom* for 'my descendant', a form that parallels Rasles's *n8dařnka8in8diak*, also listed as an alternative under the above 'mes déscendants' gloss.

112 *na·tt'·eht*: The 1918 version suggests *na·tte ttekehsi-kisihatawa*, with the *-tte-* component unexplained. It is possible that the sequence *na·tte·eht kehsi-*, with the /-ə-/ that commonly emerges between consonants at word boundaries in Penobscot and Passamaquoddy-Malieet, that is, *na·tte·eht-ə-kehsi-*, was misheard by Speck as effectively *na·tte·eht-e-kehsi-*. Note that the uncertainty marker *·eht* is used in Gluskabe's immediately preceding question. Alternatively this could just be a false start repetition of *na·tte* 'just that' heard as just /'tte/, since the /nə/ is often reduced to a nearly inaudible minimum.

112 *yē*: *yē* 'over there, yonder' is marked extra-long in the original text, hence the gloss 'waaay over there'.

112 *etali-spatənek*: The 1918 version translates as 'where there is a peak' for what literally is 'where the mountain is high'.

112 *kehtoke*: This word is not known from other sources, but *kehte-, kehtə-* is associated with 'before, previously', and may be related to *kəht-* 'great, large, elder'. The 1918 version transcription suggests *kehtoke*, possibly in parallel to *nəwatoke* 'far away, in the distance', etc.

114 *etáki·tte*: This word is used twice in this text but is not known from other sources. It appears to be used with if-constructions to mean 'if indeed . . . , if in fact (it turns out that)'.

114 *awihkʷhəwaman*: The 1918 version's transcription suggests *awixowaman*, and Speck specifically notes "X, accidental soft gutteral [sic] spirant, resulting from the collision of ' and h" (195). This may be an over-perception of *wihkʷ-* 'pull in, grab toward self; shrink', with *-(a)h-əwama* 'carry him/her on back', perhaps because the *-ihk-* sequence often has a very saliently devoiced/fricative *-ih-* sound, and because the sequence *-kʷh-*, relatively rare in the language, results in unusual voiceless labial fricative sound. The form may also possibly be *awihkʷhowaman*.

114 *wəmače(hə)waman*: Here again the 1918 version transcription suggests *-(a)h-əwama* 'carry him/her on back', even as the original Speck notes for this form lack any indication of an *-h-*, and so suggest just *-əwama*, which is also attested in other sources. This absence of *-h-* occurs with all later instances of this stem in both versions of this text. The overall distribution of the *-(a)h-* component in these kinds of stems is unclear.

116 *kčawayəss*: The 1918 version translates *kčawayəss* as 'accidentally'. The *Penobscot Dictionary* suggests the exact opposite meaning, 'on purpose', which fits better here. Related forms in Rasles as *ketsa8aï* 'p[ou]r rire, par raillerie, par semblant' (555), and *ketza8aï* 'du bout des lèvres; pas franchem[en]t' (435, 476, 555), seem to slightly support the *Penobscot Dictionary* range of meaning.

116 *na· ... təmiləkʷanehtehsin*: Following *na·* 'then', we predict the Subordinative form *watəmiləkʷanehtehsinən* instead of simple Indicative *təmiləkʷanehtehsin*. It is possible that Speck missed the often quite weak *wə-* and missed the *-ən* on a word already ending in /n/. Otherwise, it may be that the plain Indicative form highlights the event, as if it were independent/standalone. Alternately, there may have been a break in dictation with a restart returning to the simple Indicative form here.

116 *wikəwamək*: Both the original notes and the 1918 version have /uwi . . . / here, one of a very few potential indications of a possible *wəwikəwamək* form. This could also simply be a transcription hypercorrection for *wikəwamək*, or even a mishearing of *awikəwamək*.

116 *pečohset*: The 1918 version suggests *wəpečohset*, which is an otherwise unattested and unpredicted form. Probably a typo influenced by the "u" starting the previous word and the following one.

116 *noli-ssipsohkan*: The 1918 version translation 'I shall have good duck-hunting' may likely capture the meaning better.

118 *wəlawipən*: It is striking that the text gives both *wəli-awipən* and *wəlawipən*, translated the same in the 1918 version. What nuance of difference there might be here is unknown.

118 *kəspane*: The 1918 version glosses this as 'thick', a clear error given that later in these texts it is given as 'eventually'; it may mean 'eventually (it came to) even . . .'. See the other use of this term at the end of story 12. The *Penobscot Dictionary* gives it as 'eventually, in course of time, ultimately (in a series of events); from bad to worse, in the course of deteriorating circumstances, to top it all'.

118 *akʷɑkʷaləsəpi*: This word is translated as 'scummy/slimy water'. Here the *-aləs[i]-* may refer to scumminess/sliminess from algae, etc.; compare *kaskaləsi* 'seaweed'. If so, *akʷɑkʷ-aləs-əpi* would be literally 'rotting-algaeslime-water'.

118 *eyit*: Translated as 'where NA is', this refers to the NA bird, not the usually NI wind, which would presumably use *eyik* 'where NI is'.

120 *kči-ssipass eyit*: Penobscot frequently does not require obviation (i.e., what would be *kči-ssipsal eyilit*) in cross-clausal contexts like this one, perhaps in part because the context here makes a proximate shift (from Gluskabe to the Wind Bird) both well-motivated and referentially clear.

120 *wəpəyehsomal*: The 1918 version suggests *wəpəyehsoma*, which is almost certainly a transcription error for *wəpəyehsomal* 'his hairs', as seen earlier in this text.

120 *etoči- mečími -awipək*: It is not clear if this collocation uses the near-synonymous but morphosyntactically distinct particle *mečími* or preverb *mecimi-*; we tentatively assume the first and translate as 'the wind is always so calm', not as 'the wind is so constantly calm'.

120 *tɑn·ak·a·p[a]·eht*: The 1918 version translates this as 'for the simple reason [that . . .]'. It appears often in other texts to introduce an explanation. Siebert translates it often as 'accordingly', and the *Penobscot Dictionary* glosses it as 'whereupon, in consequence of which (fact), so therefore', which do not seem to fit here. The particular use here in this direct quote seems to suggest that its daily speech use is the same as is familiar from narrative use: to appeal to the listener's expectation/sense of the situation. The translation here is provisional.

122 *·asohke*: The usually but not exclusively second-position element *·asohke* 'however', which seems generally to show a topic shift, is rare in other Penobscot texts but common in Western Abenaki as *azok(w)a* 'however'. For this, Penobscot more commonly has *·askʷe*, which appears to be a contraction of this form, albeit with an unexpected *ɑːa* vowel correspondence that could possibly simply be a persistent misidentification (by Siebert, whose *ɑ*-based transcription we follow here) of the often more mid-centralized, [ʌ]-like allophone of /a/ in closed syllables. Use of *·asohke* appears to be one of several archaisms/westernisms in Lyon's speech, but since he also uses *·askʷe*, there may be a still-unidentified meaning difference between the two.

122 *etali-spatanek*: Here the 1918 version translates this as 'where it is higher', versus earlier 'where there is a peak', from literal 'where the mountain is high'.

124 *nihkʷap pésəko·tte ípi nələkʷan*: Literally 'now my wing is just one'. Centering the quantificational expression as the main predicate is the most common Penobscot syntactic construction for indicating quantity of possession.

124    *nɑkɑ·č*: The 1918 version transcription leaves open the possibility of *nɑkɑ·č* 'and ·WILL' as instead *nɑk[ɑ]·ɑhč* 'and ·also', but the previous line's *nəyɑ·č* 'I ·WILL' more strongly suggests a parallel use of ·*č* '·WILL' here.

126    *nə·*: The 1918 version suggests *ne*, again possibly representing unreduced *ni·*, but most likely just the near-universal *nə·* with "e" as a typo inverting intended "ə," possibly influenced by the word-complex itself ending in "e"—especially given that Speck's original notes here indicate *nə* rather than *ne*.

126    "*nehe*": The word *nehe* is difficult to translate simply. It is generally used to call someone's attention, but English "Hey!" seems too sharp and rude to fit here, and so we leave it here untranslated as a fundamental feature of Penobscot communicational norms. Elsewhere it often functions as the equivalent of English "come on!"

126    *akʷečilɑkʷanewi*: Body-part-incorporating verbs are ambiguous as to singular versus plural of the body part, so Speck's translation may be overly specific, even though only one of the wings needs to be tested.

126    *wətakʷečilɑkʷanewin*: The 1918 version suggests *wətakʷečilɑkʷanewi*, missing the Subordinative form's final /n/, a relatively common error by Speck, presumably because it is not acoustically salient.

126    *kipɑlɑmsoke*: The 1918 version suggests *wəkipɑlɑmsoke*, which would only be well-formed as *wəkipɑlɑmsokən*, which is not suggested by the end of the wordform. Compare earlier Speck hypercorrection/overuse of *wə*- in [*wə*]*pečohset*.

128    *etotɑlɑmsək*: It is not clear if this reads as part of the end of the previous phrase, i.e., as '. . . they cannot hunt for themselves, the wind blows so much', or at the start here, as 'the wind blows so much when you . . .'.

128    *kisípaye*: Negative *ahtɑmɑ awen* 'no one' is typically accompanied by a negative-concord verbal form. Here *kisípaye* appears to be another of Lyon's distinctive contrastively accented negative concord forms; the more commonly attested pattern would be *kisípayewi*.

130    *nɑnɑkʷɑč*: Lyon uses this for 'some; sometimes', while other Penobscot sources generally use *ɑnɑkʷɑč*, in parallel to Passamaquoddy-Maliseet *anqoc*.

130    *nɑ·kətɑtalahsimin*: The 1918 version suggests only *nɑ·kətɑtalahsimi*, while *nɑ·* 'then' regularly predicts Subordinative *kətɑtalahsimin*. Here Speck may have missed the /n/ due to the immediately following /nk-/.

130    *eləwe·tt'eht*: The exact breakdown is provisional: it appears that the intensifier ·*tte* unusually precedes the dubitative/uncertainty element ·*eht*, possibly for prosodic/phonotactic reasons.

130    -*mečimɑlɑmsáno*: Another of Lyon's distinctive contrastively accented negative concord forms; the more commonly attested pattern would be -*mečimɑlɑmsánowi*.

## 5 palenəskʷ | nɑn

PAGE

136    *tɑn·ɑskʷe*: Here is the first instance in these texts of the usually but not exclusively second-position element ·*ɑskʷe* 'however', which very often apparently serves to mark a shift to a new topic. Contrast the much rarer form ·*asohke*, possibly a variant of this, discussed in the notes for story 4. This element also seems to be used with questions asked out of the blue to someone (i.e., perhaps as a topic shift), hence we see them again in later stories when Gluskabe asks Woodchuck where Winter is and where Summer is.

136    *wətamɑweyi*: This is the first instance of *wətamɑweyi* 'tobacco' as NA, in matching *eyit* 'where NA is', which is then consistent through this story. *wətamáweyi* in the *Penobscot Dictionary*, and '*tomawey* in Francis, Leavitt, and Apt, *Passamaquoddy-Maliseet Dictionary*, however, are both listed as NI. Day gives Western Abenaki *odamô* 'tobacco', as NA (393); Rasles gives *8dámaĩ* (505); and Aubery *8damaĩ* under the heading "pétun" (401), but only Aubery under the heading "tabac" confirms it as "noble" (492), i.e., NA, and there gives both *8damaĩ* for 'tabac' and

*8damañ8ié* as 'du tabac', the latter being directly cognate to the Penobscot and Passamaquoddy-Maliseet forms. This NA gender for tobacco is perhaps another example of more western (Caniba, etc.) affinities in Lyon's speech.

138  *wətamɑweyɑl*: Similar to the issue discussed in more depth for story 11 regarding *wətamɑkanal* 'pipe (obviative)' versus *otamɑkanal*, 'his pipe (obviative)', the 1918 version transcription leaves us uncertain as to whether this is *wətamɑweyɑl* 'tobacco (obviative)' or *otamɑweyɑl* 'his tobacco (obviative)'.

138  *olihton*: The *Penobscot Dictionary* only lists *nólihton* 'I repair, fix it (after being broken or damaged), clean it', but common usage of *wəlihto-* is often simply 'make NI, complete the process of making NI', as in Day for Western Abenaki *olito* 'make something' (406). This is tied to the less frequent but consistent use of *wəl-* 'good' as 'ready, readied, finished'.

140  *tepi-kəsihkɑwíhle*: Not only does this appear to be another of Lyon's distinctive contrastively accented negative concord forms (i.e., the more commonly attested pattern would be *tepi-kəsihkɑwíhlewi*) but the stem is one otherwise only attested so far for Passamaquoddy-Maliseet (*ksi-hkawiye* 'she/he/it goes fast'), not Penobscot. If the 1918 version vowel is in fact correct, the form may be *kəsihkɑwíhle*; here we retranscribe with /ɑ/, this being the usual vowel corresponding to Passamaquoddy-Maliseet /a/, under the assumption that Speck once again confused the /ɑ/-/a/ distinction.

140  *wətəlihton*: The forms *wətəlihton* and *olihton* both get loosely glossed by various sources as 'she/he made it', but the latter form, along with *wəkisihton*, seems to consistently suggest a completive aspect, i.e., 'she/he finished making it, completely made it'. Alongside *wəl-* 'good' having a secondary use 'ready, readied, finished' (such that *olihton* may be closer to 'she/he fixed it up, got it fixed up and ready'; see earlier discussion, plus 'he fixed it' gloss in story 6), the element *kis-* regularly means both 'can, able' and 'have done/been' as the primary marker of perfective aspect in Penobscot. In contrast, *wətəlihton*, based on *əl-* '(going) to . . . ; in . . . way', seems to appear mainly in contexts where the making is viewed as incomplete (or potential/prospective). Very often the onset of making something (a canoe, etc.) is first indicated with this stem, and then its subsequent completion with the one based on *kis-*.

142  *wətamiltehkamən*: The 1918 version suggests only *amiltehkamən*, but the expected form is *wətamiltehkamən*; compare *nɑkɑ wətamiltehkamən* later in this same text.

142  *nsəta tekakɑpimək*: Notice that this third time around, the phrase *nsəta tekakɑpimək* 'three looks' is especially focused, and so now comes before rather than after the verb—in contrast to the first two repetitions. This highly extended chiasmus perhaps now prioritizes the distance rather than the motion itself, which is by this point well-established.

142  *nɑkɑ sípi*: The collocation *nɑkɑ sípi* 'and/so finally' in Siebert-collected texts is always followed by the Subordinative, as expected after *nə-* 'then', and its derivant *nɑkɑ sípi* 'and'. Here perhaps *epakʷahč* '(and) even . . . !' may possibly give the verb standalone prominence, overruling the usual Subordinative pattern and retaining its simple Indicative form.

144  *kiwohse*: This bare Indicative *kiwohse* 'he walks wandering', rather than Subordinative *wəkiwohsən*, as the complement of a causal verb is unexpected. Possibly this is just a separate quotative Imperative "Walk wandering!" Alternatively, the relative root *əl-* 'in . . . way' in the causal verb may be able to take an Indicative complement.

144  *-nəkihkɑnɑt*: '(that) he (could) get all of it'; contrast the 1918 version gloss 'secure it'.

144  *pečohset nəmɑ*: Typically this common collocation is attested in the reverse order.

144  *pečohset . . . áyi*: In Speck's original notes, this sequence is a later insertion after *weči- nekəma -nəkihkɑnɑt wətamɑweyɑl*. This may partly explain the uncertain syntax of the phrases before and after it, since they originally formed a direct transition. Without this insertion, the original sequence *weči- nekəma -nəkihkɑnɑt wətamɑweyɑl, məsi kehs(ə)lɑt čɑləss, péči-tte . . .* alone reads easily as 'so that he [Gluskabe] could get all the tobacco, all that Grasshopper had of it, even the . . .'.

144 *kehs(ə)lat*: This form is provisional, as no comparandum has been attested elsewhere. Given that Speck's original notes transcription suggests *kehsəlat*, it is possible that this is *kehslat*, with the same meaning, assuming an old -*(ah)la* 'have NA' as the NA equivalent to the stem in Wampanoag *ohtauun* 'it [NI] is owned, kept'. Goddard and Bragdon, *Native Writings in Massachusett*, 681. A Penobscot element -*(ah)to* for 'have NI', used in verbs referring to the quantity had, seems to be directly attested, forming a stem with *m(ə)sel-* 'many, much' in (retranscribed) *wəmasseltonal* 'it [yellow birch] had a lot of [them = branches]' in Andrew Dana's handwritten version of the Uugulubemo story (see story 7). (A less likely candidate is *kehselət* 'NI be so many', especially since in this text, tobacco is mostly treated as NA.)

144 *wətahkihkanak [kəloskape/čalass]*: It seems at first that a verb is missing here, since both the 1918 version *kəloskape* and original notes version *čalass* (crossed out and amended to *kəloskape*) at the end of this phrase are then difficult to relate to the event. Given the insertion noted above, however, a possible reading for the earliest sequence would have *wətahkihkanak čalass* 'in Grasshopper's garden', with *čalass* as possessor, and the original sequence would now read '. . . even the ones of his/the tobacco growing in Grasshopper's garden', then maintained simply as an argument (object) of the verbal complex *weči- nekəma -nəkihkanat* 'so that he [Gluskabe] could get all of [it]', discussed above. The initial replacement of *čalass* with *kəloskape* (which then still does not read easily here), combined then with the original sequence being split by the insertion, may be the source of this otherwise confusing segment.

146 *wətepihasin*: -*hasi* generally seems to show a sharp, quick onset of the motion/event: 'he got right into it'.

146 *wətahsitəmomək*: The 1918 version suggests *wətahsitəmonək*. This is a miscopying from Speck's original notes, which directly suggest the expected *wətahsitəmomək* form for what we have glossed as 'his shore-strip', following the 1918 version notes that report, "In the old days each hunter had his own strip of beach where his canoe could be kept, and where he always landed when returning home. Beach rights are still preserved among the Montagnais and Naskapi" (198).

146 *kənatawihokowina*: Literally 'it [will never again] cause us (to feel) scarcity [of it]'. Lacking or missing someone/something is usually expressed in Wabanaki languages as that person/thing causing the lack/absence to be felt.

146 *n·wəpečipəyehlan*: The gloss here assumes that -*hla* 'go, move, change' when added to motion verbs implies faster than usual pace, as in *pítike* 'he enters, comes in (a dwelling)' versus *pitíkehle* 'he rushes in, hurries in, enters hastily, he enters in a lively fashion, makes a grand entrance'.

148 *kənəkka-kəmotənamin*: The 1918 version suggests *kənəkka-kəmotənami*; again the final -*n* element (marking the tobacco as a secondary object) is expected here and perhaps just missed by Speck because of the following word-initial /n/. The form may also possibly be *kənəkka-kəmotənamin*.

148 *notamaweyim*: The expected form is *notamaweyam*, but *notamaweyim* is a logical leveled alternative.

148 *wənotehlan, onaskawan*: 'Gluskabe went outside (and then) he met Grasshopper'. Here the -*n* for *onaskawan* suggests either simple 'and then . . .', or perhaps a tight connection between these two events, like 'he went out and met . . .' or 'he went out to meet . . .', as the 1918 version gloss suggests.

148 *kohsəssanawak (·ahč nékəma)*: Speck's original notes include this ·*ahč nékəma* 'also they'; why this is omitted in the 1918 version is unclear, especially since emphatic/contrastive pronominal constructions like this, i.e., '[that] our descendants, they too [can . . .]', are common in Penobscot.

148 *kolalóhke*: Another of Lyon's distinctive contrastively accented negative concord forms; the more commonly attested pattern would be *kolalóhkewi*.

148 *kətali-sakeləman*: *sak-* 'difficult' versus *nəkəm-* 'easy' appear in several stems referring to stinginess versus generosity. This also may be a rare case of a secondary object with a morphologically simple transitive stem (rather than ditransitive), if it is not somehow just a Subordinative form.

152 *kʷenapemat*: Here glossed as 'however long you benefit from it' versus the 1918 version's 'it will support you'.

152 *n·wəpisənəmawan*: The 'for him' is not in the 1918 version translation but is implied by -*awa*- here.

152  *watahpskʷanse*: The 1918 version suggests *watahpskʷansi*. It is possible that this is a very irregular sound change, but it is more likely an error from Speck's frequent transcriptional variation between /i/ and /e/.

154  *"yok . . . kalakʷanak"*: Note the discontinuous constituent *yok . . . kalakʷanak* 'these wings of yours', with apparent Subordinative *kkisihtolan* 'I have made you them' rather than Indicative *kkisihtolanak*. It is possible that the form is instead based on *yo·ka* 'this/here· KA', with a presentational sense akin to English "Here!" (in handing something to someone). Another possibility is *yo nihkʷap kkisihtolan . . .* 'here now I have made you . . .', if the /-k/ in *yok* is spurious.

## 6 nakʷətɑs

158  *makʷasapemal*: The 1918 version and original notes both have *nakʷasapem(al)* for expected *makʷasapem(al)* 'lake(s)'. This may be a genuine variation—the word appears not to have a clear synchronic etymology, which may make it more prone to reshaping—or it may be that Speck misperceived (pseudo-) syllabic /m/ before /k/ as a placeless or velar nasal, then transcribed simply as /n/. In this edition we consistently restore the /m/-based version.

160  *nsahihkač*: The translation '(don't) worry about me (facing danger)' is unsure, but the form is clearly based on *nsa-* 'danger(ous)' and *-ha* 'cause NA to . . . , make NA . . .'. So it may literally be just 'don't think me in danger'.

160  *n·waposin*: The stem *posi-* seems generally to be used to mean 'leave by boat' but here may emphasize the first step of embarking, in contrast to *wamačepayan* '(then) he paddled off', from *mače-* 'leave, depart, start (off)' and *-paye* 'paddle, go by paddling'.

160  *wapihthihlanal*: See earlier notes re. *pihth-*. This is also an instance of the somewhat rare locatum secondary object with a *-hla* 'go, move' stem and notably with plural argument visibly marked.

160  *masi . . . sipawal*: A discontinuous constituent for 'all rivers'. May also possibly mean 'all the openings of the rivers on the ocean'.

160  *olihton*: Here 'he fixed it' may be plural 'he fixed them (i.e., places/river)', since a Subordinative verb form (unlike an Indicative) generally does not mark NI plural *-al*, nor does the if-clause form *sakikke* 'if it was difficult'.

162  *masi . . . wanikanal*: A discontinuous constituent for 'all portages/carries'.

162  *weči-walawatassak*: These forms do not distinguish singular versus plural, hence 'it/they' in the translation.

162  *pesakʷan*: Could be translated as 'there was (a certain) one [river] . . . that he paddled into', or just 'when he paddled into a certain one [river]'.

162  *pihthipayet*: In Speck's original notes, the text immediately transitions from here to the start of story 7, so possibly suggesting an original intent that the village Gluskabe finds there is on this particular one river. The material following it here (and in the 1918 version) is an insertion, though it does not look to be later and may be an on-the-spot addition by Lyon.

162  *wakatakʷahton*: The *Penobscot Dictionary* form *kʷatakʷahte* 'it lies/sets upside down' with *-ahte* 'NI sit, be positioned' suggests that the form here is indeed *wakatakʷahton*, with the somewhat rarer but corresponding element *-ahto* 'put, place NI' and not putative *wakatakʷahaton/ wakatakʷahaton*, with the much more common *-hato* 'move, change NI'. *katakʷani-* 'stay over night' uses a similar and possibly distantly related root (varying only in proto-Algonquian short non-high vowels, which sometimes alternate), suggesting possibly that the fundamental picture of staying overnight is the traditional practice of flipping over one's canoe (and sleeping under it). Numerous forms from Siebert suggest the initial element is *kʷatakʷ-*, as do Western Abenaki forms like *gwedegwakôla* 'throw some one over, overturn someone' (227). Note the same issue for the forms *wakatakʷahkan, n·wakatakʷahlan,* and *wakatakʷapin* in story 8. Given the consistency in Speck's transcriptions as *katakʷ-* across separate texts, however, we retain his forms as potentially genuine variants.

162   *etali-pənahpskʷihlɑk*: The 1918 version suggests *etali-pəmahpskʷihlɑk*, which could possibly be from a stem *pəmahpskʷihlɑ-* 'go along as (or turning into) stone, turn to stone going along'. Speck's original notes, however, have the /n/ expected for a stem based directly on *pənahpskʷ* 'stone, rock'.

164   *eskʷa*: Speck's original notes suggest *eskʷa·tte* here, as *eskʷa·tte nihkʷɑp·te*. A sequence of two instances of intensifier *·tte* in a row like this is rare, which may be why the first one is omitted in the 1918 version.

## 7 tɑ́pawɑs

PAGE

168   *amɔskamən*: This text is unique in this volume in that it comes from a separate set of notes that were integrated in the 1918 version as laid out below. Distinctively, the notes contain a title *weči-kisi-təpihlahətisa namehsak nɑkɑ čɑkʷalsak nɑkɑ toləpak* 'where the fish and the frogs and the turtles have come about from', omitted in the 1918 presentation. (Note here the use of *-sa*, an element that seems to be used by speakers to show that their relationship to the past event is only indirect, i.e., not directly witnessed, etc.). On the facing page here in Speck's original notes is written, "Note the People + earth have always been in existence. G. [= Gluskabe] discovered them + transformed [them]"—possibly recording a comment from Lyon. The separate-notes version begins with *nɑwat talotenesánik alɑnɑpak elɑmi-nalɑmɑwik ɑkɑləpemo*... 'long ago | they lived in a village there | the People | away upriver | Uugulubemo...'. In this version, it is not entirely clear if 'away upriver' refers to where the People live or to where Uugulubemo is as he forbids them water. Numerous versions of the story confirm the latter, but this may not necessarily exclude the former as well. The 1918 version omits everything before *elɑmi-nalɑmɑwik* above but then follows the separate-notes text directly from there. As noted in the previous story, the 1918 version material preceding *elɑmi-nalɑmɑwik* is not from the separate-notes document but instead appears directly after the end of the preceding text and seems to transition directly from it. Note that there is also a still-unpublished version of this story, handwritten by Penobscot speaker Andrew Dana, in the Frank Siebert Papers at the American Philosophical Society.

168   *ɑkɑləpemo*: *ɑkɑlo-* 'grudgingly, sparingly, only in small portions' is only attested with final /o/ in Siebert documentation. Here an earlier *\*ɑkɑlopemo* might have been reduced to *ɑkɑləpemo*, following a labial dissimilation process similar to what produces *wikɑpi* 'brown ash tree; basketweaving splint' from a Proto-Algonquian form with *\*-kwe-* or *\*-ko-*. Either *ɑkɑləpemo* or *ɑkɑlopemo* would both have primary accent on the vowel in question, and Speck might simply have misheard *ɑkɑlópemo* as *ɑkɑlápemo*. Andrew Dana's highly precise transcription in his handwritten version, however, repeatedly confirms the form as *ɑkɑlápemo*, including the accentuation noted here. It is possible that the *ɑkɑl-* component, with or without *-o*, may be from a dissimilated reduplication of the common root *kɑl-*, associated with binding, holding fast/ fixed, and also with disallowing, not permitting, holding back. We have created the anglicized form "Uugulubemo" with double "uu" to try to capture/draw attention to the distinct sound of the original Penobscot vowels.

168   *nɑpi*: The 1918 version includes the second *nɑpi* 'water' here as the start of this sentence (as do the original notes), glossing the phrase as 'some died thirsting for water'. This may be possible, but the word order like *nɑpi nɑnɑkʷɑč kʷaskʷi-katawɑssɑmolɑtɑwak*, with *nɑpi* in initial position, is otherwise rarely seen. Another option may be that *wɑkɑlhamawɑn nɑpi alɑnɑpa* 'he forbid the People water' was repeated in dictation as the possibly more information-structurally natural *wɑkɑlhamawɑn alɑnɑpa nɑpi* 'he forbid the People water', or that *nɑpi* was just repeated as a corrective afterthought. Either scenario would result in a slightly fragmented bit of syntax being recorded.

168   *kʷaskʷi-katawɑssɑmolɑtɑwak*: This could be 'they (group) died of thirst' or 'they (group) were dying of thirst'. Here we follow the 1918 translation.

170   *"tɑn ali-təpihle?" itamohɑtit*: The original separate-notes document has here instead *"tɑn kɑtali-təpihlana?" wɑtihlɑkon*... '"What has happened to you (pl.)?" (Then) they said to him...'. The difference is minimal: the wording we use here (and also in the 1918 version) is the text mate-

170   *n·wətəlohsanα sakəmαl*: We follow the 1918 version translation in assuming that the plural form *wətəlohsanα* '(then) they go there' can be used with an obviative argument like *sakəmαl* 'chief' to read as '(then) they go together with [the obviative]'. This reading is specifically supported by the original-notes gloss of the latter as 'with the chief'. It is conceivable that *sakəmαl* 'chief' instead refers to Uugulubemo, i.e., 'they went to see the chief, Uugulubemo, where he was' (with *αkələpemo* in proximate form, as common in appositives of obviatives), but that reading would require a rarer and much less certain use of this verb with Uugulubemo/the chief as a secondary object of the relative root *əl-* 'to . . .'. Unexplained either way is exactly why the verb here is not the group-plural form *wətəlαpαsinα* expected, if more than a minimal group (i.e., the people of the village) is walking there.

170   *eyit*: The 1918 version notes, "Supposed to have been at Chesuncook Lake": Chesuncook = *kči-sαkok* 'at the great (water-body) opening'.

172   *kohsəssənawak*: The 1918 version again has *kohsəssənawa* for expected *kohsəssənawak* 'our descendants'.

172   *kohsəssənawak*: See immediately above re. *kohsəssənawa*, here again in the 1918 version for expected *kohsəssənawak*.

172   *wətəmαhikanephαn*: The 1918 version suggests *wətəmαhikaniphαn*, but normal body-part incorporation patterns predict *təm-* 'sever' plus *-αhikan-e* 'spine' ('spine' is mostly attested as *-αyikan*, but *-αhikan* is not unsurprising for a /y/-dropping variant; see *spətáhi* below) plus *-phα* 'quickly/sharply grab NA'. The 1918 version is likely another /e~i/ transcription error by Speck.

172   *weči-*: The usual/expected *nα·* 'that' for 'that is why . . .' is missing here. This may have been missed in transcription or is possibly genuinely omissible.

172   *kəpalαmak*: The use of a plural form here may be a miscorrection from Speck, since the verb is singular, apparently referring to *məsi kəpalαm* 'every frog' instead of *məsi kəpalαmak* 'all frogs'. The original notes show no sign of any miscorrection/emendation and have the same singular verb with plural noun as here. Compare the similar issue in story 12 with singular verb *pemαkαt* 'as she/he danced along' matched to plural noun *nákskʷak* 'two young women'.

174   *kči-apasi*: That the form *kči-apasi wikʷesk* is not obviative *kči-apasəyal wikʷeskal* (or possibly *wikʷeskol*) suggests either a late or parenthetical insertion (not suggested by the original notes), or it is simply a proximate appositive of an obviative, a common pattern in Penobscot.

174   *wəkawəhαn*: This appears to mean '(so/then) he felled it [the tree] on him [Uugulubemo]', but the syntax is unclear. Speck's original notes gloss this as 'cutting so', apparently implying 'cutting [the tree] so [that it fell on him]'. See also the discussion in the following note.

174   *wəkʷaskʷtəhαn*: Both *wəkʷaskʷtəhαn* '(then) he/it smashed him to death' and impersonal-agent *kʷaskʷtəhαn* '(then) he was smashed to death' are possible. Some Algonquian languages are reported to disallow trees as agents of a Direct verb acting on a human patient (and require instead an Inverse), but this restriction may possibly not apply in Penobscot. It is possible that the original note gloss 'it killed him' is just an indirect interpretation of the impersonal-agent form, but the obviative form *αkələpemαwαl*, while not impossible with an impersonal-agent construction, more readily suggests a simple proximate-acting-on-obviative pattern, where the proximate may be the tree or possibly even Gluskabe. This last possibility is supported by the relevant line from Andrew Dana's handwritten version text, retranscribed here as *kaloskαpe wəkisihatawαn wətehsi-kipihlαlin yol αkələpemαwal, weči·pa -kisi-nlαt* 'Gluskabe made it [the yellow birch] fall onto this Uugulubemo, so that he could kill him'. Dana's English version is even more explicit: "Glooscap made it fall on Aglabemo to kill him."

174   *nα·weči- . . . sipo pαnawαhpskewtəkʷ*: Or possibly 'that is why it became a/the river, the Penobscot River'.

176   *nα·məsi sakətehtəkʷal*: Since the element *nα·* 'then' usually triggers Subordinative, which in turn usually does not mark NI plural *-al*, it is possible that instead the *nα·* here has its basic reading 'that (NI)' and forms a discontinuous constituent with *kči-sipok* 'at the great river', or just has its locative reading 'there'.

176   *wəčawpikətaholətinɑ*: *čawp-* is a contracted variant of *čawahp-* 'into the water'.

176   *nə·nanəkʷəč*: Speck's original notes suggest *no·nanəkʷəč* here, but glossed simply as 'some'. This may be overgeneralizing the very common sequence *n·wə-* 'then· 3rd.person', to a place where it is evidently impossible. See the next note for further discussion.

176   *namehsihlɑwələtəwak*: Strikingly, after *nə·* 'then', *namehsihlɑwələtəwak,* 'they (group) turned into fish' is not the expected Subordinative *wənamehsihlɑwələtinɑ*. This suggest that the *nə·* 'then', originally transcribed as /no/ before *nanəkʷəč* 'some', may be a false start or mishearing, perhaps for the first syllable of *nanəkʷəč* itself (or some as-yet unidentified secondary reduplication thereof). Note especially the string of similar Indicative verbs that follows, strongly suggesting that there is no Subordinative trigger.

176   *wahkehsəwak*: Literally 'only a few were those who survived/came out alive', where 'survived/came out alive' apparently means 'did not transform; stayed in human form'. Note that *pamɑwəsáwino* 'human being' literally means 'live-er = one who lives' and is based on the same element *-ɑwəsi* 'live, be alive'.

178   *weči*: Here *weči-* lacks the expected Conjunct verb normally co-occurring with it. It may be a false start for the next line. Or a Conjunct was intended for the verb, but a performance break resulted in it finally being said as Independent *wətetakʷapihtámənɑ* instead.

178   *wətetakʷapihtámənɑ*: Speck's original notes give this as 'they inhabit the length of the river', but the form may mean 'they sit/occupy on both sides (ends) of it', if related to *ehetaw-* 'on both sides of', or as a reduplicant of *takʷ-* 'both, double', i.e., as *tetakʷ-*. The latter might refer instead to both ends of the length of a river, a possibility that the original gloss might reasonably fit. Toward either or both readings, compare also the comparable line in the Andrew Dana handwritten version (retranscribed): *ni pɑnawɑhpskewtəkʷi-alənɑpak wətayinɑ məsi ni kki wəč iyo pɑnawɑhpske{k,wtəkʷ}* 'Then the Penobscot People had all that land from here at Penobscot/from this Penobscot River'. Dana first writes *pɑnawɑhpskek* 'at Penobscot', then emends to *pɑnawɑhpskewtəkʷ* 'Penobscot River'. His accompanying English version is "The Penobscot Indians had all the country of the Penobscot River."

178   *wətalənɑpeməwɑka*: The 1918 version suggests *wətalənɑpemənaka*, which matches no known form. This is a misreading of the original notes, which here have / . . . muaga/. Here Speck's handwritten "u" was evidently later taken to be an "n" for the 1918 version. The original notes form matches well the expected *-ɑwa* 'their' plus absentative *-ka*: compare also *Penobscot Dictionary* form *ohsássəwaka* 'their deceased kinfolk'.

178   *-wihkʷənəmohatit*: The 1918 version suggests unattested *-wihkʷəmohatit*. The predicted *-wihkʷənəmohatit* here likely has had its /-ənəm-/ sequence misheard as /-əm-/, as often happens.

178   *ehkihkikit*: This stem is often used in singular form with a plural argument, as per the discussion of *msel(ət)*, *kehsit,* and Passamaquoddy-Maliseet *elinaqsit* above.

## 8 nsɑsək

PAGE

182   *alənɑpa*: Here again, it is uncertain if this the original use of the term to refers to humans in general or to the People, etc.

182   *kči-məkʷasəpemək*: The 1918 version suggests *kči-nəkʷasəpem*; we restore the locative assuming this is not a secondary object and noting that there are apparent omissions at the end of this word and the start of the next.

182   *etali-*: The 1918 version suggests only *tali-*, but the Conjunct ending generally requires the initial change form *etali-*, which in turn could read as 'where [he . . .]' or could possibly even be reduced/misheard from *n·etali-* 'that is where [he . . .]'.

182   *nəkisi-katonkasolətippəna*: The 1918 version suggests *nəkisi-katonkasolətipəna*; Speck may have missed this in part because the relatively rarer unaspirated geminate /pp/ could easily be mistaken for the /b/ of his original transcription.

184 *oči-mačehlan akʷiláwəhan kči-mosol*: Here again it is possible that these are two separate clauses: '(then) he started off from there; (then) he looked for the great moose'.

184 *aməskamən*: Speck misglosses as 'he found him' when this verb cannot apply to the NA moose, only the NI yard.

184 *awəssanoti*: Despite the superficial similarity and the decent chance that the often highly velarized Penobscot /l/ could be misheard as a /w/, all evidence suggests that *awəssanoti* is the form for 'moose/deer-yard' and is not directly related to the *aləssin-, -aləssin-* 'NA lie there' stem also seen here. Siebert's fieldnotes in fact have a form *aləssanoti* that is explicitly corrected by two cited speakers to *awəssanoti*, i.e., Siebert too may have mistakenly connected these two stems at first. Speck's original notes write out both the noun and verb stems here a second time on the facing page, suggesting that he too was confirming the difference.

184– *eləmiphəkʷet . . . osəwehlan*: This entire section describing the first incident with Jug-Woman is a separate insertion at the original direct transi-
192 tion between *n·wənohsohkawən* and *maləm yewokənahkiwik*.

186 *kamač kkati-pəlikʷewi*: The 1918 version suggests *-pəlikʷeyo* but has '[y]ou are very haughty'; we follow the translation here and assume the expected pattern for 'you' was simply slightly misheard. It is also possible that the form is *kamač kati-pəlikʷewo* 'He wants to be all proud-faced' instead. That is, Jug-Woman first makes an observation to herself about Gluskabe, and then in the next phrase shifts to rhetorically speaking to him directly.

188 *pənihlat*: The 1918 version suggests *pənihlač* here, but the next line, with *mina* 'again', has *pənihlat*, so we restore it here. Compare the Penobscot Dictionary's *pánihle* 'it gradually opens, he goes into the open, passes into view'.

188 *nawəpaməkʷek*: This is more likely to be *nawəpaməkʷek* with *naw-* 'middle', as there is no attested element *naw-* and that form would otherwise be expected to have initial change as *newəpaməkʷek*. We leave it as is, however, as these points are not certain, especially given that there are at least extended roots *nawat-* 'along the way, in passing' and *nawət-* 'hither', where the first might potentially relate to the form in question. A 1918 version footnote explains this as '[a]n opening in the woods where a view can be had of game'.

188 *senape*: Speck's translation at this point seems to combine a small mishearing with a big misreading: "She said, 'That Gluskɑ́ʹbe is a very swift man'. When she reached the mouth of the river, looking across a rocky point, she saw him going along after the moose" (204). Here we suspect that Speck missed the sentence break at *[n]·askʷe kəloskape . . .* 'then [changing the topic] Gluskabe . . .'. The element *·askʷe* 'however' is very commonly used in Penobscot literature to turn attention (or topic status) from one character to another, and *n(ə)·* 'then' (argued in the note below to precede it) is itself nearly always clause-initial in its use as a temporal linker. When Speck missed these markers of a new clause with topic shift, he ended up misreading the subsequent verbs to refer to Jug-Woman rather than Gluskabe, all the way to "she saw him going along after the moose." That translation does not fit *n·wənamihan eləmihlɑ̆ličil mosol* 'then she/he saw the moose going away', which matches better as the final thing Gluskabe does at this point. The overall translation we offer for these lines also fits better with the rest of the text, since a few lines later, Jug-Woman is described as following this very same path and seeing the same landmarks. That description would be redundant if the lines discussed here referred to her but would not if they instead refer to Gluskabe.

188 *[n]·askʷe*: As with *(nə)·tte* earlier, *·askʷe* is generally, though not exclusively, a second-position clitic, so it is likely though not certain that Speck missed *n(ə)·* 'then' preceding it here.

188 *sakətehtəkok*: The 1918 version suggests *sakətehtəkohč*. Unless this is the very rare *-ohč* 'disliked thing', this is a mishearing either of *sakətehtəkok* 'at the river mouth' or *sakətehtəkʷek* 'here the river has its mouth'. Speck's original notes to this word say "Penobscot River near Castine."

190 *pohkačinskʷehso*: The 1918 version and original notes have only *pohkačinskʷehs*. While this superficially resembles the normal final vowel-drop forms of Passamaquoddy-Maliseet, it is more likely that Speck missed the final *-o* in Penobscot; his accentuation matches the expected Penobscot antepenultimate high pitch for *pohkačĭnskʷehs[o]*.

192 *pekəssik*: The 1918 version suggests *apekəssik*. This *a-* may likely be Speck's hearing of the epenthetic schwa that often occurs between two consonants across a word boundary. Note too Lyon's historically regular use of the *-k* allomorph of the NA Conjunct ending after a consonant-final stem: this is leveled to the postvocalic allomorph *-t* for most later-generation speakers, as it also is in Passamaquoddy-Maliseet.

194 *mosolakəsəyal*: The 1918 version suggests *mosolak*ʷ*əsəyal*, but all other sources for *-əlakəsəyal* '-guts' suggest a plain /k/, rather than the /kʷ/ that occasionally crops up as a clear hypercorrection in other Speck transcriptions.

194 *wəlakəsəyal*: Related to the above, the 1918 version suggests *wəlak*ʷ*əsəyal*, but again, all other sources for *wəlakəsəyal* 'guts' suggest a plain /k/ rather than Speck's /kʷ/.

194 *n·aləmoss wəmitsin*: The 1918 version translation "His dog ate as far as they went" captures the apparent implication of this construction, apparently referring to the three "looks" behind Gluskabe where he threw the guts. At this point in Speck's original notes, there is a brief sequence that Speck marked "Omit": *nə·tte kəloskape wətəlakk*ʷ*asin[;] wətahtawəkk*ʷ*asotəyal wəpassanlən mosiye* 'Right away then Gluskabe cooked for himself[;] he filled his kettle with moose meat'. At this point in the original notes, the original transition from *wəmitsin* to *kisəkk*ʷ*asit* has a facing-page text insertion of the *nə·tt' eləpektek . . . n·eləkk*ʷ*asit* sequence, which apparently expands the original omitted component.

194 *nəkα tali-kətahle*: The Subordinative blocking of NI plural *-al* here means this could be either 'and (then) they sank there' or 'and (then) they were sinking (there)'.

196 *wαpahpəsk*ʷ: This might specifically be quartz; the *Penobscot Dictionary*, however, also only glosses it as 'white rock'.

196 *wewinαk*ʷ*atol*: Speck's original notes and 1918 version suggest *wewinαk*ʷ*ato* (and so perhaps *wewinαk*ʷ*áto*), but the most likely possibility is that he simply missed the expected final *-l* here referring to 'them', i.e., the guts.

196 *etali-pənahpsk*ʷ*ihlαt*: The original notes and 1918 version both suggest *etali-pənahpsk*ʷ*ihlαk*, which does not fit with *aləmoss* 'dog'. The NA form *etali-pənahpsk*ʷ*ihlαt* would be needed instead. Here Speck may have overgeneralized the immediately preceding *etali-pənahpsk*ʷ*ihlαk* referring to the NI guts.

196 *pótəki*: Or perhaps just *pətəki*.

198 *pečohse*: It is possible that *pečohse* is a mishearing of *pečohset* 'when he arrived', which would set up a common correlative pattern with the following *etalαkk*ʷ*asit* 'then/there was where/when he cooked for himself'.

198 *wəkətək*ʷ*ahkαn*: As noted in story 6, Penobscot forms from Siebert and Western Abenaki cognates both suggest the initial element might be *k*ʷ*ətαk*ʷ-, here and for the subsequent forms *n·wəkətək*ʷ*ahlαn* and *wəkətək*ʷ*apin* in this text.

198 *n·wəkətək*ʷ*ahlαn*: The 1918 version translates as 'then he upset it', which seems to closely repeat the earlier *wəkətək*ʷ*ahkαn* '(then) he sharply flipped it over'. This might be an unintentional restart in the dictation or some nuance of meaning that has been lost in translation. We reconstruct as *n·wəkətək*ʷ*ahlαn*, using *-ahlα* 'put/place NA', since typically the form *-ahαlα/-ahəlα* is only found when *-halα* 'move/change NA (especially, quickly)' follows an element ending in /α/ or /e/, which appears not to be the case here. See also the argumentation for the parallel form *wəkətək*ʷ*ahton* used with a NI object in story 6. If *n·wəkətək*ʷ*ahlαn* is correct, then this may be a more contextually appropriate 'then he placed it there flipped over'.

198 *na nihk*ʷ*αp wačo ali-wiso kkiniyo*: The 1918 version has this as '[i]t is the mountain called Kineo', but the syntax here is uncertain. It may possibly be two sentences, i.e., *na nihk*ʷ*αp wačo* 'that is now a/the mountain' and *ali-wiso kkiniyo* 'it is called Kineo'.

200 *-ntamólənα*: This accentuation pattern, where an open penult schwa apparently is counted for primary accentuation on the antepenultimate stressable vowel, remains poorly understood but is noted here (as with several—but likely not all—similar cases elsewhere in these texts, especially when backed up by alternating secondary-stress documentation) as it is explicitly supported by the 1918 version transcription.

200 *wəlitαhαsolətəwak*: The 1918 version form suggests *[n·]wəlitαhαsolətəwak* 'then· they (group) were happy', but *n(ə)·* 'then' not followed with the

expected Subordinative form *olitəhasolətinα* is highly unusual. On top of this, discourse linker *n(ə)·* is almost always the first element in the clause and essentially never found preceded by particles like *kamαč* 'very'. It seems more likely that Speck mistakenly added *n(ə)·* as an over-generalization. If it is however correct, it could be a rare case of an Indicative following *n(ə)·*, perhaps to highlight the event in some way.

200 *kolihalipəna*: The stem here, discussed earlier for story 1, again is cognate to that in Mi'kmaw *wela'lin* 'thank you', literally 'you do good to me'. Compare *nolihala* 'I prepare him, fix him, give relief to him, allay him, assuage him, benefit him, I like his ways, am used to his ways, am accustomed to him', from the *Penobscot Dictionary*, and also in these texts, *kətalamihi*, literally 'you make me grateful/thankful', but used to express 'I thank you'.

200 *tepəne·pa·na*: Here *na* may be cliticized to the preceding word, a point never documented by Siebert but common in Algonquian languages and occasionally apparently detectable in some extant Penobscot sound recordings.

202 *kətalamisəwαməlápəna*: The 1918 version notes, "A very formal expression."

# 9 nóli

PAGE

206 *pečihlan*: May be *pečíhlan*, with a contraction-based accent.

206 *saki-kisαwəsolátəwak*: *saki-kis-*, literally 'with difficulty (be) able to . . .', i.e., 'have a hard time being able to . . .'.

206 *msel . . . kʷaskʷalαmolátičik*: Here again, a singular form for a verb of quantification that refers to an explicitly plural argument, as per *kehsit*, etc.

206 *etotαkʷahtek*: It is not clear if this is meant to be read as part of the end of the line here or the start of the next.

208 *wanəhokhatəwak*: The 1918 version suggests *wawəhokhatəwak*; this is a miscopying of what appears to be an "n" in Speck's original notes.

210 *makαlipəwewayiyαk*: The ending *-ewe*, seen as *-eway-* here in *makαlipəwewayiyαk, nolkewayiyαk, mosewayiyαk,* etc., refers to a hide with the fur still on, a pelt, as opposed to *-atekən* for hide/skin with the fur removed. It seems surprising at first that snowshoes might be made of skin with the fur still on, but perhaps this is specifically for greater traction in facing ice.

210 *wəmehtkawα*: The 1918 version suggests *mehtkawα*.

210 *mosewayiyαk*: As this form is a proximate plural rather than the expected obviative plural, it may be a parenthetical/appositive or an after-thought. NA proximate plural *-iyαk* and NI plural *-iyαl* forms for the element *-iye* 'of . . . material; -meat' are well-attested, but so far it has been difficult to locate in the Penobscot corpora clear and certain examples of a distinct obviative plural. The Passamaquodddy-Wolastoqew/Maliseet cognate *-ey(a)* does attest its expected obviative plural *-eyà*, but it is not clear if a directly corresponding form *-iya* is in fact the actual Penobscot equivalent. Compare *makαlipəwayiye* and *nolkewayiyαk* below, for which we also expect an obviative plural form, even as they instead seem to show a proximate singular and proximate plural respectively.

212 *wəmehtkawα*: Here the 1918 version does in fact suggest full *wəmehtkawα*, contrary to the *mehtkawα* forms elsewhere, suggesting that Speck simply had difficulty reliably hearing the initial *wə-* here and supporting its restoration in the forms noted elsewhere.

212 *nolkewayiyαk*: As this form is not obviative plural, it too may be a parenthetical/appositive or an after-thought. Compare *mosewayiyαk* above and *makαlipəwayiye* below.

212 *wəmehtkawα*: The 1918 version suggests *mehtkawα*.

212 *makαlipəwayiye*: Again, an unexpected apparent proximate singular rather than the expected distinctive obviative plural. Compare *mosewayiyαk* and *nolkewayiyαk* above.

214 *(kis)*: In Speck's original notes, this first *kis* is written together as a single word with the preceding word, suggesting that it might be treated

as an enclitic: not unexpected for a monosyllabic particle. It is also possibly a simple performance error, though in audio recordings, speakers seem to naturally repeat phrases like *kis·ahč* 'already·also', as they use them to transition from one situation to the next. It may also be a bit of both, that is, a genuine clause-final clitic anticipating the immediately upcoming *kis* of *kis·ahč*.

214 *wəpitikαn; pkʷamikamikʷ*: The 1918 version translation offers 'it was an ice-house' as a completely separate sentence, hence the gloss here. Locational secondary object constructions (which use the *wə-…-n* marking seen here) seem to be used when the locatum is noticeably discourse-established and/or focal; otherwise, the far more common pattern of a simple locative-marked nominal occurs. Since the latter is not evident here, and the house has just been introduced and established as a clear focus of attention, this reading of the verb is supported, though whether *pkʷamikamikʷ* should then be seen as an appositive of the verb-marked secondary object ('[then] he entered it, an ice-house') or as a wholly separate predication ('it was an ice-house') remains uncertain. And since the Subordinative is itself derived from secondary object morphology, the verb's form is also ambiguous with '(then) he entered'.

214 *kəpətehtehsən*: The 1918 version gives 'closed tight'; we translate 'slammed shut' based on *-əhtehsən* 'NI fall with a striking action'.

216 *wəkisi-notessewən*: The 1918 version suggests *wəkisi-notessαn*. This is likely either a mishearing or miscorrection by Speck.

216 *pkʷaməyαl*: Since the original notes and 1918 version both gloss this as 'of ice', the form may possibly be *pkʷamiyαl* '(made) of ice', based on the *-iye* element discussed earlier. As Speck does not fully reliably transcribe the *a:α* distinction, it is difficult to determine between this option and a simple appositive obviative *pkʷaməyαl* 'ice'.

218 *nə·kəloskαpe itam*: A rare case of *nə·* 'then' followed by a non-Subordinative *itam* 'he said'. This could possibly be a fragment/restarting, but such uses specifically with *itam* are occasionally attested elsewhere, perhaps due to its frequency as a quotative verb.

218 *awihkʷinawαn*: The 1918 version translates this as 'he laughed at him'. The literal meaning of the stem here seems to be 'see NA as funny, laughable': *wihkʷ-*, which elsewhere means 'pull in, grab toward self, shrink', seems to have a consistent use as '(find to be) funny, humorous, laughable', then *-nawα* 'see, view NA as …'. Hence the *Penobscot Dictionary* offers *nəwíhkʷinawα* 'I look upon him as comical, view him as a laughingstock'. Compare also *wihkʷínahso* 'he laughs (at something)' and *wihkʷínakʷəso* 'he is ludicrous, comical, a laughingstock'. The 1918 version gloss 'laugh at', however, matches the *Passamaquoddy-Maliseet Dictionary* gloss *wihqinuwal* 'she/he teases him/her playfully or laughs at him/her (e.g., cute child)'. It is not clear if these latter English glosses represent a genuine shift in the meaning or just a looser translation that more easily fits English usage.

220 *nə·tt' eləssik*: Possible translations may be 'right there he/Gluskabe lay' or 'he/Gluskabe just lay right there' or 'he/Gluskabe lay right there'. As with *pekəssik*, this *eləssik* is a further example of Lyon's conservative treatment of *-n-* final stems with the postconsonantal *-k* allomorph of the NA singular Conjunct ending, rather than the postvocalic *-t* allomorph generalized to these stems in most of Siebert's documentation and in Passamaquoddy-Maliseet as well.

220 *ččehe*: The exact meaning of this form is unknown (Speck's original notes give 'why', as in 'Why, there I have been asleep!'), but it sounds affectively similar to two sound-symbolic families of interjections attested in the *Penobscot Dictionary*, namely *nèhe* 'now, well now, come on! Come now!' e.g., *nèhe máčehla* 'Now go!' and then also *ččèka* and *ččèna*, as in *ččèka nə̀ya* 'let me try'; *ččèka nači-akʷetskəhʷátone* 'Well, let's go try to do it'; *ččèna nə̀ya* 'Let me try!'; and *ččèna àpi* 'Sit right down!'

222 *awikəwaməwαk*: This is one instance of an explicitly transcribed *a-* prefix for this form, even as most of the other 1918 transcriptions suggest *wikəwaməwαk* (or possibly even *wəwikəwaməwαk*, if that latter form genuinely exists).

# 10 mətala

226    *wənəpahkatawɑnɑ*: The 1918 version suggests *wənəpahkatawɑnɑl* or *wənəpahkatawɑnal*. Both are possible forms but do not fit the context of proximate plural external argument 'foxes', obviative singular 'Woodchuck' primary object, and N-marking for either Subordinative or secondary object: either of these last two elements normally blocks obviative singular marking for the primary object. More likely is that Speck, who often missed coda /l/ after /a/ and /ɑ/, hypercorrected one into existence here.

226    *sɑkhɑpilite*: This form is ambiguous between an 'if . . .' or 'when . . .' translation.

226    *wsisəkok*: 'face' and 'eye(s)' are the same word in Penobscot, usually distinguished mainly in that 'eyes' are referred to using the plural form, while 'face' and 'eye' both use an identical singular *wsisək*ʷ. The locative form *wsisəkok* may only refer to the singular 'face' but may also apply to the eyes, even without using the usual locative pluralizer *-ihk*ʷ-, given that the 1918 version translates this as 'in her eyes'.

226    *nə·č*: The 1918 version suggests *nis*; most other attestations of this collocation here support retranscription as *nə·č*.

228    *wɑtɑpɑteləmohkɑsin*: The final stem element here might be *-ɑsi*, *-ɑssi*, *-ahsi*, or even *-asi*. We assume simple sound-correspondence with the *Passamaquoddy-Maliseet Dictionary* form *(y)alelomuhkasu* 'she/he goes around laughing' and reconstruct *-ɑsi*.

228    *kisi-msáwihɑ*: Besides evidently being another of Lyon's distinctive contrastively accented negative concord forms (i.e., the more commonly attested pattern would be *kisi-msáwihɑwi*), the stem here is not found in the *Penobscot Dictionary* or in available Passamaquoddy-Maliseet materials. Rasles, however gives *nemesaðakazézi* for 'Je suis trop brûlé, je n'y retourne plus, je ne m'expose plus à être brûlé [I am too burned, I return there no more, I expose myself no more to being burned]' (400). The bare impersonal-agent pattern used with *-ihɑ* here suggests 'she is [not] caused to . . .', so the sense of *msaw-* on its own may be something like 'have a bad experience you don't want to come back to'. Thus, the full sense here may be something like 'she could not be made to give up hope/become averse to'. This also fits with the next few lines, especially *sɑkhɑpihaso* 'she stuck her head quickly out to look', which seems to emphasize her quick response/reaction, i.e., that she still has not been made to give up on looking outside for her grandson's arrival.

228    *etoči-k*ʷ*ilomɑt*: The 1918 version has 'anxious for', but the *Penobscot Dictionary* has *nək*ʷ*ílomɑ* 'I long for him, I year[n] for him', and the *Passamaquoddy-Maliseet Dictionary* has ''kilumal, 'qilumal* 's/he misses h/, is homesick for h/, longs or yearns for h/'.

230    *kɑloskɑpe*: It is not clear whether this word belongs to the preceding or following clause.

230    *kkeləpi-mɑčin*: The 1918 version suggests *kkeləpi-mɑčin* 'you hurry up and go away'; compare with Rasles, *nekérbar8kké*, literally, 'I hurry working', under the heading "dépêcher" (431).

230    *kənihlipɑ*: The 1918 version suggests *kənihlipa*, which again may be a genuine form retaining the archaic *-a* rather than leveled *-ɑ* for the second-person plural.

232    *kkisi-nəpahkatawippɑ*: The 1918 version suggests *kkisi-nəpahkatawiləpa*, where Speck mishearing an [l] for the labial onglide of geminate [pp] in *-awippɑ* is not unexpected, as the Penobscot /l/ is quite often heavily velarized. In coda position this means it is often not heard by transcribers or is mistaken for a distinct vowel quality. See also the discussion of *wənəpahkatawɑnɑ* for the 1918 version *wənəpahkatawɑnɑl / wənəpahkatawɑnal* in this story. And here even emended to *kkisi-nəpahkatawippɑ*, the 1918 version suggests *-nəpahkatawippɑ*, which (as noted above in stories 2 and 3) may be a genuine archaic form.

232    *nɑta*: Nearly all of the 1918 version transcriptions (including Gluskabe's own first protest that he is not a fox) suggest *ɑta* rather than *nɑta*, but this transcription looks closer to *nɑta*. The distinction between the two, if any, is not clear in Siebert's documentation. Western Abenaki also attests both *ôda* and *nda*, even as Jesuit-era documentation seems to have only a single *maïda* form, and Passamaquoddy-Maliseet has verbal negative *má(-te)* versus (primarily) nominal negative *kàt*.

232 *ipa waˇckawihptinewi*: The 1918 version suggests *ˇckawihptinewi*. The easily missed initial /wə-/ is restored here as *waˇckawihptinewi*. The form *ipa* is not attested as such in Siebert's documentation, though it may be connected to Penobscot *ksipa* 'so you see' and related Passamaquoddy-Maliseet *ipa, sipa* 'hey! listen! hark!; look! give heed! pay attention!' It is uncertain why this *ipa* is omitted in the 1918 version; we restore it here with the gloss 'just' used in Speck's original notes.

234 *peˇcihlan*: May be *peˇcíhlan*, with contraction-based accent.

238 *watahkʷəˇcihtəhɑn*: '(Then) he spared him' is unattested in the *Penobscot Dictionary*. Rasles gives *nedak8tsitéhañ* 'Je l'epargne, je ne le tue pas, je ne lui fais rien [= I save him, I do not kill him, I don't do anything to him]' (448). Aubery offers *mañda kég8i akk8tsitt8ï* 'Il n'a rien épargné [= he has not saved anything]' (237). The original dieresis might be *8i*, i.e., over *8*, not *i*, as per the predicted negative ending *-owi*, not *-wi*. Passamaquoddy-Maliseet *'t-asqihtahal* 'she/he spares h/ when hitting or picking, leaves h/ untouched; she/he deflects h/; (boxing, fighting) she/he deflects or parries h/ blow, punch, etc.' seems not to be directly related, though it may be indirectly, through some kind of reanalysis.

238 *kətɑpenkɑtassin*: Passamaquoddy-Maliseet attests forms with both *apenkat-* and *apenkot-*, i.e., corresponding to Penobscot *ɑpenkat-* and *ɑpen-kat-*, and without a clear distinction in meaning/use. As Speck's transcriptions of the /ɑ/-/a/ distinction is often unreliable, the *-kat-* here is therefore only provisional.

240 *ehkʷtahi*: The 1918 version suggests *ehkʷtahe*, which would be 'stop beating him/her/them'. This is a clear example of Speck's recurrent difficulty with the /i/ versus /e/ contrast.

244 *-ahkʷɑləmit*: The 1918 version suggests *-ahkalami-*, but the *Penobscot Dictionary* has *áhkʷɑləmo* 'he is instinctively shy, wary (most often said of an animal, such as a fox, but can be applied to humans, especially children)'. The *Passamaquoddy-Maliseet Dictionary* has *ahqalomu* '(wild animal) she/he is shy, hides when people come near', which together suggest the *-ahkʷɑləmit* form restored here, though the etymological breakdown of this stem is still unclear.


# 11 nəkʷətɑnkaw

PAGE

248 *kohsəssənawak*: The 1918 version again has *kohsəssənawa* for expected *kohsəssənawak* 'our descendants'. Here this would be an otherwise unattested mismatch with *nətahčəwi-alohkewək* 'I have to work for them'.

248 *-otehkkawɑ*: This may possibly be *-otehkawɑ* or *-otekkawɑ*.

248 *kohsəssənawa*: This is in this case the expected obviative plural.

248 *wesɑmi-awehket*: The original notes and the 1918 version both suggest *wəsɑmi-awehkat*. This suggests a rare unchanged Conjunct, but the likely impossible /a/ for the final vowel in *awehke-* 'use' suggests it is more likely that this form was overall just imperfectly heard by Speck. An alternative is that Speck misheard *osɑmi-awehkɑn* 'he overuses it', which would be possible if the final *-n* was partially devoiced, as can happen at the end of an utterance in Penobscot.

248 *wesɑmi-awehket eləhɑnɑtəwit*: Here the season *pəpon* 'Winter' is personified and so treated as NA rather than the usual NI. We see this again with *nipən* 'Summer' and also with *kəsəlamsən* 'Wind' in reference to the Wind-Bird.

250 *eyit*: This NA form again refers to *nipən* and is treated as NA.

250 *saki-nenawelətɑso*: Here *nipən*, though treated as NA elsewhere in this text, may be reverting to its usual status as NI, as *-ɑsi* stems are the main Penobscot construction for impersonal agent acting on NI. For NA, we would expect *saki-nenawelɑmɑ*. That said, *-ɑsi* stems are occasionally attested with NA arguments, though typically not for impersonal-agent constructions like these.

250 *wənenaweləmɑwɑl*: Starting with this NA-object verb, Woodchuck, who in the previous line may have treated Summer as NI, unambiguously refers to Summer as NA from here onward. We approximate this shift by using 'it' in the previous line and 'him' in this line only, though we have no indication of a gender for Summer. Again, Summer is NA possibly because it is personified, even though later it is spoken of as a liquid- or jelly-like substance in a container, which is likely to be NI unless it is very thick or gummy.

250 *spətáhi*: The 1918 version suggests *spətáhi*, where the generally expected form is *spətáyi* 'during the day, in daytime'. However, sequences conventionally transcribed as /ayi/, /awo/, etc., are often acoustically more like [ai], [ao], etc., and there occasionally seem to be instances of emergent /h/ between vowels in these and other vowel sequences, though the overall set of evidence remains unclear.

250 *ahč*: This form, meaning 'also, too', is one of the small set of elements that is most commonly a second-position clitic but also can occur free/ without a host. Here the latter seems to be the case, though not for sure.

250 *alɑpehsəmawi*: The 1918 version suggests *alɑpesəmawi*, but the *Penobscot Dictionary* form *nətəlɑpéhsəmawə* 'I cut out rawhide strings for him' (*sic* /sam/ for expected /səm/) and Speck's explicit marking of preaspiration in *wətəlɑpehsikən* in the next line both support restoring /hs/.

252 "*nɑkɑ . . . alihtawi*": The original notes and 1918 version both miss that this is a second request from Gluskabe and instead conflate it with the preceding line describing Woodchuck's work, glossing *alihtawi* as 'she made' (rather than 'make them for me'), which would also make the following line oddly redundant.

252 *wətəlhɑkəman*: The 1918 version has *wətəlhɑkəman* as 'filled the snowshoes', while the *Penobscot Dictionary* has *álhɑkəme* 'he makes snowshoes (thus)', in contrast to *aləskánawe* '(1) he weaves, fills (snowshoes); (2) he weaves ash wood strips, wicker, rushes, rattan; (3) he weaves mat'. Rasles has *nederhañghemé* as both 'je fais des raquettes [= I make snowshoes]' and 'je la [= babiche] passe en faisant la tissure [= I weave in the babiche in making the webbing]' (518), so it may well be that the term refers both to the specific crucial action of weaving in the webbing and to making snowshoes in general.

252–254 *nápi·tte·č . . . wəmɑčehlɑn*: In Speck's original notes, the material between these two points, where Woodchuck tells Gluskabe how to recognize his father, is a separate insertion.

254 *pahpɑkʷɑkʷahte*: Speck's original notes have this as 'less depth of snow'. Related forms in Siebert documentation suggest that *pahpɑkʷ-* describes a thin/sparse level of covering and a reduction, lull, or abatement in rain, storms, or snow.

254 *[mam]tahkamike*: The 1918 version suggests only *[C]tahkamike*, i.e., showing only an initial voiceless and/or tense /t-/ that hints at a preceding consonant. From *Penobscot Dictionary* forms like *mamtahkʷikánehle* 'he goes barelegged', *mamtálamsən* 'the wind renders it visible', and Passamaquoddy-Maliseet *mamciw* 'in the nude, naked', we see an apparent Penobscot element *mamt-* 'bare, exposed, visible'. The fact that Penobscot and Passamaquoddy-Maliseet share the same vowel here is unexpected but may reflect independent paths of reduplication from an earlier *mt-* (which could be the original element or even the actual one Lyon used)—of which Speck then missed the acoustically low-energy nasal CVC /mam-/ component.

256 *wətahsapkʷɑn*: This stem is not found in the *Penobscot Dictionary*, but is seen in Rasles, under the heading "cache" in *sabk8añgan* 'Espèce d'armoire dans un arbre [= a kind of wardrobe/cupboard in a tree]', along with *nedasabaʿk8añn*, apparently 'I cache it in a tree' (401–402). Notably Rasles here also has *nedag8* (= *nətakʷ*) 'Je mets dans le cache [I put into the cache]', and third-person *ag8* (= *akʷ*, possibly *ako*) with *ág8né* 'Cache dans la terre [cache in the earth]', suggesting still another distinct stem, *akʷ-*, for caching in the earth. (Compare also *nemanág8* 'Je vais la lèver, je la lève [I go to raise it, I raise it]', suggesting *manakʷ-* as 'remove from an earth-cache'.)

256 *kənenawɑpatəmən*: The 1918 version suggests *nenawɑpatəmən*, an otherwise unattested form, even as *kənenawɑpatəmən* '(so) you keep a watch on it', is a common use of the Subordinative as a less-direct Imperative. A simple Imperative would be *nenawɑpata*; for 'keep watch on it for me', *nenawɑpatamawi* would be expected.

256 *[ma]mčəsitáhi*: The 1918 version suggests *məčisitáhi* as 'on foot', a form and meaning that is otherwise unattested. The original notes, however, give it as 'on foot (without snowsh[oes])'. Gluskabe asked for two pairs of snowshoes and has now worn out one set and just hung up the other. This initially suggests that this form means something like 'with feet exposed', likely not literally 'barefoot' (compare *amehsakəsítehle* 'he goes barefooted'), and perhaps more specifically meaning 'not wearing snowshoes'. Regarding the form itself, Rasles's use of *mesaghesi-daïði* 'aiant les piés [ . . . ] nud' (557) for 'barefoot' suggests *-əsitáyi* 'with foot/feet in . . . way' (for *-áhi* here, see discussion of *spətáhi* vs. *spətáyi*), with the *mamt-*, *mamč-* 'bare, exposed' discussed earlier. *Penobscot Dictionary* forms offer *mamčəsítehle* 'he goes with worn-out shoes, with his feet showing', *mamčəsítesse* 'he walks with worn-out shoes, with his feet showing from his shoes', and *mamčəsítewo* 'his feet stick out/show out of his shoes, he has worn out shoes', which firmly support an element *mamč-əsite-*, albeit with a slightly different meaning than that suggested by Speck's glosses. So it remains unclear whether this describes Gluskabe as going along without snowshoes at all or simply going along in his first worn-out pair, with his feet sticking out.

256 *eləmihlɑt*: Note parallel to previous *eləmihlɑt*. This expression is common as a transition in stories as a character literally heads off/onward to the next location.

256 *ketəwəkɑmək*: The 1918 version superficially suggests *kətəwəkɑmək*, a possible rare instance of unchanged Conjunct, but is instead evidently a simple misreading of Speck's original notes, which directly suggest *ketəwəkɑmək*.

258 *kəpetotehkkawi*: As per earlier notes regarding this element, this may be *kəpetotehkawi* or *kəpetotekkawi*. Here the original notes and 1918 version both clearly indicate a geminate /kk/ (unlike *-otehkkawa* above, recorded with a simple /k/) but again do not mark any preaspiration before it.

258 *apehkʷihlɑməkowəya*: This verb, not found in the *Penobscot Dictionary*, has a Passamaquoddy-Maliseet equivalent in *'pehqiyamal* 'she/he welcomes him/her; she/he comes back to him/her after a long absence'. Note also that despite following *nə·* 'then', the form is not Subordinative. This is perhaps because the non-welcome is not viewed as a logical consequence of preceding events, making *nə·* a mere default linker, not interpreted as tied directly to this event.

260 *wəkatonalɑko*: An independent Indicative complement of direct perception is rare compared to Conjunct forms. Alternatively, this may be two separate sentences—'Right away he recognized them; they were after him'—forced together by Speck.

260 *otamɑkanal*: The 1918 version transcription rarely distinguishes *wə-* from *o-* at the start of a word. This obscures the well-established contrast between obviative *wətamɑkanal* 'the pipe (given/taken/in relation)' versus third-person possessed *otamɑkanal* '(his/her) pipe'. Here the 1918 version translates this as 'his pipe', but Speck's original notes give 'the pipe'. Possessor-raising constructions, which here would be Indicative *(a)wihkʷənəmawanal* or Subordinative *(a)wihkʷənəmawɑn* (compare story 10: *nə·kɑloskape (a)wihkʷənəmawɑn wpɑtin* 'Then Gluskabe took her paw') are not always used even when the possessors are distinct, and so their use versus nonuse cannot necessarily be diagnostic here.

262 *wətamɑkanal*: Another instance of the *wətamɑkanal* 'pipe (obviative)' versus *otamɑkanal* 'his pipe (obviative)' ambiguity. Here we follow the 1918 version English gloss.

264 *otamɑkanal*: With *nekəma* 'he, his (own)', this form is very likely *otamɑkanal* 'his pipe'.

264 *kataweləmawal*: The 1918 version glosses this as 'smile', but we go with the literal interpretation supported by the cognate Passamaquoddy-Maliseet form in the *Passamaquoddy-Maliseet Dictionary*: *Peciyay yut eltaqsi, psi-te wen kotuwelomu* 'The way I've come to sound, everyone wants to laugh'.

264 *awihkʷitəhɑmal*: The 1918 version translates as 'he scorned it in his mind'. Regarding *wihkʷ-* here (with *-təhɑmɑ* 'think/feel regarding NA'), see the earlier discussion of *awihkʷinawɑn* for story 9.

264 *otamɑkanal*: Again ambiguous with *wətamɑkanal* 'pipe (obviative)', and again we retranscribe following the 1918 version gloss 'his pipe'. Note again that the verb is not in Indicative or Subordinative possessor-raising form, that is, neither Indicative *awihkʷitəhatamawanal* nor Subordinative *awihkʷitəhatamawɑn*.

266   *(a)wihkʷipəkətenalɑl*: This form is provisional, as the final element here is not clear. The collocation *-nahəlɑ* from *-ne-halɑ*, 'tear/destroy', possibly related to *-ne* 'NA be ill, in pain; NA die', seems unlikely. Alternatively, this could be the form *pəkate-n-* 'smoke', with the linking *-n-* seen with some verbs of its type, followed by either *-alɑ* or *-ɑlɑ* for acting on the NA pipe.

266   *wəlahsənal*: The 1918 version has 'sweet flavor', literally, 'it is a good stone', wherebe *-ahsən* 'stone' in combination frequently serves to refer to pipes. The accent may be *wəláhsənal*.

268   *nə(h·ə)nn·ahč*: The 1918 version form initially suggests something like *nehnahč* with the 1918 gloss 'then also' related to *ennahč* 'and that one', *nina* 'then at that', and *neh na* 'then then the' later in this same story and *nəna ahč* 'then also', at the start of story 12. Patterns like this have not been found in Siebert's documentation, and so the reconstruction is uncertain here. Western Abenaki has forms *enna* and *enni* apparently as fully stressable versions of the often clitic *na* 'that (NA)' and *ni* 'that (NI)'. These are unattested in Siebert's documentation of Penobscot, though what he transcribes as the collocations *wən na* 'that one' and *wən ni* '[that one] [sic: gloss omitted from ms.]', based on *wən* '(1) a certain, a particular, the very one, the special one; (2) (defining) that was, it comprised, composed; (3) he/it is the one', may possibly be equivalent variants. Since all three contexts suggest a strong deictic contrast ('then HE too . . .'), it may be that we have *nə(h·ə) nn[a]·ahč* 'then THAT ONE too' for the first and last of the forms noted above, with an intervocalic *-h-* common in clitic clusters, and then similarly *nə(h·ə)nna* 'then THAT ONE' for the third and fourth cases. For the second case, we suggest simple *enna·ahč*, where its use with non-Subordinative *pahtaso* 'he got sick on smoke' suggests that there is no Subordinative-triggering *n(ə)·* 'then' missing from the transcription, i.e., this is just 'THAT ONE too'.

268   *awičaya*: Contrast this *a*-form (and an earlier instance on page 258) with *wičəyal* earlier in the text. The variation may be from Lyon, but it may also be Speck simply missing the unstressed initial /a/.

268   *nəkihkə-pahtasolətəwak*: It is common for obviatives under possession to show proximate marking on an intransitive verb as here, or this may be an editorial hypercorrection by Speck.

268   *mehč·ətte*: The 1918 version has as 'lest certainly'; we follow the common and consistent English translation of *mehč(·ətte)* as 'still, nonetheless'.

270   *wəčəskawɑlɑwal*: Speck's original notes explain specifically that they were jealous of Gluskabe "on acc[ount] of [their] father making a pet of him."

270   *wəlatehəmhatine*: May represent more archaic/earlier *wəlatehamhatine*.

270   *wəlatehəmɑkanal*: This too may possibly be more archaic/earlier *wəlatehamɑkanal*.

270   *wəlatehəmɑkanal; pənahpskʷiye*: Here is a further example of a proximate shift. Unlike later with *awɑlatal*, the form matching *wəlatehəmɑkanal* is not obviative singular *pənahpskʷiyɑl*.

272   *kehčayiwit*: Possibly *kehčayəwit*.

274   *awɑlatal: piwsəssəwal wapikaniyɑl*: The syntax here is unclear, i.e., it is not certain if the two modifying predicates are separate clauses or not. Note earlier the parallel scene, where the wording appears to explicitly involve separate clauses: *piwsəssəwal, kenok wapikaniyɑl* '[his pipe] was small, but made of white bone/ivory'.

274   *nə(h·ə)nna*: See the above discussion of *nə(h·ə)nn[a]·ahč*.

276   *n·etali-sehkalot*: This could also possibly be 'that/there was where he was defeated', but the pattern [*n(ə·)* plus time-Conjunct plus Subordinative], as 'then when X happened, (then) they did Y', is extremely common in these texts and fits the 1918 translation as well.

278   *ičəye*: This form without *n-* is elsewhere unattested (it occurs both in Speck's original notes and the 1918 version), but it is hypothetically possible (and perhaps somewhat more informal/intimate), assuming it parallels Passamaquoddy-Maliseet *uhkomi* 'grandma!' in dropping first-person marker *n(ə)-*.

278 *pəkʷánɑ*: 'It is (not) successfully lifted' versus other speakers' *pəkʷánɑwi*, i.e., another of Lyon's distinctive contrastively accented negative concord forms; the more commonly attested pattern would be *pəkʷánɑwi*.

## 12 nisɑnkaw

282 *wənɑči-witəkɑn*: The 1918 version transcription suggests *n·oči-witəkɑn* 'then he joined in dancing from there', an odd meaning. *n·wənɑči-witəkɑn* 'then he went to join in dancing' makes more sense in the context and matches a two-step narrative pattern common in Penobscot, of describing a character first as physically heading to a place, and then with *nɑt-*, *nɑči-* 'go (off) in order to . . .', describing what they are going there to do.

282 *-kikimətonkahətičik*: A mismatch with the preceding obviative plural, either as a Speck editorial miscorrection or likely just a genuine proximate shift.

282 "*tɑn mina ali-təpihle?*": With the question 'what is happening, has happened?' *mina* 'again' is often used, not literally but in some idiomatic or affective sense not fully understood.

284 *kekʷəss alihtɑkʷat*: Literally 'What does it sound like?' the 1918 version glosses it as 'What is being done?'; the same phrase appears elsewhere in various Penobscot (and related-language) sources with glosses suggesting that it is an everyday expression comparable to English 'What's the news?' or 'What's up?'

284 *ččəsči*: The fact that the *Penobosct Dictionary* has instead *ččìsči* highlights the relative phonetic closeness of /i/ and /ə/. Schwas in Eastern Algonquian languages tend to be somewhat high and front, i.e., often impressionistically in the [i~ɪ] area), especially when adjacent to coronals. The contrast is complicated further by the frequent laxing of /i/ to [ɪ] in closed syllables. The two vowels mostly get very different prosodic treatment, however, with /i/ as a fundamentally accentable vowel and /ə/ as a weak, often accentless or unaccentable vowel, and in many (though not all) cases, accentual behavior can be enough to distinguish them.

284 *kəya·p'·eht . . . kəwewelətamən . . .*: Might possibly be a single line together and translate as 'As if the likes of you would know what's going on!'

284 *nə(h·ə)nna·ahč*: The 1918 version suggests *nana ahč*; see the discussion of *nə(h·ə)nna·ahč* in story 11.

284 *nipənal*: The 1918 version consistently gives apparent *nipənal* rather than the expected *nipənol* for verb-based nominals of this type. In contrast to *mənəlɑmsənal-manəlɑmsənol* case in story 4, we do not amend to the *-ol* form, though it is possible that Speck (rather than Lyon) may have overgeneralized the *-al* plural here as a miscorrection.

284 *kči-pkənačok*: The 1918 version suggests *tepapo kči-pkənačo*; we expect locative *kči-pkənačok*. Compare this to the *kči-mɑkʷasəpem[ək]* issue discussed earlier. This may again be a recurrent type of mishearing by Speck.

286 *peməkahətit*: The 1918 version suggests *pəməkɑt*; it is possible that Speck missed the unstressed *-həti-* sequence here expected for a NA plural form. Alternatively, this may be still another type of genuine verb-to-noun number mismatch, possibly relatable to those discussed earlier, and/or to the phenomenon of Arabic and Welsh (etc.) singular verbs preceding plural subjects. The 1918 version /ə/ for the first vowel here is a misreading of original notes /e/.

286 *awihkʷinɑko*: The 1918 version translates as 'they made fun of him'. See the discussion of *awihkʷinawən* above.

286 *wəsamihpskʷanenɑn*: The 1918 version glosses as 'because he stroked them on the back', mistaking *wə-sami-* 'he touched . . .' for *wəsami* 'because'. The restored (but still uncertain) /h/ is as in the *Penobscot Dictionary nətasonihpskʷánena* 'I rub his back'.

286 *pesəkʷəta*: The 1918 version translates as 'at once' but probably '[danced] around away one time'. Hence also the next line 'before . . . again'.

286 *máskkak*: This transformation of dancers recalls a different story of dancers turned to rattlesnakes, recounted in *Penobscot Legends* (*sihsihkʷak*).

286   *nisəwa máskkak epičik*: The form here again has a mismatch between obviative plural *nisəwa* 'two' and proximate plurals *máskkak epičik* 'toads sitting' (the second element may be *epihətičik*). We might otherwise expect full obviative plural concord as *nisəwa máskka epiličihi*. Possibly these forms come as a dictation break, stopping and restarting.

288   *pəsəkáhtahasič*: 'Let it turn dark (suddenly)'. Here again, -*hasi* seems to refer to events with sudden/sharp onset or instant change. The form may also be *pəsəkáhtahəsič*.

288   *n·wəkisi-nimiphən*: This can mean either 'then he grabbed it' or 'then he was able to grab it': *kis*- means 'have done' or 'can do'. Most contexts make it clear which one is meant, but here it could potentially be either; we follow the original English translation.

288   *amače-kʷakʷəmahlən*: The 1918 version and original notes suggest *amače-kʷakʷə́ma*. The expected final syllable /-hlən/ -*hlan*, which is supported by the accentual transcription and needed for stem *kʷakʷəmahlɑ*- 'run' with Subordinative, appears to have been missed. This is likely because the original notes transcription of this word runs right up into and against the very bottom corner of the notebook page. Note too that *mače*- can also mean 'heading off, away', so this could be glossed as '(then) he ran off/headed off running'.

290   *mekʷeličil*: This is one of the few independent instances of a stem *mekʷe*- 'NA groan', which has in some sources been given as an etymology/literal meaning for *mekʷe* 'Mohawk/Iroquoian/Onkwehó:nwe/Haudenosaunee person'.

290   *wəkisi-čilənal*: The 1918 version gloss '[s]ome one has succeeded [in] snatching away' appears to have misglossed what the *Penobscot Dictionary* gives as *nàčiləna* 'I make a mark on him (handprint, bruise)'. The implication may be that Gluskabe scooped out the main chunk of Summer, leaving just an imprint behind.

290   *piləwi-alənape*: This literally means 'strange/different Person' (i.e., unfamiliar Indigenous person), and in Penobscot literature is often used to refer to new/unknown people from outside the Wabanaki community.

290   *n·elalohket*: The 1918 version suggests *n·elalohke*, with Speck missing the final -*t* of the NA singular Conjunct.

292   *nohsohkəkohči(či)hi*: The 1918 version and original notes transcription suggest *nohsohkəkohčičihi*, an unclear form. For 'the (obv. pl.) ones who were following him', we expect instead *nohsohkəkohčihi*. The transcribed form could be a mishearing of *nohsohkəkohətičihi* 'the (obv. pl.) ones who were following them (prox. pl.)', as per story 1's *ketonaləkohətičəhi* 'the (obv. pl.) ones who were hunting/seeking after them (prox. pl.)', but this does not fit the context. Much more of a stretch would be a form *nohsohkəkohčiličihi*: this would involve a further unexpected /i/ (and palatalization) for more expected *nohsohkəkohtəličihi* (= expected *nohsohkəkohčihi* with additional obviative marker -*əli*-, as in *ekhočinəličihi* 'the [obv. pl.] ones that were hanging up', seen later in this story). It is also possible that Speck simply misheard an extra syllable. Lacking further conclusive evidence, we provide both the 1918 version original and the expected options here.

294   -*ɑpihtahpote*: The 1918 and original notes transcriptions have the first vowel here as /a/. This form is so far unattested in other sources but may very likely involve the element *ap*- seen in stems of reversal, untying, etc., and so is retranscribed accordingly.

296   *n·wənaskatəhasin*: The 1918 version glosses as 'gave up'; the stem *naskatəhasi*- seems to convey strong discouragement; giving up may be just an implication.

296   *pesəkʷən elihlat kəloskape; elapit*: It is possible that *kəloskape* 'Gluskabe' belongs at the start of the following clause.

296   *wkʷáhli*: The 1918 version only suggests *(k)kʷáhli*, while one form in Siebert's notes suggests *wkʷahl*- as the key element here. However, Day has *kwahliwi* 'near, nearby' for Western Abenaki (260), and Aubery has *k8arriði* 'prime abord [at first]' and *k8arriði api* '[sit nearby]' (416), so the exact initial sound sequence remains provisional.

298   *n·wəpatəkitəwihalətina*: In other attestations, the group-plural stem for -*təwi-hla* 'fly' is -*təwihlawəlati*. This alternative element -*haləti* resembles the unusual construction of the group-plural for -*hal-əkʷe* 'float in the current', which simply replaces its final component with reciprocal -*ati* to form group-plural stem -*hal-əti*. It is not clear if this is a dialectal variation or might have some special meaning.

298 *kačəkikilahsəwal*: The 1918 version suggests *kčikikilahsəwal*; *kačəkikilahsəwal* is restored based on the earlier form in this text, plus the *Penobscot Dictionary* form.

300 *tihtəkəli*: A rare instance of a word shared with Kanien'kéha/Mohawk: *tsihstékeri* 'owl' (Maracle, *One Thousand Useful Mohawk Words*, 94; possibly also *tsistékeri*). Contrast this with *kwareró:ha* 'barn owl' and *ko'khó:wa* 'big grey/white owl/moth owl', e.g., *Katsi'ten'serí:io ne ko'khó:wa* 'The white owl is a nice bird' (First Voices: Kanien'kéha, https://www.firstvoices.com/explore/FV/sections/Data/Kanehsatà:ke/Mohawk/). Note also the close similarity of *ko'khó:wa* here to Penobscot *kohkóhkhahso* 'Barred Owl, (Strix varia Barton)' and *kóhkohkhe* 'white-owl, snowy owl'.

300 *(a)wihkʷimən. wəpečitəwihlan*: The 1918 version suggests *wihkʷiman*; *pečitəwihlan*.

300 *kʷaskʷáyī*: The 1918 version glosses this as 'it grew colder', but the *Penobscot Dictionary* has *kʷaskʷáyi* as '1) by successive stages, 2) by degrees, 3) step by step, piece by piece, drop by drop, 4) a little at a time, 5) gradually, progressively'. It is possible that Speck missed a 'grew colder' verb here, particularly if it was the monosyllable *tke* 'it is cold'; alternatively, this may simply have been implied from contextual use of the form above.

302 *nə·mlohsəssis epit*: The 1918 version suggests *nə·* here, which makes sense as *nə· . . . epit* 'there/that was where [he] sat', but it is possible that the form is *na* 'that (NA)'.

304 *nətapamalsin*: It is unclear here if this is a Subordinative 'so I feel hot' or a secondary object 'I feel hot from it', or both.

306 *wpətinal*: The 1918 version mistranslates *wpətinal* 'his hands' (or 'his arms': like Passamaquoddy-Maliseet *'pihtinol*, the Penobscot term apparently can cover just the hands or the entire arm with the hand) as 'his legs'.

306 *nkaskəmehlal*: The 1918 version mistranslates *nkaskəmehlal* 'they [his hands] melted away' as 'he melted away'.

## 13 nsαnkaw

PAGE

312 *nəkisi-wəlihton αta·č mina atoči-sakipponowi*: This may simply be two separate sentences, *nəkisi-wəlihton* 'I have fixed it' and *αta·č mina atoči-sakipponowi* 'it will not/never again be so hard a winter', or the second is an unmarked in form Subordinative linked directly to the first, i.e., 'I have fixed it so that it will never again be so hard a winter'. We follow the 1918 version in going with the latter translation.

312 *kohsəssənawak*: The 1918 version again suggests *kohsəssənawa* for expected *kohsəssənawak* 'our descendants'.

312 *mehtakʷičihlak*: The 1918 version glosses this as 'the extreme end'. Some attestations of this stem seem to suggest *mehtakʷečihlak*, though *akʷič-* would transparently mean 'float, be in water', as per viewing the (main)land or even the whole world as a great floating island. (Compare also Passamaquoddy-Maliseet *metoqiciye* '(something floating; figuratively, an island or faraway land) it comes to an end'.) The 1918 version notes "Surmised to be at the eastern end of the world" (215).

314 *nə·či nihkʷap . . . nətalalohkαn*: The 1918 version suggests *nə·č etalalohkan*, which is literally 'then/there (is when/where) you will be working'. The two possibilities that fit the context are *nə·č etalalohka* 'then/there (is when/where) I will be working' or *nə·č nətalalohkαn* 'then/there I will be working'. Speck may have simply modeled *etalalohkan* after the *etalihtawa* that immediately follows it, but it is not clear which of the two possibilities suggested above is more likely here. It is also unclear if the *nə·* elements here should be read as 'then' or 'there', particularly since *tal-* 'in . . . stretch of place/time', also frequently used for progressive/ongoing aspect, is equally ambiguous for a place versus time reading. The 1918 version seems to go with the time reading, especially in glossing the preceding component *nə·či nihkʷap* as 'from now on' (but literally just 'then ·WILL now'). Compare *nə·č nihkʷap noli-ssipsohkαn* 'so now I will hunt ducks well' in story 4, with what may be a similar '[since I have] . . . (so) from now on . . .' sense. We offer both options but lead with that suggested by the 1918 version.

314   *kči-awotin*: The 1918 translation of *kči-awotin* as 'a great war' is disputed by elders who report that this word can refer to a contest between two champions for resolving conflict. Note too that the same expression is used to refer to a contest between two *mɑtewɑlɑnɑwak*.

314   *mikahkehɑtihɑtit*: The 1918 version and original notes suggest an uncertain *mikahkéhití[hɑ]tit*. Forms from Siebert like *amikahkhatinɑ* and *wɑmikahkhatinɑ* 'then they (group) fight' together lead us to expect *mikahkhatihɑtit* 'when they (group) fight'. But it is possible that here Lyon uses the group-plural variant -*hɑti* instead, giving *mikahkehɑtihɑtit*. (An alternative reading might be *mikahkehɑtite* 'if/when they fight'. While lacking the group-plural element [which is not always present in forms that clearly do involve substantial groups], it would match the semantically and discursively parallel *awotimɑke* 'if there is a contest' following it. This however requires assuming that Speck misheard a final -*e* as -*it*, or miscorrected it so.)

316   *pemɑkisɑkahk*: The 1918 version suggests *pemɑkisɑka*, highlighting Speck's difficulty with some final consonants.

316   *n·wɑtapaskʷasin*: This form, suggested in the 1918 version as *n·wɑtapaskʷasin* and glossed as 'raises his head', is not clearly attested elsewhere. It is possible that the -*kʷasi* represents -*kʷahɑsi* from -(*o/ɑh*)*kʷe-hasi*, referring to a quick motion of the face or even head (e.g., the *Penobscot Dictionary* has *nɑkʷɑtalakíkʷahɑso* 'he winks' and *pɑsɑkɑlakíkʷahɑso* 'he blinks'; compare also Passamaquoddy-Maliseet *pisqewu* 'she/he inserts head'). The original notes translation '[he] throws his head up' perhaps reflects this 'quick motion' component even more closely. If so, the (*t*) *apas*- remains uncertain, since the only known similar element is *tapahs*- 'low', which would suggest the opposite gloss, 'he lowers his head'. Attested terms for raising and lowering the head are quite distinct: the *Penobscot Dictionary* offers *ačitawɑmkʷétotam* 'he moves his head downward, hangs his head down' (or *kčitawɑmkʷétotam* 'he moves his head low [in dejection, sadness]') and *čikɑlɑmkʷétotam* 'he raises his head from a prone or lying position'.

# Works Consulted and Suggestions for Further Reading

Alger, Abby L. *In Indian Tents: Stories Told by Penobscot, Passamaquoddy and Micmac Indians to Abby L. Alger.* Boston: Roberts Brothers, 1897.

Aubery, Joseph. *Father Aubery's French-Abenaki Dictionary* (1756). Edited and translated by Stephen Laurent. Portland, ME: Chisholm Brothers, 1995.

Day, Gordon. *Western Abenaki Dictionary,* vol. 1, *Abenaki-English.* Hull, QC: Canadian Museum of Civilization, 1994.

Eckstorm, Fannie Hardy. *Indian Place Names of the Penobscot Valley and the Maine Coast.* Orono, ME: University Press, 1941. Reprint Orono: University of Maine at Orono Press, 1978.

——. *Old John Neptune and Other Maine Indian Shamans.* Portland, ME: Southworth-Anthoensen Press, 1945.

——. *The Penobscot Man.* Boston and New York: Houghton Mifflin, 1904.

Francis, David A., Robert M. Leavitt, and Margaret Apt. *A Passamaquoddy-Maliseet Dictionary: Peskotomuhkati Wolastoqewi Latuwewakon.* Orono: University of Maine Press, 2008.

Goddard, Ives, and Kathleen J. Bragdon. *Native Writings in Massachusett.* Philadelphia: American Philosophical Society, 1988.

Haviland, William. "Local Indians and the End of the Last Ice Age: Part I of II." *Mt. Desert Islander,* November 29, 2012, 5.

Kolodny, Annette. "A Summary History of the Penobscot Nation." In *The Life and Traditions of the Red Man,* by Joseph Nicolar, 1–34. Durham, NC: Duke University Press, 2007.

Krashen, Stephen D. "The Input Hypothesis: An Update." In *Georgetown University Roundtable on Languages and Linguistics 1991,* edited by James E. Alatis, 405–431. Washington, DC: Georgetown University Press, 1991.

Laurent, Joseph. *New Familiar Abenakis and English Dialogues.* Quebec City: Leger Brousseau, 1884. Reprint Vancouver: Global Language Press, 2006.

Leland, Charles G. *The Algonquin Legends of New England; or, Myths and Folk Lore of the Micmac, Passamaquoddy, and Penobscot Tribes.* Boston: Houghton Mifflin, 1884.

Leland, Charles Godfrey, and John Dyneley Prince. *Kulóskap the Master and Other Algonkin Poems.* New York: Funk and Wagnalls, 1902.

LeSourd, Philip S. "Enclitic Particles in Western Abenaki: Form and Function." *International Journal of American Linguistics* 81 (2015): 301–335.

——. "The Passamaquoddy 'Witchcraft Tales' of Newell S. Francis." *Anthropological Linguistics* 42, no. 4 (Winter 2000): 441–498.

——, trans. and ed. *Tales from Maliseet Country: The Maliseet Tales of Karl V. Teeter.* Lincoln: University of Nebraska Press, 2007.

Maracle, David Kanatawakhon. *One Thousand Useful Mohawk Words.* Guilford, CT: Audio-Forum, 1992.

Masta, Henry Lorne. *Abenaki Indian Legends, Grammar and Place Names.* Victoriaville, QC: La Voix des Bois-Francs, 1932. Reprint Toronto: Global Language Press, 2008.

Nicolar, Joseph. *The Life and Traditions of the Red Man.* Bangor, ME: C. H. Glass, 1893. Reprint edited by Annette Kolodny. Durham, NC: Duke University Press, 2007.

O'Brien, Jean M. *Firsting and Lasting: Writing Indians Out of Existence in New England.* Minneapolis: University of Minnesota Press, 2010.

Penobscot Nation. *Penobscot Dictionary.* Orono: University of Maine Press, forthcoming.

——. "Penobscot Legends." Vols. 1–2. Unpublished digital manuscript, 2021.

——. "Transformer Tales: Stories of the Dawnland." Unpublished script, 2016.

Prince, J. Dyneley. "A Passamaquoddy Aviator." *American Anthropologist,* new series, 11, no. 4 (1909): 628–650.

——. "The Penobscot Language of Maine." *American Anthropologist,* new series, 12, no. 2 (1910): 183–208.

Rand, Silas Tertius. *Legends of the Micmacs.* Edited by Helen L. Webster. New York: Longmans, Green, 1894.

Rasles, Sébastien. Dictionary of the Abenaki Indian Language, 1691–1724. MS Fr 13. Houghton Library, Harvard University, Cambridge, MA.

Rasles, Sébastien, and John Pickering. "A Dictionary of the Abnaki Language in North America" (1833). Book Collections at the Maine State Library, Augusta. 103. https://digitalmaine.com/books/103.

Roeder, Amy, Carol Dana, Carmella Bear, and Margo Lukens. "The Production of *The Transformer Tales Play.*" Interview by Donna Loring. *Wabanaki Windows,* WERU, August 16, 2016. https://archives.weru.org/wabanaki-windows/2016/08/wabanaki-windows-81616/.

Senier, Siobhan, et al., eds. *Dawnland Voices: An Anthology of Indigenous Writing from New England.* Lincoln: University of Nebraska Press, 2014.

Siebert, Frank T. Frank Siebert Papers. Mss.Ms.Coll.97. American Philosophical Society, Philadelphia.

——. "The Suprasegmental Phonemes of the Penobscot Dialect of Eastern Abenaki, an Eastern Algonquian Language." In *In Honor of Mary Haas: From the Haas Festival Conference on Native American Linguistics,* edited by William Shipley, 715–763. Berlin: Mouton de Gruyter, 1988.

Speck, Frank G. "The Functions of Wampum among the Eastern Algonkian." *Memoirs of the American Anthropological Association* 6, no. 1 (January–March 1919): 3–71. Reprinted as *The Functions of Wampum among the Eastern Algonkian.* New York: Kraus Reprint, 1974.

——. *Penobscot Man.* Edited by David Sanger. Philadelphia: University of Pennsylvania Press, 1940. Reprint Orono: University of Maine Press, 1998.

——. "Penobscot Tales." *Journal of American Folklore* 28, no. 107 (January–March 1915): 52–58.

——. Penobscot Texts, no. 9049. Cornell University Library Division of Rare and Manuscript Collections, Ithaca, New York.

——. "Penobscot Transformer Tales." *International Journal of American Linguistics* 1, no. 3 (August 1918): 187–244.

——. "Wawenock Myth Texts from Maine." In *Bureau of American Ethnology, 43rd Annual Report,* 165–197. Washington, DC: U.S. Government Printing Office, 1928.

Voorhis, Paul. "Grammatical Notes on the Penobscot Language from Frank Speck's Penobscot Transformer Tales." *University of Manitoba Anthropology Papers* 24 (October 1979): 1–83.

# INDEX